FAMILY
AT WAR

Swain's

FAMILY AT WAR

THE FOLJAMBE FAMILY AND THE GREAT WAR

JOLYON JACKSON

FOREWORD BY RICHARD HOLMES

Haynes Publishing

Dedication

To Serena, Alicia and Thomas

First published in 2010

A catalogue record for this book is available from the British Library

ISBN 978 1 84425 943 2
Library of Congress control no. 2009936940

Published by Haynes Publishing,
Sparkford, Yeovil, Somerset BA22 7JJ, UK
Tel: 01963 442030 Fax: 01963 440001
Int. tel: +44 1963 442030 Int. fax: +44 1963 440001
E-mail: sales@haynes.co.uk
Website: www.haynes.co.uk

Haynes North America Inc.
861 Lawrence Drive, Newbury Park,
California 91320, USA

Design and layout by James Robertson

Printed in the USA

FRONTISPIECE *Francis Foljambe.*

Contents

FOREWORD

Professor Richard Holmes

The generation that endured the First World War was strikingly literate. Across the whole spectrum of rank, officers and soldiers wrote letters and kept diaries, while their families exchanged news, congratulated, commiserated, waited and worried. There is such a rich seam of primary source material that a historian could spend a busy career simply burrowing his way through it. Most manuscripts sit in great collections like the Department of Documents at the Imperial War Museum or the Liddell Collection in the Brotherton Library at Leeds, or remain in private hands. Occasionally a set of correspondence is so illuminating that it bursts through the accessibility barrier and genuinely deserves to be made available to a wider audience. The Foljambe papers are so self-evidently in this category that it is a real delight to see them in print.

The extended family of Francis John Savile Foljambe ('the Squire') played exactly the sort of role that one might expect from an upper middle-class family of the age. The Squire's son George had commanded a Territorial battalion of the Sherwood Foresters and, although over-age and unfit, was re-employed to train volunteers for the first two years of the war. His younger brother Hubert, a Regular officer in the King's Royal Rifle Corps, was killed on the Aisne in 1914: 'A better man never wore a Rifleman's jacket,' lamented his regimental journal. George's eldest son, Ted, was reported wounded and

missing at the Battle of Cateau, and it took anxious months for his family to discover that he was alive and in German hands. The other son, Francis, had been commissioned into the Royal Field Artillery in 1912, and was in the battery that fired the first field artillery shell near Mons on 23 August 1914, losing his popular battery commander, shot through the throat in this opening action. There were more military connections as the family circle rippled outwards. One of George's brothers-in-law, Henry Warre, was another Regular rifleman, and Victor Yeats-Brown, his son-in-law, married to Rachie, midway in age between Ted and Francis, had served in the same battalion as Hubert.

Francis's letters form the main thread in this rich braid of correspondence. By the time that he was posted home to work in the Ministry of Munitions in the summer of 1917 he had been mentioned in despatches, won a Military Cross and was commanding a battery as an acting major. In the process he had fought at Mons, Le Cateau, the Aisne and Ypres. His letters are full of the sort of practical detail that illuminates a gunner's world, from gripping tales of battle to the more humdrum narrative of daily life, interleaved with requests for food, toiletries and whipcord breeches to replace those worn out by life in the saddle. He had certainly felt war's hard edge, but described his departure for Britain as 'the end of a most enjoyable three years'. Ted was eventually released to internment in Switzerland, where his preoccupations became sartorial rather than military: 'I want a new *black* serge coat,' he told his parents, 'in place of my old green one.' He urged them to hurry, for 'this coat does stink'.

Many of George's former subordinates kept him apprised of the fate of the men he had trained. 'Sorry our casualties are now 400 from the old battalion,' wrote one, while another regretted that newly commissioned officers really had no idea of their 'entire responsibility' for all aspects of the life of the men they commanded. Victor Yeats-Brown was invalided home – 'Some fellows crack under the strain,' wrote a brother officer, 'and others control themselves during the strain and crack on the reaction' – but commanded a company in North Russia in 1918–19. Although this is epaulette history, there is extraordinary sympathy for the soldiers who appear in it, and it is impossible to read a Sherwood Forester's account of the 1917 Arras offensive – *The men were glorious, and the officers also*' – without being reminded, yet

again, of the tensile strength of the men who shouldered rifle and pack in this terrible war.

The quality of editing rises marvellously to meet the merit of the text, and judicious use of unit war diaries helps put individual stories into collective perspective. The fact that Francis, who lived till 1987 (his last years darkened by the accidental death of his son), survived to add a reflective gloss to his account of 'the Kaiser's war' is an added bonus. His description of his last night at the front, in a forward observation post, catches the feel of the moment majestically. It was: 'A typical "All Quiet on the Western Front" night with Very lights lobbing up to light up no-man's-land, and occasional outbreaks of small arms fire here and there, and the faint rumble of transport taking supplies up to the forward areas. I realised then that I was looking at this "strange world" for the last time ...' Thanks to this book we can now look into this world through the eyes of that now-vanished generation who inhabited it.

Richard Holmes

Author's acknowledgements

This book has taken a while to write and I want to thank a few people who have supported me throughout the project. From the family, Caroline Yeats-Brown and Ann Boileau. From the regiments, Will Townend and the staff at 'Firepower', the Royal Artillery Museum; Oliver Hackett from the Worcestershire and Sherwood Foresters; General Christopher Wallace from the Royal Green Jackets Museum, which looks after the heritage of both The Rifle Brigade and King's Royal Rifle Corps. I gained much from reading the old chronicles and

dipping into the war diaries. Richard Holmes, the eminent historian, who also read an early draft, has encouraged me and kindly written the foreword. Donald Sommerville, with his editorial skills, tore through the early draft and has given it a better sense of shape and order. Alison Miles, with her eagle eye, and Jonathan Falconer from Haynes who has brought the book both to life and fruition.

Finally, I must thank Michael Foljambe, who has allowed me to tell the story of our family.

Author's Introduction

I was given the diary of Francis Foljambe by his son Michael (my cousin) who, knowing that I was a serving soldier, thought I might be interested in the exploits of his father in the Great War. I had not seen the diary before and as I thumbed through the pages with the text so understated and phlegmatic and the sketches of the trenches and gun positions that were so immaculately executed, there came a dawning realisation that I was looking at something rather special. Not only had Francis Foljambe been there at the beginning of the war (he claimed to have fired the first 18-pound artillery round for the British Army in the war across the Mons Canal, and I can find no reason to doubt him – the first 13-pound round was fired by the Royal Horse Artillery (RHA) earlier in the day), but he stayed in northern France and Belgium for the next three years. As I talked to Michael about his father I discovered a side of the family I had never met and all of them had been involved in the war.

Even as a regular soldier I suppose much of my knowledge of the war began with the Kitchener Armies and the famous poster featuring Kitchener's stern face with bristling moustache, finger pointing directly at the potential recruit. I then knew something more of the conscripts, the horrors of stalemated trench warfare, the works of the war poets, the courage, bravery, sacrifice and death that permeated that four years of European history. However, I had almost forgotten that a small and experienced professional Army deployed in August 1914 – faster than we could do today in those numbers, cheerfully smashed itself against the advancing Germans and checked them (of course with the French throughout). It then carried out a difficult retreat, turning to the attack and then stood firm against a new German advance. In these battles the small Army that deployed to France and Belgium in August 1914 was shattered almost beyond recognition.

I never knew anyone who was there at the beginning. My grandfather was there in 1916, having lied about his age (he died while I was in my twenties), but he went through training from instructors who had already served in the trenches and learnt much about the art of survival. Amongst those there in August 1914, many had been through the Boer War and others had fought on the North-West Frontier or in other skirmishes around the Empire. But many had not faced battle and I wondered what they were like, what their values and standards were, how they saw their duty and how they thought.

I discovered from Michael that there were other family papers and letters, all of which had languished in an archive since the end of the war, unseen and unknown.

As I unravelled the letters and other diaries, I discovered that four of my cousins had been regular soldiers at the beginning of the war, three of them serving in the antecedent regiments of my own regiment, The Rifles. And there were other soldiers, both within the family and amongst their friends. Who the various family members were and their positions, in and out of service life, are explained in the family tree on page 19.

Of course, the war in Europe was not the whole story (there was fighting elsewhere) and what was happening at home was of equal importance, so I was thrilled to find letters from the women of the family, showing many of their hopes and fears and their bravery in the face of terrible events to come. There were other letters from family friends discussing the stresses and strains of all their lives and the costs that were being borne by the communities at home.

As well as including material from the various letters and diaries, I have written a brief historical commentary linking the various pieces and setting them in context. For this purpose I have also drawn on a variety of sources, including war diaries and regimental histories.

I have also made some minor corrections to the spelling, grammar and punctuation of various of the original documents, many of them written in haste from the front or in the difficult conditions of prison-camp life, in the interest of making them clearer and easier for the modern reader. In particular, place-name spellings have been corrected as far as possible and made uniform. In all cases where emphasis is shown in quoted matter this appears in the original document.

The family's varied history is in a way representative of the range of experiences encountered by many British families of the time, and indeed families in other combatant nations. One is killed in action and a second is wounded and taken prisoner. A third serves for over three years at the front, while another makes an early and perhaps fortuitous transfer to a staff job. Older family members see war service at home but all, in uniform or out of it, are affected in many significant ways.

The transition from an officer's relatively pleasant pre-war routine with hunting more of a concern than serious training is also well charted. The ferocious intensity of First World War combat is then vividly described by family members and other correspondents at First Ypres, Loos, Arras and other notable battles. The changing nature of warfare is also clearly set out. Even in the opening weeks of the war the importance of air reconnaissance is plain to family members, while Francis's diary and its drawings chronicle the increasingly scientific nature of artillery work. His early actions are fought over open sights but soon his writing is peppered with expressions like 'registered' and 'bombardment'. His first use of the word 'barrage' is in his description of the Battle of Loos in September 1915.

Away from the fighting, the family's domestic experiences are also illuminating. Like many others in the early weeks of war they are concerned by reports of German spies and taken in, too, by accounts of Russian troops passing through England. Rather less predictably, Francis's brother Ted develops a relationship with the Polish nurse who tended to him as a wounded prisoner of war and in due course they marry. There has been ample literature published on prisoners' experiences in the Second World War, but far less, like Ted's letters reproduced here, on this aspect of the Great War.

Family members clearly had very different personalities and views. Some write in a mainly formal style, very much of the stiff upper lip of traditional British stereotype. Others are more openly loving and prepared to show their vulnerability – and even to criticise the conduct of the war. But this story is about a family and I want them to tell it in their own words. It is not for me to impose my 21st-century views on these men and women who grew up in the Victorian and Edwardian era, but for them to talk to you from the pages of this book. I feel I know them now and hope you find the same by the end of the story.

PREFACE

Francis Foljambe Looks Back, 1965

When I happened upon this diary which I had kept during the Kaiser War 1914–18 and re-read it after the lapse of half a century I wondered how it was that I could have, in the concluding sentence, described those times as 'enjoyable'. The tragic elimination of a large proportion of a generation, including the best of the young men at that time, undoubtedly resulted in the poor leadership by lesser men from which this country has since suffered and which led it into a Second World War. How then could I have described the times of the First World War as enjoyable?

I was twenty-two years old in 1914 and a 2nd lieutenant serving in the 120th Battery (5th Division) at Newbridge in Ireland. When war was declared a small nucleus was detailed to remain at the station to wind up affairs. I can remember that those people who were detailed to stay behind were in a state of despair because they were convinced that, by the time they joined up again, the war would be over! The one thing of which the ordinary person was certain was that no modern war could last for more than a few months on account of the expense.

Promotion in those days was slow; one could expect to reach the rank of captain in not less than fifteen years of service, so it is not surprising that one felt a little proud to find oneself commanding a battery at the age of twenty-three! The command of a battery was perhaps the pick of all regimental commands. By reason of the tactical role, a Gunner automatically enjoyed certain privileges; for example he had to spend a considerable portion of his time in observation posts, chosen as places which gave the best view of what was going on.

When trench warfare set in, a broad strip of France and Belgium, about 6,000 yards deep, became a sort of 'world apart'. Living in this world was undoubtedly dangerous but there were many compensations. The peculiar circumstances and the common purpose seemed to bring out in most people their very best characteristics: courage, unselfishness, good humour and so on; and then there was the total absence of all the conventional and social worries of ordinary civilised life. In spite of having to sleep for months on end in a hole in the ground and in spite of the appalling mud in winter, I kept in excellent health during the whole of the three years I was at the front, except for a couple of days in the exceptionally severe winter of 1916, when we were in action at Marrières Wood on the Somme. I had to spend a long time at a forward observation post for a wire-cutting task and came back very cold. Later, aches and pains got so bad that I could not move and I had to send for the brigade medical officer. He produced some pills which brought me out in a muck sweat and in 48 hours I started to get better again. Perhaps I mentioned this indisposition when writing home, and

OPPOSITE Francis in his 'best kit' with 120th Battery Royal Field Artillery (RFA) in Ballincollig in Southern Ireland, 1914.

it may have caused my mother to have spoken to her relative (Sir Francis Bingham) who was head of the military side of the Ministry of Munitions. Anyway, in the late summer of 1917, I unexpectedly received an official order directing me to report forthwith to a department of the Ministry of Munitions.

I remember that I spent my last night at the front at the battery observation post. A typical 'All Quiet on the Western Front' night with Very lights lobbing up to light up no-man's-land, and occasional outbreaks of small arms fire here and there, and the faint rumble of transport taking supplies up to the forward areas. I realised then that I was looking at this 'strange world' for the last time, and it was with regret, and feeling rather like a deserter, that on the following

BELOW Francis and Mary Foljambe as children in 1905.

morning I handed over command of the battery, said goodbye and rode away.

The word 'enjoyable' in describing these times was obviously not the right one but it was probably intended to record the many privileges and unique experiences which participation in the events at the front had afforded.

The years since 1914 have seen such prodigious changes in every aspect of life that it becomes more and more difficult to believe that one was an eye witness to the appearance and methods of war in 1914: the French *cuirassiers* with breastplates and plumed helmets, the *poilus* with blue and red uniform and their enormous packs, the long rifle with outsize bayonet of the French territorials, the first military aeroplanes with rival airmen shooting at each other with revolvers, the Boer War pom-pom as the official anti-aircraft gun, the German soldiers in their *Pickelhaube*, the mass of horses and wagon lines stretching in a band at a reasonably safe distance in rear of, and roughly parallel to the front lines – wagon lines came in for an occasional shelling (my groom Driver Crease was killed in that way) but generally speaking during trench warfare they were not much molested. It was at night when ammunition and supplies were being taken up to the front that the horses and transport dropped in for a bad time.

In recalling memories of those times one is tempted to think back still further and compare conditions under which one has lived with those of the present (1965). I was born at Brackenhurst near Southwell. The house is now the Notts agricultural research station. We went to live at Cockglode in 1898 when I was only six years old and I remember very little about Brackenhurst except the large cedar in front of the house (still there I believe), my father's pack of beagles, the Jersey house cow (Beatrice) and the gobbler turkey at Holloughton, which used to attack us on nursery walks. Cockglode was leased by my parents from Lord Manvers and at that time was about as isolated and remote as any place in the whole country. [The nearby] Ollerton village consisted of the church and vicarage (Mrs

Paley Reade), Dr Wright and his family (Muriel, Dimples, and Willy who was a Harrovian), a store (Mr Appleby) and a greengrocer (Miss Booth), also Mrs Morris at the post office who always came and hunted with the Rufford hounds whenever the meet was near. My mother probably quite rightly considered that Cockglode was too quiet for my sisters and in about 1904 a London house (89 Queen's Gate) was acquired. Cockglode, however, suited my brothers and myself well enough – we spent our Easter holidays shooting jackdaws out of the old hollow oak trees of Sherwood Forest, and ferreting with Mr Woodcock the Edwinstowe rabbiter; the summer holidays were spent at Sundet in Norway, fishing and shooting, and the Christmas holidays shooting at Osberton.*

My parents had the opportunity in about 1902 of buying the Sundet property in Norway when Mr Dick the former owner died and I think it was a question of [my father] choosing between taking over the mastership of the Rufford hounds (a great ambition) or buying Sundet. Greatly to our own benefit he chose the latter course. The Sundet property covered about 100 square miles of mountain, field, lakes and rivers. Altitude of Sundet was 3,000 feet. Besides the big lake (Miovaud) there were numerous other lakes and two rivers, all well stocked with trout, and ryper [a type of grouse] abounded, especially on the *fjeld* and wooded ridges on the south side of the big lake. Edmond, my brother, and I achieved an ambition one day when we got fifty brace of ryper. This was quite an accomplishment since we had only our old setter (Hector)

BELOW The Foljambe family spent every summer at Sundet in Norway. Rachie is on the right with Mary standing next to her. The rest of the group are Norwegian staff and friends.

ABOVE *Rowing on a lake near Sundet. Ted and Francis would collect their 'bag' of Ryper by boat.*

RIGHT *Francis was a friend of Prince George of Battenberg and it is thought this photograph from his album is of the armoured cruiser* HMS Drake, *which was the flagship of George's father, Admiral Prince Louis of Battenberg, when he commanded the Royal Navy's Second Cruiser Squadron before the war. Francis and George were regular visitors to the ship.*

and had to carry our cartridges as well as the birds. My brother at one time of the day was shooting while carrying twenty brace on his back. I was able to manage ten brace. We made dumps of birds at the lakeside and at the end of the day picked them up in the boat. Besides Sundet we had another group of huts at Varmviken on the south end of the estate, a lovely place with a lake with a lot of islands in it and full of trout. Then there were single huts and three other places where we stayed a couple of nights when shooting and fishing in those neighbourhoods. It was indeed a boys' paradise on earth and fortunately there are a number of watercolour paintings of Sundet, painted by my mother, as a record.

After two years at St David's, Reigate, I went to Osborne which suited me well; I think that there, and at the youthful age of twelve, I attained the peak of my 'career'! I was captain of football and hockey and in the cricket eleven, and became cadet captain and then chief cadet captain. My particular friends there were a boy by the name of Pym, and Prince George of Battenberg [older brother of the future Earl Mountbatten]. The latter used to take us to Osborne cottage and when his father's flagship (*Drake*) came to Cowes we were on several occasions invited to go on board. Prince Louis of Battenberg [Prince George's father] used to show us over his fine ship, provide enormous meals and play card games and drawing games with us in the evening. I cannot think why he should have been so kind. We looked up to him as a sort of god!

Alas, it was not too long before I tumbled off this 'pinnacle' of glory. In my first term at Dartmouth I injured myself playing football. At first I was not very much incapacitated but my back and neck became increasingly painful and it was with difficulty that I struggled through the rest of the term. Christmas holidays at Osberton followed and soon I reached a stage where I could only get up out of bed by rolling into a kneeling position on the floor.

I got 'noticed' and taken off to a doctor in London who discovered that the injury was a severe one, that I was lucky (he said) to be still alive and I was ordered into a long stay in bed with sandbags round my head to prevent movement. After about two years of treatment and convalescence I was sent to Clifton, which in comparison with the discipline, smartness and glamour of life at Osborne, seemed to me to be a very poor sort of place. I hated the time I spent there! I was not allowed to play football but could play cricket and how I managed to get into the school 1st XI I have never been able to understand. I was too weak to hit a ball past any fielder in front of the wicket so I must have made the few runs I got by gliding the ball to leg or even through the slips!

I was in the Army class and evidently paid some attention to studies since I managed without any special coaching to pass into the Royal Military Academy about half-way up the list. In Woolwich, in the rather Spartan life one led at the 'Shop', I regained much of my lost health. I took up hockey and was one of a side which included several players who later played for the Army. Due chiefly to them we distinguished ourselves by beating Sandhurst and winning every match in a long list of fixtures.

Another set-back was in store for me. Shortly before the end of the last term I got enticed into playing a game of football and again injured my neck. Then I was in hospital with exams coming off within a few days. I have to be grateful to the authorities who allowed me to take the exams in bed. It was a serious handicap not being able to revise work during the last few days and awkward to use pen and ruler when propped up in bed. I had hoped to pass out well but in the circumstances was perhaps lucky to pass out at all; in fact I had to be content with a position about half-way down the list, practically the same as when I passed in. Anyway, and at almost the earliest possible age of 18½ years, I got my commission and, after a month's course of gunnery at Shoeburyness, was posted to 120th Battery at Ballincollig in southern Ireland. My battery commander, whom I thought was a silly old man, took an instant dislike to me and it was fortunate for me

that his time for retirement came along a few months after I joined.

He was replaced by Major Holland and things for me there began to look up again. Major Holland was the very finest type of regimental officer and we subalterns should be grateful to him for his wise leadership, his efficiency and innate kindness to us (he was the first Gunner officer to be killed in the war on the very first encounter with the Germans on 23rd August 1914).

It is astonishing to think back to the circumstances of the young officer in 1914. He had to provide his own uniform and equipment which was comprehensive: 2 suits service dress, full dress, frock coat, mess kit, blue patrol tunic, sword, belt, revolver, uniform and boot cases, etc., etc. My parent [his term of address for his father] kindly paid for my outfit which I think cost about £100. The pay of a 2nd lieutenant was 5s. 7d. a day which amounted to approximately £100 a year and my parent gave me an allowance of £160 a year. Then there was, if lucky, two month's leave during which I could live free. On the debit side there was the mess bill which absorbed an absolute minimum of £6

10s. a month, and one had to pay for laundry and give soldier-servant and groom each 15s. a month.

This remuneration for a job involving responsibility, after having to provide all own clothing and equipment, not to mention having to pay for all the preliminary education, does not seem to have been exactly generous; however it sufficed then to permit of a very full life. I was never in debt and cannot remember ever feeling short of cash. In spring, summer and autumn one was very fully occupied with training, practice-camp and manoeuvres, but winter was the time when furlough could be taken and at Christmas time in 1911, 12 and 13, I spent my two months each year at Osberton.

In those days the horse was the end-all and be-all of life. I had a good government charger and General Bewicke-Copley (Commander South at Cork) very kindly gave me a black hunter mare (Biddy) and still better my grandfather gave a chestnut hunter (Marourene). I shipped the latter two horses and groom to England each year and to back up hired a horse from Bellamy of Grantham as well; and so it was (frost permitting) four day's hunting and two day's shooting each week of one's leave. More hunting of course on return to Ballincollig. Everyone hunted whenever possible, even the orderly officer who, however, was required to inform the orderly sergeant where the meet was!

When I returned to Ireland early in 1914 I hadn't a notion that the country was heading for a major war, training started as usual and my parent came out in June to see our practice camp at Glen Imaal in County Wicklow. It was soon after his visit that the Curragh Mutiny happened, a most peculiar affair in which a meeting of all officers was called and presided over by some high-ranking officer from the Army Council. At this meeting officers were required to choose between obeying orders to march against Ulster, or being dismissed from the service. Exception was made for anyone whose home was in Ulster and any such could 'disappear' for the period of hostilities! Also 2nd lieutenants were required to seek their

parents' advice before making a decision – my father cabled back from Portugal where he was staying at the time 'Cannot advise fighting loyal Ulstermen'. Thus it came about that every officer (bar one) chose dismissal and we put on mufti and command of the brigade was handed over to the regimental sergeant-major.

Within a few days, however, the whole position changed; war with Germany became imminent, the dismissals were declared to have been all a mistake, officers gladly put on uniform again and all thought turned to the matter of mobilisation. And so in due course to France and Belgium when on 23rd August 1914, the 120th Battery found itself with the advanced guard at the Mons Canal and fired the first 18-pounder rounds of the 1914–18 War.

* Brackenhurst, Southwell, Cockglode, Ollerton and Osberton are all situated in Nottinghamshire, east and north-east of Nottingham.

BELOW *The 8th Battalion Sherwood Foresters digging trenches at Scarborough Camp in 1911.*

FAMILY TREE

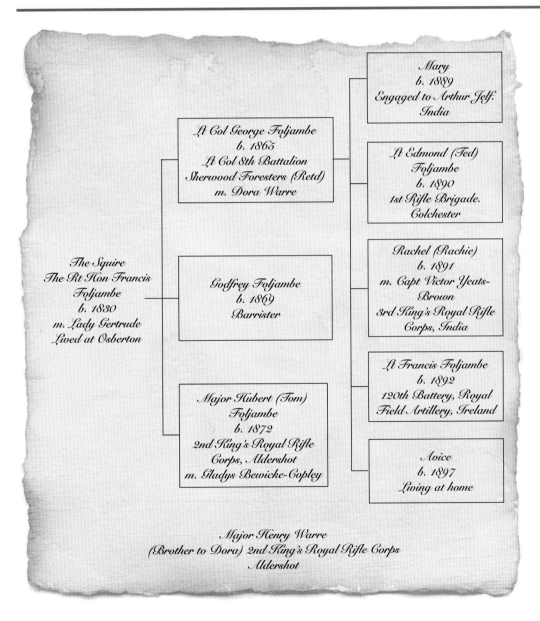

The Squire
The Rt Hon Francis Foljambe
b. 1830
m. Lady Gertrude
Lived at Osberton

Lt Col George Foljambe
b. 1865
Lt Col 8th Battalion
Sherwood Foresters (Retd)
m. Dora Warre

Godfrey Foljambe
b. 1869
Barrister

Major Hubert (Tom)
Foljambe
b. 1872
2nd King's Royal Rifle
Corps, Aldershot
m. Gladys Bewicke-Copley

Mary
b. 1889
Engaged to Arthur Jelf.
India

Lt Edmond (Ted)
Foljambe
b. 1890
1st Rifle Brigade.
Colchester

Rachel (Rachie)
b. 1891
m. Capt Victor Yeats-
Brown
3rd King's Royal Rifle
Corps, India

Lt Francis Foljambe
b. 1892
120th Battery, Royal
Field Artillery, Ireland

Avice
b. 1897
Living at home

Major Henry Warre
(Brother to Dora) 2nd King's Royal Rifle Corps
Aldershot

OPPOSITE *The Foljambe family. Front, left to right: Avice, Lady Gertrude, Francis Savile (the Squire), Rachie, Ted. Rear, left to right: Dora, Mary, George and Miss Egerton. Francis is not present.*

CHAPTER 1

The Foljambe Family

The head of the Foljambe family was the Right Honourable Francis John Savile Foljambe, known affectionately by all as 'The Squire'. Born in 1830, he had large estates in Nottinghamshire and Yorkshire and lived in some style in a country house at Osberton in north Nottinghamshire. The family had originally come to England in 1068 from Normandy as part of William the Conqueror's garrison troops and had spent the centuries consolidating their estates and marrying well. By the end of the 1800s the Foljambes were a wealthy land-owning family and firmly linked into and leading the local community.

The Squire had been MP for East Retford and High Sheriff of Nottingham and was a man of high morals and principles, determined to look after his estates and workers with benevolence, with Osberton as the centre of family life. It was a privileged life, particularly considering some of the deprivations of parts of Victorian England, but it brought with it great responsibility, commitment and a duty of care. He was married to Lady Gertrude Acheson, a daughter of the Earl of Gosford, with whom he had three children. At the outbreak of war he was 84 and had been married for 58 years. He was becoming very frail and the family were growing increasingly concerned about his health.

George Foljambe was the Squire's eldest child and was brought up initially as an only child at Osberton (his brothers Godfrey and Hubert were much younger) with his German nanny Freda. His parents were deeply fond of him and wanted to ensure that he was raised to understand and accept the responsibilities that would come from being the heir to the estates. He was sent to Bush Hill prep school at the age of 8. Most of his letters were from his mother and Freda, full of gossip and news of the family, but at some stage he seems to have transgressed and received the following missive from his father.

My dearest boy,

I was sorry to hear from Mamma that you had been very naughty at your lessons the day after you arrived at Bush Hill. It gave me great pain to hear such an account of you, and it must have given Mamma a great deal of pain to write it. You are not fulfilling the charge I gave you when I left, 'to take great care of dear Mamma'.

For every time you allow your temper to get the better of you, you give Mamma great anxiety; and nothing makes people ill and old sooner than anxiety. I am sure that you would be very sorry if I was to find Mamma looking sad, when I come to you next week, and to think you were the cause of it. You know that we hope and pray to see you grow up to be a good man, and able to be useful to those around you. You can never be this, unless you learn whilst you are young not to be the slave of your

OPPOSITE *The Right Honourable Francis John Savile Foljambe (the Squire) and Lady Gertrude Foljambe. The family can trace its roots back to 1068 when it came to England from Normandy, with William the Conqueror's garrison troops.*

Passions and of the Devil who likes to see you give way to them. You can not either be of much use, when you are a man, unless you learn now to think for yourself, and to use the talents that God has given you for improvement.

He will require an account of them in the Day of Judgement. Do you remember the Parable of the Talents? Now I must say goodbye, trusting, and with many prayers, that I may hear a better account of your conduct, and when I come that I may find Mamma pleased and happy with you. Give her my best love, and many kisses,
Your affectionate Father.

BELOW *Francis Foljambe (the Squire) with his eldest son George in about 1910.*

Poor George must have been quite struck by his father's letter, but it did not squash his character and he developed into a thoroughly decent young man. After prep school he moved on to Eton, which he enjoyed and it was there he first met Dora, the eldest daughter of the Revd Dr Edmond Warre, who was his housemaster and later headmaster and then provost of Eton. Dr Warre was one of those educated, humane, intimidating and moral men that the late Victorian era managed to produce. Dora remembered her first meeting with George in about 1878:

About this time George Foljambe came to Eton and fell ill from inflammation of the lungs – he was moved to our side of the house – Henry [Dora's brother] and I called him 'the little boy in bed' and as a great treat were taken to see him; one day when he was better we each took a pillow, evaded the nurses and threw them at him. We had a fine pillow fight. For the remainder of his time at Eton I do not remember seeing him till he came down on his return from shooting in Tibet and we married in 1888.

George was the heir to Osberton and the estates and was settled with a good income. He was very much a country gentleman who was both a keen huntsman and a good shot. George's great passion was the Volunteer Army. He had joined the local Nottinghamshire Volunteers in 1875 and each year attended the annual summer camp. The regiment was reorganised in 1905 and became the 8th Battalion, The Sherwood Foresters. It became part of the Territorial Army on its formation in 1907. George was eventually promoted to lieutenant-colonel and commanded the 8th Battalion, which he viewed as very much his. When he retired in 1913 at the age of 57 he had been with it, and its predecessor regiment, for 38 years. He knew every individual and had nurtured and encouraged the battalion through all its life. All the soldiers were local to north Nottinghamshire, the depot being at Newark, and many of the officers were his friends. The *Regimental Chronicle* for 1912 gave him a fond farewell:

Colonel Foljambe, during his eight years of command, has won the devotion of all the officers, non-commissioned officers, and men who have served under him, by his kindness and consideration for their well-being, and it is the greatest wish of the battalion that he may as an Unattached or Reserve Officer be a frequent visitor at Annual Training Camps. Under his command we have passed through the difficult transition from the Volunteer to the Territorial Force, and it is due to his untiring energy and enthusiasm that the battalion stands where it does today – the strongest in the Division.

George was 13 years older than his brother Godfrey and 16 years older than Hubert, so he had already left Eton by the time the younger two went to prep school (and later to Eton). Godfrey's greatest passion was cricket. A giant of a man at 6ft 6in, he played cricket for the Eton Ramblers for 14 years and was a renowned slow bowler. He went on to Cambridge University and became a barrister, practising in Herefordshire. At the outbreak of war he was 45 and was married to Judith Wright.

Hubert, the youngest, decided on a career in the Regular Army and after Eton joined the King's Royal Rifle Corps in 1895. He was a popular man with officers and soldiers alike and was known as 'Tom' amongst all his friends. His first taste of active service was in South Africa in the Boer War, where he served in 1901–2 as a captain with his regiment's 3rd Battalion. He acquitted himself well and saw action in Natal and Transvaal. He married Gladys Bewicke-Copley, daughter of a fellow Green Jacket officer, Brigadier-General Bewicke-Copley, in 1909 and at the outbreak of war was 42 and a major in command of B Company, 2nd Battalion, The King's Royal Rifle Corps, at Aldershot.

The final member of this generation was not a Foljambe but a Warre. Dora Warre, George's wife, came from a large family. She was the eldest of seven of whom only two were girls. Her favourite brother was Henry (whom she often called Harry) who was only four years her junior. One of Dora's early memories was of her father lecturing on Marlborough's campaigns and Henry inheriting masses of tin soldiers that had been used to show the disposition of the armies. From then on Henry's future was cut out; the schoolroom became a battlefield and Henry commanded an army mounted on a stick horse. It was no surprise when he became a Regular soldier and joined the King's Royal Rifle Corps in 1887, the same regiment that Hubert Foljambe would join seven years later. It is not known if Hubert joined because his brother-in-law was already serving but family connections mattered. Henry was on the staff in the Boer War and was awarded the Distinguished Service Order for showing considerable skill and leadership during the campaign. He later moved with the 3rd Battalion to India and was there in 1914. At

ABOVE The 8th Battalion Sherwood Foresters at their annual camp at Hindlow near Buxton in 1910. George was commanding officer and attended every year. Even when he handed over command he continued to visit right up until the outbreak of war.

ABOVE *Hubert Foljambe plays chess with his mother at Osberton in about 1885.*

the outbreak of war he was 48 years old.

The next generation of the family began with George's and Dora's children. George and Dora had a strong marriage and had three daughters and two sons. The first four children were born one a year, starting the year after George and Dora were married. Mary was the eldest, then came Edmond, known as Ted. He was followed by Rachel, whom they all called Rachie, and then came Francis. At the end came Avice, born six years later and very much the younger sister to them all.

Around 1902 George bought an estate at Sundet in Norway to which the whole family migrated each summer (though George always attended his unit's annual camp). All the children loved it and roamed free amongst the fjords and fells. Life at Sundet was quite basic but was bracing and energetic.

Dora had been brought up in an intellectual, dynamic and energetic house

dominated by her father at Eton. She had been exposed to intense debates and famous people from a young age and was a strong-willed woman, but did not apply the same standards to her daughters. Mary and Rachie were both taught at home and, although they had a happy childhood, were not allowed to follow their own paths. Mary had a love of music and was accepted as a student at the Royal College for Music. When Dora realised it would clash with her coming out for the season she withdrew her and Mary was launched on the social scene intellectually unfulfilled.

For Ted, the elder son, life was much more clearly mapped out. As the first grandson of the Squire, he would be the heir to the Osberton estate after his father. He went to Eton and then on to Oxford University, where he joined the Officer Training Corps. He then decided to join the Regular Army and was commissioned into

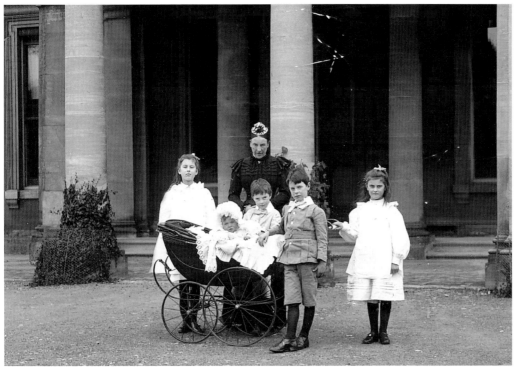

ABOVE *The Warre family. Henry Warre is standing on the right. Back row, left to right: A.F. Warre, GL, Rachie Foljambe, Mary Foljambe, Major Henry Warre, (King's Royal Rifle Corps). Seated centre is the Rev Warre, Provost of Eton. Avice and Dora Foljambe are seated second and third from the left.*

LEFT *The Foljambe children with their mother at the front of Osberton. Left to right: Mary, Avice (in pram), Francis, Ted and Rachie.*

ABOVE *A family group of Ted, Mary (at the rear with dog), Rachie (centre) and Avice (grinning), with a friend.*

the 1st Battalion, The Rifle Brigade, the sister regiment of that of his uncles, and joined his unit in Colchester in 1913. As his 1965 note has already explained, Francis had also decided to join the Army and in 1912 went to Woolwich to train to be an officer in the Royal Field Artillery. He had a fairly undistinguished tour, passing out in the middle of the field, but had made the hockey team. The RMA magazine reported he: 'has

filled the hard-working position of centre-half very well; very quick on the ball, seldom stopping it with anything but the stick; but when he does so, however, with his hand he is very apt to "hand ball", a trick which once acquired it is difficult to cure.' Whilst he was there he had his 21st birthday and was sent a travelling suitcase full of useful camping things by the Squire. Francis was very fond of his grandfather, who was also his godfather and wrote to him to thank him for the present. He got the following good advice with his reply:

I am much gratified to know that your suitcase gives you satisfaction; and I hope it may prove very useful and handy to you. On the other piece of paper, I have copied out for you the advice old Polonius gave his son Laertes, on his going into the world, and I would ask you to not be in a hurry to throw it away, but even to commit it to memory. For the affairs of this world no advice could be truer, and straighter, to elevate and strengthen the character, for the yet deeper and more important things that belong to Eternity. I have obviously commended the passages in Ecclesiastes *beginning 'Remember thy Creator in the days of thy youth' which I hope you will occasionally refer to, for all that can give happiness now, and peace at the last is contained in it. There is a great deal too much ignoring of the important relations that bind man to his Maker, and too little regard for the things that belong to our duty to God. For they and they alone shall bring a man to peace at last, and we can none of us know when that 'last' may be. Never be ashamed to confirm Jesus as your Master, as he is your Friend and your Redeemer. Before him, if you hope that he will confess you before his Father and be careful to say and do nothing that can imply a reproach against those, who are carrying his cross and banner through the unconverted world. There is a great chance for China now that her leading statesman is a Christian.*

God bless you my dearest Grandson and Godson and grant that the career you have now entered may be one of worldly honour and credit, and one in which you may serve your Creator as truly and faithfully as many of the distinguished soldiers who have borne the Cross, as well as the Union Jack.

Francis joined 120th Battery, Royal Field Artillery, stationed at Newbridge in Ireland at the end of 1912.

The End of an Era

The Foljambe family had a busy year in 1913. George had just retired from commanding 8th Sherwood Foresters and had more time on his hands, although he was determined to go to the annual camp in the summer. Francis was in Ireland with his battery and had been sent on a course in Limerick which

ABOVE *Ted Foljambe, the eldest son of George and eventual heir to the estates.*

had not much pleased him, as he relayed to his father:

I see Ted got his [cricket] Blue all right. Did you see the match on Saturday last? Pity there was so much fog on.

I hope you have got rid of your influenza. I can fully sympathise with you, as I have got an awful cold myself, from standing about on these dreadful ranges. Thank goodness we leave this on Saturday. They add injury to insult by making one pay to come on these courses! And it's not as if they taught us anything new. Everything so far I learned the first day I was at Woolwich. We shot Tables A & B the other day with the new rifle and pointed ammunition. It is an awfully good weapon. Far better than the old one and shoots very accurately indeed.

In spite of our touching a rifle once a year, our scores were far better than what the infantry here make which rather surprised them I believe. An examination ends the course tomorrow.

There hasn't been a drop of rain since I came here, most unusual at Limerick which is one of the wettest places in Ireland. I heard from Ballincollig that last week they had four extremely good hunts.

Ted I suppose will join at Colchester. They are due for foreign service in about two

BELOW *The 8th Battalion Sherwood Foresters marching at annual camp in 1911, led by the drums.*

year's time, so our instructor who is Rifle Brigade told me. That will be about the time I shall be going abroad I expect too. I sent back all the clothing to Bellamy before I came here. I suppose he has got it safely by now. I hear that the mare is very well indeed and getting wonderfully clever over banks. She has been schooled once or twice by a very good man at B'Colly, so I hope to get some more hunting when I get back.

With much love to Mother and Rachie
Yr affectionate son
Francis
P.S. I was nearly forgetting to congratulate you and Mother on your Silver Wedding!

The Squire was still on good form and corresponding regularly with Francis:

My dear Francis,
Thank you for your letter telling me of your arrival in Ireland, and having joined your battery. I am glad Bewicke-Copley is still at Cork. I should think he would be able to give you some useful and pleasant introductions.

We received your portrait yesterday and consider it a great success – perhaps a little stiff in the neck. I have no doubt you were so after a long sitting.

The Coal War has not yet produced an assault on Osberton or any other

BELOW *The Squire, Ted and George. Three generations of Foljambes at Ted's 21st birthday celebration in 1911.*

ABOVE *Osberton near Worksop in Nottinghamshire. It was known as 'the barracks' by the family. The meet is on the lawn with the hounds.*

OPPOSITE *Victor Yeats-Brown married Rachie Foljambe in 1914.*

'Castle' and I sit like a baron of old ready to summon my 26 retainers in defence if needful. The suffragettes are the more serious infliction; as if any man is rash enough or fool enough to marry them they will 'mox daturos progeniem vitiosiorem' – which, oh unlearned young man, means breed still more sinful offspring. Unrest and violence is more widespread over all the world than I ever recollect and China, which I hoped had settled her reforms, seems breaking out afresh in violence and murder. Still I hope they have begun a new era, and that under Sun Chang Yung, their Christian President, humanity and good will may be promoted.

Your father returned here on Monday. His leg is much better and he was able to ride with the hounds yesterday without any inconvenience or bad result. I hope you and your charger will soon part company, not in the field but by mutual consent.

We are having our regular March winds

and there is a great promise of apricot blossom which I hope may ripen in July. The grass is very green but hardly enough of it to make the lambs grow, of which we have a good crop. Granny sends her best love. She is very grateful to you for having sat to Lionel Fawkes.

There were two big family excitements. George and Dora had decided to go to India to visit Dora's brother, Henry Warre, who was serving with 3rd King's Royal Rifle Corps (3 KRRC) at Meerut. They decided to take Mary, who was now 25 and still unmarried. They were to set sail in October 1913 and planned to get back to England in May 1914, returning via South Africa and the Victoria Falls.

The second excitement was Rachie getting engaged. Her fiancé was Captain Victor Yeats-Brown who had served with Hubert Foljambe in South Africa and had been best man at his wedding. He was about to finish a posting in England and was then due to move out to India to rejoin 3 KRRC in Meerut. Rachel would then start married life in India and the family all decided to go out together. Victor's father was Monty Yeats-Brown who was British Consul in Genoa and subsequently Boston. He was godson of The Princess Royal, the eldest daughter of Queen Victoria. She, of course, became Empress of Germany and was the mother of Kaiser Wilhelm II. So Victor had complicated royal connections. For his part Hubert was particularly delighted that Rachie, his niece, was going to marry one of his best friends and wrote:

You little villain, my dear Rachie, running off with my best friend in this sort of way, and adding yet another nephew to my establishment of nephews – how dare you do it? Nevertheless you have acted very wisely, for I have very accurate knowledge of the virtues of your young man, to whom (if by chance you should see him) give my love. The exigencies of the pursuit of knowledge of musketry prohibit any longer letter writing at the moment, but this takes all my best wishes for your happiness now and always, and my congratulations to two very dear persons.

On 26th June, Rachie wrote to tell Francis her news:

I write off at once to tell you that your old prediction of the country parson has not come true.
    I was engaged yesterday to Captain Victor Yeats-Brown of the 60th. We hope to be married early in October, and go out to India by the same ship that Mother and Father and perhaps Mary go by. Mary wrote this week to say her second escort had failed her, so she would probably stay on till August.
    Father and I go to Sundet on Saturday week, the 5th. Victor is very likely coming too. We have to get back by the boat of the 30th for Father's camp which is to be in the Dukeries. I hope you have a good and dry time while in camp this summer. So far it has certainly not been so wet as last year.
    I can't help wondering what Grandpapa

will say to this news. I do hope you will get a few days' leave early in the autumn. I should hate to go away for good and all without seeing you.

George, Dora, Mary, Rachie and Victor all set out for India. They had a good trip out and Victor and Rachie went off to join 3 KRRC in Meerut and George and Dora went travelling, as described in a February 1914 letter to Rachie from Peshawar:

Thanks for your letter. The last I heard from your uncle was that we were going out on the 15th (my leg permitting). I am much looking forward to my first proper visit to your home and I will turn up for breakfast with Mother on Friday morning. This has been a tour full of interesting events and happenings. Though one has read of the frontier, one can hardly realise what life on the frontier means till one sees it. It gives one to think, when you go everywhere with armed escort. It is a lovely place and the officers of the local force were most kind and such good fellows. It unluckily elected to snow the night we got up to the Peiwar and we could not get up to the top.

We came here on Wednesday last, after one false start, as we ran into a bad storm on the Kobat Pass. Broke down and were hauled up by a crowd of hill men to the fort at the top, whence we telephoned to Mr Jelf to send us transport to bring us back to Kohat. Next day we successfully surmounted it. Friday we went to the Khyber and were allowed to Lundi Kotal and had a peep into Afganistan. Hope the Hindustani is getting on well. I'm afraid I have come to a deadlock. We are just going to some point-to-point races.

No time for more, being mail day. Ted had what might have been a serious adventure. He was staying in Suffolk and the house was burnt. He lost all he had but luckily his guns were saved. I hear he did

BELOW *Rachie (centre) and Victor Yeats-Brown (right), photographed on holiday in Sundet in the summer of 1914, soon after their engagement.*

good salvage work, which I was glad to know, but [he] has never written a word to his mother and me since we left England and it is difficult to keep up interest in his doings under the circumstances.

George and Dora Foljambe had had a fantastic trip in India, exceeding all their expectations and with the added bonus of seeing Victor and Rachie firmly settled into their bungalow in Meerut and Victor taking command of D Company, 3 KRRC, as a captain. In addition Mary was in love and engaged to a man of whom they thoroughly approved, and they left her behind with Victor and Rachie to follow on later. The man of Mary's choice was Arthur Jelf, who was with the Indian Civil Service, and they were engaged at the beginning of 1914. George and Dora came back through France to Portugal (they were unable to find passage to South Africa), with a wedding to plan in November. Mary and Arthur were to follow. Arthur had a brother Rudolf, who was also in the King's Royal Rifle Corps and was serving with Hubert in Aldershot.

Francis was settled into regimental life in Ireland. As he says in his 1965 note, he had taken a while to settle in, as he had not got on with his battery commander but the arrival of a new one, Major Holland, had changed his life for the better. He now had a battery commander he liked and respected and he was beginning to turn into an effective officer. Much of an officer's life in Ireland revolved around hunting, which was considered an essential accomplishment for artillery and cavalry officers. It taught them to use ground, identify and tackle obstacles, choose places of observation and fields of fire. Francis commanded a section of two guns and knew that in war they would be galloped into and out of action and it would be for him to choose the route and assist in the placement. The hunting had another serious purpose too, as training for the endurance required for spending long hours in the saddle on active service. The ability of the battery to survive rested on its mobility so the training and care of the horses was of particular importance – no horses and the battery would be next to

useless. In addition, much time was spent on section drill so that coming into and getting out of action became second nature to all the men.

Political events in Ireland were always in a considerable state of flux. The Liberal government was proposing an Irish Home Rule Bill and in March 1914 matters came to a head when it seemed set to become law. This threw the Protestant majority in Ulster into ferment at the prospect that the Catholic majority in the rest of Ireland might rule them. Volunteers were raised and armed and there was every prospect of a civil war. The Army might then be forced to intervene, but the natural loyalties of many officers were with the Protestants; many officers came from the Anglo-Irish community and many of the others were opposed on principle to the Liberal government. On 20 March the Commander-in-Chief Ireland, Sir Arthur Paget, made an alarmist speech to his senior officers which left them with a strong but false impression that they would be shortly ordered into Ulster to coerce the population into accepting Home Rule. The officers were offered a choice of being prepared to move to Ulster or accepting dismissal. The affair became known as the 'Curragh Mutiny'. Francis wrote about it to his father on the 24th:

Many thanks for your telegram just received. You will have seen in the papers all about this mess which the Govnt have got the country into, though half of what is reported is only a pack of lies. What happened as regards officers here was this. They handed round a paper which they said was from the War Office, giving all officers the choice between fighting Ulster or taking their dismissal; three-quarters of an hour to decide. After thinking it over I chose the latter course. Afterwards they gave us time for a reconsideration and as soon as I was allowed I wired to you. Next morning various generals came down and made speeches. The result was that most of the officers here changed their minds and agreed to go to Ulster. I stuck to my original decision. Soon after this we heard that the whole cavalry brigade had refused to move.

I see now in the papers that General Sir A. Paget denies stoutly that any ultimatum was ever offered to officers. Things seem to be at a standstill now and I hope the Govnt realise that they are in a rather ludicrous position.

The government backed off and, although there were many calls to 'discipline' the Army, much effort was put in place to calm down the officers and correct many misconceptions.

Dora and George were still on their travels. Dora was determined to keep in touch with Rachie and wrote a series of letters that often spanned days to keep her abreast of family news and gossip. Her first was started on 21 March on the train from Marseilles:

Here we are at last and very thankful I am – since Port Said we have had an odious time, very cold and very rough as the ports shut nearly all the time – and to make matters worse Father has got a bad chill which is still affecting him very much – he can take nothing but milk and is very weak, it began on board with one of his usual colds and then turned to fever. He was 100 degrees one day and 103 the next. I had to get in the doctor. With a crowded ship and rough sea and absolutely no place to go that was not cold, you can imagine it was not a happy time. I decided that we must go to an hotel on our arrival yesterday. We had sumptuous apartments with a sitting room and bathroom and a huge fire of logs – and today his temperature has been normal and I think he is better. We are now going to the Villa Albemarle and I hope he will soon be better. I too have got a cold so I hope we shall not prove too unwelcome guests for Cousin Charlie and Serena! Father is interested in the Daily Mail which gives an account of the excitement in the house over the Home Rule question, Sir E. Carson has gone off in a dramatic way to Dublin to direct operations.

I have been thinking much of you all and Arthur Jelf's visit which I hope was able to come off and I hope you and Victor like him and that the Easter visit will also

be able to be managed. I must send this to Ranikut – I expect you will soon be thinking of flitting and I am so glad you have Mary with you to help you with packing. The temperature here is 63 degrees inside my despatch box, but there is a cold wind outside and Father is abusing the cold tremendously and constantly regretting Africa. We have had it 86 in the Red Sea so there is a difference to contend with. We heard of snows in England so I am glad we are able to stay about here for a bit and look forward very much to seeing Victor's father and mother before we go to England. After our experiences I am not very keen about the journey home from Genoa by sea, especially as it loses half Avice's holidays. We shall hear from you by next mail I hope.

22nd March   Father went straight to bed on arrival and has had milk in a Thermos throughout the night. I have kept a fire going and this morning he is certainly better and is going to have some breakfast for the first time for four or five days! I trust now he will soon be better, but he will have to be careful as it is very cold here.

Please give my love to Mary and tell her I cannot write separately today but tell her Cousin Charlie and Gemma are enthusiastic about the Jelf family. I received a wire from John Jelf at Port Said and have written to him and now do not know how to send it as I cannot remember whether he is in the Egyptian Army or Civil Service.

I found letters from Grandmama and Avice here, I must say goodbye with very much love to you all.

Father is certainly better since breakfast but will be very difficult to keep quiet and warm, as he always thinks he is short of exercise. I have a horrid cold myself but have not had time to trouble much about it. Thunder and rain this morning.

Dora and George finally reached Portugal and were staying with the Yeats-Browns before moving to stay with Dora's Warre relations, who had settled in and established a considerable port business in Portugal. Dora started a new letter to Rachie on 6 April:

No one thinks or talks now without the subject of Ulster and the Army and Home Rule cropping up. The Govt. now try to make out that no questions were or should be asked before giving an order, but we know the question was asked and hostilities against Ulster were seriously contemplated, else why were Francis and the rest asked whether they would 'fight or be dismissed!' and given the choice. I am very glad this did happen as it shows the feeling in the Army against being used as a political tool – for one party against another – if there is to be civil war the Army must break up or stand in a body for the King; it is impossible they should fight side by side with and for the Nationalists who cheered every Boer Victory in the South African War. Our Army is not made up of paid levies. I do hope Ted's brigade will not be ordered to Ireland. I wonder if by the time you get back to England there will have been a revolution. I trust the Ulster people will keep calm. The meeting in Hyde Park seems to have been a success and very orderly.

7th April   We got a wire from Uncle Ernald to say he has started Avice [Avice had been left with one of Dora's brothers during their trip to India] with Harvey [a maid] off! How glad she will be and how I am longing to see her dear little face. It was very lucky she could get to Eton two days earlier to collect their things and start.

8th April   We expect Avice tonight, she goes to the Torre to sleep. I have been rather knocked up lately and have had four days more or less in bed which I consider too great a waste of such a nice place as this.

9th April   Avice has arrived half a head taller, thinner, smiling rosy and so happy to have at last got here. She came late last night and slept at the Torre where we shall join her on Saturday. Poor Harvey has had a toothache on the journey and must have been most agitated at having suddenly to come off to unknown lands! I have not seen her yet. Avice and I are sitting in the little garden house on the terrace garden at the Castello. Everything is so lovely that

one cannot help looking about instead of writing. With many kisses to you, my dearest, I must stop.

Someone told us a story that amused the aunts very much. During a debate in the House of Commons the other day on the Home Rule Bill, Mr Asquith speaking, Lady Londonderry made audible exclamations – 'What lies, what a pack of lies!' – Miss Asquith, also in the Ladies' Gallery, got very much annoyed and wrote 'you perhaps forget it is my father who is speaking' on her visiting card and sent it round. Lady Londonderry took no notice, but ejaculated more than ever – Miss Asquith then wrote a note hastily to the Speaker, asking for 'some objectionable people to be removed' and received the reply 'I regret I am too much occupied with the devils below to attend to the angels above.' A snub no doubt well merited. Though Lady L. is quite mad on the subject of H.R.

Meanwhile, back in Ireland, Francis's battery was soon back to work, as he wrote to his father on 24 April:

Many thanks for your letter. I am glad you have got back safely from your travels and I hope this will catch you before you leave Osberton. At present we are pretty hard at work, getting ready for camp early next month. Then more work getting ready for the main camp in July, but between those dates we shall have a few things like musketry and bridging which are not taken very seriously. If you were thinking of coming over, that would be the best time, but I will let you know later and also find out whether it is possible to put up in Newbridge which I doubt; if you do, bring a good supply of Keating! After July camp there is a fortnight of nothing to do and I think I shall get some leave there to see how my 'stud' is getting on and start getting things ready for next hunting season. When is Mary going to be married? I must make an effort to get over this time and make the acquaintance of one brother-in-law.

I heard from the Squire yesterday. I am glad he has decided to go away for the spring cleaning; at Xmas he was talking of not moving. Please thank him for his letter and tell him I am glad he has got a good foal out of his brown mare.

I have been studying prospectuses of ranching and farming in the colonies lately; I don't think the Army will be fit to stay in much longer! Edmond I suppose will be pushing off at the end of the year.

George visited Francis at the end of June, before the July camp, and was looked after, amongst others, by Francis's new battery commander, Major Holland, who wrote back to George after the stay:

Thank you for your kind letter. I'm afraid we didn't do much for you all the same. I did not exaggerate at all about Francis, who is quite one of the best young officers I have known. He is the greatest help to me.

We came down from the Glen today – had two quite good days' shooting to finish up. I see they talk about a deadlock again about Ulster. I wish the beastly thing was settled.

Back in England, Ted had settled in to 1 RB, though the battalion was short of officers. He started his regimental life as a platoon commander. Much of the training revolved around route marches, bayonet fighting (mostly for the men), musketry (which the regiment prided itself on), signalling, scouting and generally the education of the soldier in his duties. Ted also had time to pursue an active social life as London was within reach. His greatest passion was still cricket and in July every year the Green Jackets descended upon Winchester, their regimental home and training depot, to play cricket for a week against a number of opponents. The team was selected from the best of both the Rifle Brigade and the King's Royal Rifle Corps. Ted played all week, but there was one special game where the RB played the KRRC. Hubert came down to play for the KRRC and bowled his nephew for 29 in the first innings and caught him for 7 in the second, but the match still ended in a draw.

The spring and early summer passed peacefully but events in Europe were moving into crisis. In July Henry Warre came back to

BELOW *Practice camp at Glen Imaal in County Wicklow for 120th Battery RFA.*

England from 3 KRRC for some well-earned leave and was due a posting, so it was not yet clear if he would return to India at the end of his leave.

Dora was still writing from England to Rachie in India and her letters in July give a flavour of family events and gossip, with the occasional mention of wider events:

17th July   Uncle Henry arrives in time for breakfast from India looking well in spite of the tremendous heat he has been through. He stays at St James's Court as Ted is occupying our extra room together with Mary's trousseau and trunks. Father and I go to Holy Trinity Church in the evening. I had not been there since your [Rachel's] wedding and it all came back to me. We are now arranging for Mary's wedding to be there on October 5th, as Grandpapa's health is too precarious to allow it to be at Eton.

20th July   Mary and I lunch at Carlton Grill Room with the uncles and I go on to Bennington and Morse in the City with Uncle Harry and Avice to see about the black buck heads [shot in India], a good wholesale place.

21st July   Gwen [Henry's wife] arrived from Durham; she and Harry have an early tea and go down to Finch.

22nd July   Go to the oculist, Dr Ernald Clarke, and have my specs inspected. Father comes with me. My goggles are to be for reading only, the divided glasses made into pince-nez and the gold lorgnette made for reading so I shall be well fitted out soon. Father goes to fish at Walton with the Butlers.

24th July   Frank Bingham comes back from the War Office and says 'Ulster is nowhere. By this time next week we shall be mobilising!' A true prophecy, as after events show. I drive with Gemma to Hurlingham, sit by the river and then have tea. Then we drive on to Roehampton and watch some polo. We talk over arrangements for Mary's wedding – the Clarkes have most kindly lent us their house for the reception and we shall be at 21 De Vere Gardens.

25th July   Father, Mary and I go to St Margaret's Westminster. Father and Mary go to stay at Lennox Gardens.

27th July   Mary and I have a good deal of shopping to finish so we have a Daimler car morning and afternoon. Ted arrives for dinner.

28th July   Mary has a bad cold and I am tired so we decide not to go today to Bemerton [where Avice was at school]. Father goes to Osberton.

29th July   Mary in bed – I decide to go to Bemerton to see the Morris dancers this afternoon, am met by Nelly, Sybil, Mrs Fisher and Gwen, we drive up to the school. Lovely day and very pretty sight it is, a great surprise to Avice to suddenly see me – Miss

Douglas gives a very excellent report of her.

War-like news from Europe today, Austria has sent an ultimatum to Serbia and Russia and Germany may be drawn in. Henry fishing.

30th July *Stop in bed for fast. I am getting too fat with all this eating. Bemerton is very pleasant and nice and the dear presence of Aunt Nelly seems to be there always. Avice goes to Hove this morning with Lilian King for a week. Henry and Gwen go to Wilbury for tea.*

31st July *Sit out in N Shanty and Harry, Wen, Nell and I all go to sleep there in the afternoon, but are disturbed first by Mrs Fisher then by Lady Glengower who stops to tea and buys three of Nell's pictures – Mary arrives, having got rid of her cold.*

1st August *Rain, write letters, H. and G. go to Finch, H. has caught grayling and trout every day. We hear the fleet reserves are being called in.*

With this combination of domestic news and concern over international events Dora described the last days of peace. Menfolk throughout her family were already embarked on military careers and would soon see action.

ABOVE *Heathfield School's Ascension Day picnic at Burnham Beeches in 1910. Avice is here with the rest of her school.*

CHAPTER 2

Mobilisation – August 1914

The assassination of the Archduke Franz Ferdinand of Austria on 28 June 1914 sent shockwaves around Europe and, despite intense diplomatic efforts, war was becoming inevitable. The Army had quietly been preparing for this eventuality since 1910 and mobilisation had been very carefully planned.

In the years leading up to war the Army had been organised as never before to participate in a European war. The proposed British Expeditionary Force was to include most of the Regulars in six infantry divisions and one cavalry division. Hubert Foljambe and 2 KRRC were in 2nd Brigade of 1st Division; Ted Foljambe and 1 RB were with 11th Brigade of 4th Division and Francis Foljambe was with 120th Battery in 27th Brigade, Royal Field Artillery, in 5th Division. (Artillery brigades and infantry brigades were different organisations; in 1914 an infantry brigade had 4 battalions, usually from different regiments, each of roughly a thousand men; most Regular artillery brigades had 5 batteries, with 76 guns of 3 different types, and roughly 800 men in all.) Hubert, Ted and Francis would all go to France at the outbreak of the war. When war began the Regulars then serving with the colours would be reinforced by reservists recalled from civilian life.

The next source of reinforcements for the Army came from the Territorials. These part-time volunteer soldiers served in county regiments which in turn were formed into 14 Infantry Divisions and 14 Cavalry Brigades. A depot system of training battalions was set up to improve training standards and ensure there was a strong link between the Regulars and the Territorials. Military committees were created in each county which were responsible for the administration of the Territorial Force. George Foljambe's 8th Sherwood Foresters was in the Notts and Derby Infantry Brigade alongside the 5th, 6th and 7th Sherwood Foresters, other Territorial battalions from the regiment. Newark was the depot of the 8th Sherwood Foresters. The Stafford Infantry Brigade and the Lincoln and Leicester Infantry Brigade completed the North Midland Division (which would later become 46th Division).

Finally, there was the large army in India, both British troops and the locally recruited Indian Army. In 1913 the government of India agreed to provide two, possibly three divisions, and one cavalry brigade in the event of a serious war between Britain and a European enemy. Victor Yeats-Brown's and Henry Warre's 3 KRRC was one of the battalions earmarked for the move to Europe.

Mobilisation instructions for Regular and Territorial units were held in a huge document known as the 'War Book'. This laid down (and there was a blank space against which one inserted the name of the enemy!) exactly what was be done to pull together all the threads to deploy the Army. In addition to calling up the reservists to make up the

OPPOSITE *Ted wearing the dress uniform of the Rifle Brigade.*

shortfall in men, all was planned to the last detail; on which day and how each battalion would move from its barracks to its point of embarkation. The detail was Top Secret but the orders were crisp and sharp, as these examples show:

> Train No 463Y will arrive at siding B at 12.35 a.m. M+6
> You will complete loading by 3.40 a.m.
> The train will leaving siding C at 9.45 a.m. M+6 . . .

In addition, the horse was the bedrock of mobility of the Army and the government had carried out a census in 1910 (which was updated) of all the horses in Great Britain and 120,000 were earmarked to be requisitioned on mobilisation. They had options to buy them all for up to £70 each (this sum compared with the shilling a day that was the pay of a soldier or an annual salary of £18 5s 0d a year).

On 29 July the government ordered 'precautionary measures' to meet an immediate prospect of war to be put in force. These affected the Regular troops only, and included the recall of officers and men on leave and the manning of coast defences. 1st Rifle Brigade was one of the units involved and Ted Foljambe found himself at Harwich for the next week with the task of defending the port, trying to stop German reservists from getting back to Germany and searching for spies. The big excitement was providing the guard of honour for the outgoing German Ambassador.

On 3 August 1914 Great Britain declared war on Germany and on the 4th mobilisation proper started.

Dora's letter to Rachie in India continues:

2nd August   *Stormy day, go to church and Mary and I stay for the Holy Communion. In the afternoon I go with Uncle Frank to Fugglestone where he does the service and preaches. Call on the Fishers, and find them sitting over a fire in great heat. Major Fisher is collecting horses. The rumours of war are increasing.*

Hear that the Reservists are being called out. Two trains of troops said to have left Salisbury for Colchester today. Germany has threatened France and Russia.

3rd August   *Sit in the shanty – serious news, Germany has invaded Luxembourg. We shall have to help France. Hire a car and drive to Stonehenge, Mary, Sybil, Nell and I. I have never seen it, it is much compacter than I expected. Many camps all around and many Territorials came to have a look at Stonehenge before leaving. They were all ordered home before mobilising and had been up one or two days. We went to Amesbury for tea. We went to see the church, which Edmond Bear had had to repair, a very large church, far too large for the parish. There had been a convent there in which Queen Guinevere lived. The Archdeacon of Dorset, Mr Dundas, comes to stay.*

4th August   *Hear that the aunts have at last got over by Flushing also Florence and Madeleine Slade who were at Bayreuth. [They had] a most disagreeable journey back, I believe, with 900 on a boat that usually takes 200. Today England declares war on Germany who has attacked Belgium. Father's camp has been dispersed and he has gone to Newark to the depot to get all ready for mobilisation. I go on the 10.23 train and arrive at Winchfield only 40 minutes late where Joan meets me. I leave Mary at Bemerton to see Aunt Margaret who is expected today. Stations full of soldiers and machine guns and stores waiting about. Find poor Grandpapa not at all well and in bed and Grandmama anxious. Uncle Henry goes up to the War Office to see if he can find something to do.*

5th August   *Drive to Wokingham to meet Ernald and Felix and to Wellington to tea with Violet. They have taken the Maconoghey's house. Grandmama comes too and I try to telephone to Bemerton in vain and am getting anxious now to meet Mary and Avice tomorrow. Harvey was to fetch Avice and Lady King find an escort from Hove and I have had no reply to my telegrams.*

Francis was sitting in Ireland and worrying what to do with his belongings:

Dear Father,

I think the best thing to do with my kit in the event of mobilisation is to get it all over to Osberton. Here it will be motheaten and probably stolen – would it be possible to send someone, Fred for instance, over to bring some of the more valuable things, like a suitcase etc. and to dispatch the rest of the stuff by goods? It is of no use my trying to send anything during the rush of mobilisation and after we have marched out there will be no one left who will have interest in the matter.

If somebody came over just before we left, he could take over the luggage and when things have quieted down a bit he could have it dispatched. I wouldn't trust the railway people to look after it – they are just like all the Irish railway people. All this stuff is insured and the policy is at Cox's. What do you think about this plan?

I don't see how mobilisation can be delayed much longer!

P.S. I have got a list of my belongings which I will send you if we go to the wars, so that you can call the roll when the things arrive at Osberton. There is also my motor bike to get over. This is also insured through Cox. It lives with Mr Wood's Garage, Newbridge, but if we go, I will try and sell it and I will let you know what I do about it.

Sorry to trouble you with all my private

ABOVE *120th Battery RFA parading at the Curragh in Ireland, 1914. At the front is Major Charles Holland, Francis Foljambe on the left, Bulteel in the centre and Lindsay on the right. Holland was killed in 1914, Bulteel and Lindsay in 1918.*

affairs but I think it just as well that someone should know of them or half of them could be lost and none any the wiser.

Four days later Francis was in Glasgow, sent by the brigade to pick up some reservists to fill the ranks. He was particularly worried about his chestnut mare at Osberton, writing to his father of his fears that the Army might buy her up:

I wonder if the government will want to take the horses at Osberton. If they do, you might stick out for the full £70 for my chestnut mare – that is the maximum they give – I have taken one of the Kildare Hunt horses as my second charger. I am here collecting reservists and am taking about 500 back to Newbridge tonight. Thank goodness by sea, so they won't be able to run away. I wonder when we will be

moved. I hope to hear some news when I get back to Ireland tomorrow morning. I heard from Edmond the other day. He has been living in a redoubt for the last week on the east coast looking for spies!

It is a horrible journey up here by rail, three changes between 2 and 3 a.m. at Chester, Warrington and Carlisle: I am glad I haven't got to go back that way. With much love to all.

I rather wish I had brought the mare over to Ireland together with the other horse. If I had to sell her to the government I would like to have had her myself – but very likely you will be able to hide her.

Francis had rather a rough trip back from Glasgow to Dublin on 7 August on the SS *Tiger*. He collected a receipt from the chief steward for refreshments for 452 men at 2s a head, the sum of £45 4s 0d. Presumably

about 50 of the 500 reservists were too busy feeling seasick to eat.

9th August 1914

Dear Father

Thanks for your letter. Just got back here from Glasgow. It would be very kind of you if you could send William over to fetch my things. The best time for him to come will be the night before we leave the station and I will wire you when that will be. Of course we have no orders yet. I will have everything packed and labelled and ready to hand over to William when he arrives, and all instructions. We have pretty well finished mobilisation now. Horses of all colours, sizes and shapes! I have spent the morning getting them into trains – a lot of them are very refractory and afford a lot of amusement. I got my draft of 500 men over alright and only lost two or three of them.

We had an awful tossing between Greenock and Dublin.

The horses they had were of high quality but were mostly hunters brought up from grass and therefore quite unfit and not trained for draught work, but the battery had to be prepared to take the field. Many of the reservists had not sat on a horse for years. The sight of a heavy handed, and now somewhat portly artillery driver on the back of a hunter, fresh up from grass and which had never been in harness in its life, was quite a trial. However, horses and men were absorbed into 120th Battery and the rest of the brigade. Francis was still trying to sort out the final arrangements for his kit, as he wrote to his father on 10 August:

I have been discussing the situation with the railway authorities and they seem very doubtful whether any luggage would arrive safely – I think now that I will warehouse the stuff here. (1) It won't cost so much as sending it over and (2) it will save you losing William. In addition I have got someone to take and look after a few more valuable things for me. When we get orders to leave (which I think will be in a day or two) I will send you a list of all the stuff and where to find it, so that when I am blown up by a German shell, you will be able to check it and claim any damage if necessary.

My motor bike, separately insured at Cox's, will also be warehoused, Vaselined and in a crate. We are about ready to move now.

The reference to being blown up by a German shell will not have pleased his mother, but he sorted out his kit, continued

the training with the battery and on Saturday, 15 August, eleven days after mobilisation, Francis set out for war.

Whilst Ted was in Harwich, great preparations were being made back in the barracks in Colchester and in the regimental depot in Winchester. The reservists for both the Rifle Brigade and the King's Royal Rifle Corps were all initially entered through the depot at Winchester, a process not without its problems. The War Book had allowed for an influx of 800 men on the first day but by the evening of 5 August over 3,000 had reported. It had proved impossible to accommodate them all in the depot itself and large numbers spent the night in churches, school and college buildings, and many even slept in the streets. To add to their discomfort it had started to rain hard early in the afternoon and continued to do so until late in the evening.

The next day the rush continued so

BELOW *Crowds outside Buckingham Palace cheer King George, Queen Mary and the Prince of Wales following the declaration of war on Germany, 3 August 1914.* **IWM Q81832**

they were formed into batches of 500 and marched to the football ground to be out of the way until they were needed. Feeding was a problem but eventually they were all given something to eat and drink. They were all in tremendous spirit, and were all very anxious to get to their regiments. Numbers of them were time-expired but begged to be allowed to rejoin and once they were processed they were sent to their battalions.

On 8 August Ted wrote to his father:

I wonder if you would settle up these bills for me out of my next allowance as I am overdrawn at the bank. My allowance will, however, cover the overdraft and these bills. There are one or two that haven't come in yet, but they are all very small.

My company has just come back from Harwich where we have been for a week. Our party were very successful and collected a lot of German reservists on Parkeston Quay, who were sent for me to look after in one of the redoubts. There was very little sleep to be had then, but it was just good fun. We are getting on splendidly with the mobilisation, and there seems a possibility of our moving somewhere tomorrow.

It rather looks as if the German scheme is a bit upset by Belgium putting up such a good show. And if Russia can get moving soon, it ought to be sufficient for them.

Had I better send my belongings back to Osberton? There are a lot of clothes etc. which are doing no good roughly packed away without any anti-moth stuff.

By the way, also could you get hold of £5 in gold for me – I can't get it here.

In Colchester they had a problem with boots. The regulation issue proved to be unsuitable (history does not relate why) and they had to ransack the local shops for civilian footwear, which they then waterproofed by soaking in oil. Many of the soldiers therefore started out with boots that were not only unsuitable but unbroken in. By 8 August mobilisation was complete and from that date to the 17th time was devoted to intensive training in barracks. It was not

without its problems, as Ted's letter of 11 August showed:

Thank you very much for sending the money. The banks are hating to part with any gold and it's the only coin worth anything I imagine abroad just now. Thank you also for seeing about those bills.

We are walking hard every day to try and get some of the beer out of the men, and are succeeding well, helped by some hot weather. I hear we are in for a heat wave. There is nothing exciting doing here except that the transport are a bit unruly occasionally. Most of the drivers have never worn spurs and none of the horses have ever been ridden with them or with blinkers, – result, one of our wagons finished up in my platoon yesterday after taking away most of the drill shed, and as we marched out of barracks this morning, one of the Hampshires' wagons was going well up the barracks.

The discomfort here is awful – bare rooms and little to eat, and I hope we get away soon.

I was inoculated the other day and am still feeling the results, and am not feeling like doing it again yet. Well, I must stop now and get on with a job of sorts.

On 18 August the battalion moved to Harrow and camped on the school playing fields where it spent three days in intensive training. On the 22nd, 24 officers and 964 other ranks entrained for Southampton before dawn.

Much the same was happening to Hubert Foljambe with 2nd King's Royal Rifle Corps at Blackdown Barracks in Aldershot. Mobilisation was ordered on 4 August and on the 6th they collected most of the horses required for the battalion transport from Aldershot. Each horse had to be fitted to its harness and two civilian saddlers and a farrier had been sent the day before by the Board of Trade to do this work– escorted by a Boy Scout.

Two batches of Reservists arrived, the first of 220 in the afternoon and the second of 350 at 10.30 p.m. They were a fine lot of men and full of enthusiasm; only a few were in soft condition or badly nourished. Reservists would form over 50 per cent of the battalion as it went to war.

The battalion was due to move on the 8th but the day before was told that it had been postponed. There was trouble with some of the horses, which were objecting to being put into draught and were unfamiliar with their drivers. The whole battalion went for a route march for 2 hours, the horses worked much better and only three men fell out, being exchanged with three others in the waiting details.

The new date for deployment was set for 12 August so they continued training, which included every reservist firing ten rounds on the range (apparently with satisfactory results). Another route march followed and

on the 11th they lined each side of the road in the barracks and the King drove through. The battalion was photographed and there was a special photograph of the 182 men who had served in South Africa.

Henry Warre, meanwhile, had been working at the War Office, trying desperately to ensure that he was not sent back to India, and managed to get orders to join 2 KRRC just as it was about to deploy. So, on 12 August, before dawn, when the battalion boarded two trains for Southampton Docks, Hubert and Henry were both aboard.

For the Territorial Army the story was rather different. The 8th Battalion, Sherwood Foresters, was at annual camp in the Dukeries at the end of July and the atmosphere was so charged that the men had found it impossible to settle down to the normal routine of

BELOW *8th Battalion the Sherwood Foresters marching at annual camp, 1911.*

training. George was no longer in command – he had handed over to Lieutenant-Colonel Huskinson the year before – but he still liked to go to camp on the Territorial reserve.

On 4 August, when war was declared, the camp was broken up and all ranks ordered home with instructions to hold themselves in readiness for any emergency. On joining, Territorials had agreed to be called up for full-time home-defence duties in the event of war. Many had also signed the Imperial Service Obligation, which meant they could be sent abroad; in the event almost all would agree to overseas service soon after war broke out.

On the 5th and 6th they mobilised by companies at various locations in the county. In all 29 officers and 852 other ranks joined the battalion. The War Book had not been completed in all instances for the Territorial Army and the first task was to try to equip the men with underclothes and other necessities. This was quite an undertaking and shops were searched throughout the area and their stocks bought up. On the 7th the battalion concentrated at Newark and was billeted in local schools. The next task was to gather together a transport train for the battalion. When buying local horses they could pick the best, but the wagons were a very eclectic collection. Floats from Warwick and Richardson's and Hole's (all local traders) formed the majority of the small-arms ammunition and tool carts, and Dicken's Mineral Water drays and Davy's brewery drays were made into general-service wagons. A furniture van full of blankets, two corporation water carts and a bread cart with a large red cross on each side completed the collection.

Whilst all this was going on, Dora wrote again to Rachie in India:

I am so glad to get your letter and telegram this morning, forwarded from Bemerton to Finch – the telegram tells us a lot we want to know. I am thankful you have engaged a nurse for October. I hope she will be a great help and support to you. It will not be so expensive as if the journey had to be paid and now, even if I had got Nana or someone else to go, it might not be possible to travel out in such times as these. It is a good thing you have received six of the eight parcels and I hope amongst them the box from Clayton and Bell? I was afraid the coat and skirt might be too large but I hope it may easily be fitted. I got a wool stuff as it might be more useful than cotton. I doubt now if I shall be able to send you any more parcels and I am glad that in the last one was included your birthday present and now you have got the cot so will be pretty well fixed up for things. I hope the binders will reach you soon.

I trust this terrible war will be over by March and all quiet again for your return. It is almost impossible to believe that all these civilised nations are grappling with each other. The feeling in England is

*splendid and the differences in Ireland
which the Kaiser and his people traded
upon have vanished. Mr Redmond's
splendid speech has done more for Ireland
and unity and good will than all the
striving after Home Rule. I am thankful
to have Mary and Avice with me again,
having been very anxious about how we
should meet, all coming from different
places. The railways [have been] taken over
by Govt. for troops and transport, and
[there are] rumours of bridges being blown
up by German spies – Avice came up with
a cousin of the King's at Hove with whom
she had been staying and this girl has come
from Paris after a fearful journey with no
luggage having lost all that she brought
with her, money and everything. She said
people were fainting from exhaustion – a
three-hour wait in Paris and six hours at
Dieppe. She is going to her home near York.*

*Uncle Henry went up on Thursday to
the War Office and, after waiting about
a long time and seeing a lot of people, he
went away and then was recalled by a
porter running after him, and given a post
immediately on the staff of the press censor
and is now on duty from 8 a.m. to 8 p.m.
I took his luggage to him today and found
him in bed trying to sleep but there was
a band playing outside so he said it was
impossible. He said he would get up and
follow me to King's Cross so we have met
and lunched there and just before the train
started Mary and Harvey arrived – raining
hard, and ages to wait at Salisbury. The
early train they were to have gone by did
not start nor the next one, and so they only
just got up in time.*

*I found Grandpapa not at all well in
bed, and with two nurses. Grandmama is
just beginning to realise how ill he is and
is very anxious, though she does not say
much. Last night I heard his bell ringing
incessantly and got up and the night nurse
said she was ringing for John to help her
to lift him in bed so I helped her with him.
He is very heavy and is given a drug at
night which makes him very helpless, poor
dear. Three more times during the night
she called for assistance and I got up but*

*the last time, 5.30 a.m., called for John as
it was pretty hard work and at last John
heard the bell.*

*Gwen was sad but philosophical about
the sad news of poor Teddy Bruce's death. I
hope Blue will be all right. Father has work
at the depot at Newark – I am so glad for
him that he is employed. Ted is at Harwich
in a redoubt. Francis I have not heard
from. Uncle Hubert may have to go with the
expeditionary force, good for him but I am
sorry for little Gladys if it is so. I trust the
3rd Battalion will not be wanted at present
for your sake, my dearest. But we must all
do our best for the Empire.*

Back in Newark, on 10 August the 8th
Sherwood Foresters paraded in the market
place. In front of a great crowd the mayor
gave a short speech and the vicar held a short
service; they then marched off down the Fosse
way to Radcliffe-on-Trent, followed by their
transport which looked rather like a travelling
circus. George was right in the middle of all
this activity and was immediately picked to run
the depot at Newark now that the battalion
was deploying. He was responsible for helping
them to put it all together and then to train
as many officers and soldiers as he could and
send them out as reinforcements.

The battalion spent two days marching to
Derby (37 miles), which was very hard on
the men's feet, and there they spent the next
three days on more marching to toughen
everyone up. They then moved to Luton by
train and ended up in Harpenden, where
they were to spend the next three months
preparing for war.

Newark and its citizens rallied around and
on 15 August the mayor called a meeting in
the town hall to consider how best to assist in
raising recruits as Lord Kitchener had asked
them to muster a second battalion. George
was there of course and the hall was packed,
with many standing. The meeting started
with the mayor describing a telegram he had
received from Buckingham Palace asking
Newark to contribute to the 'Prince of Wales's
Fund' – which was being set up to support
the Soldiers' and Sailors' Families' Distress
Fund and the Patriotic Fund.

The mayor then gave a rather long speech
about the history of Nottingham Volunteers
(going back to 1138!) and the Sherwood
Foresters before outlining Lord Kitchener's
recruitment plans. The mayor added that he
was going to seek out those men suitable for
this service, and get them to offer themselves
at this time. It would be a proud thing that
their children should know that they or
someone related to them possessed a medal
for this war, the greatest war, he believed in
history, and he hoped the last great war that
would ever occur. (Hear, hear and applause).
He then handed the stage to George, whose
speech was reported in the local paper.

Colonel G.S. Foljambe, who was the next
speaker, said that England had always been

a peace-loving country; this war was none
of our seeking, but honour and friendship,
to say nothing of self-preservation, had
drawn them into it, and once in it, he
thought they were all agreed they were
going through with it. (Applause) Germany
had been building up her fleet for many
years past with no other object than to talk
to us when the time came. Years ago it
was prophesied that about 1913 or 1914,
Germany would feel herself able to talk to
us at the gate. He had mentioned that fact
very often, but he had been jeered at for
a bloodthirsty jingo. (Laughter) But thank
goodness, providence so arranged matters
that it was not Germany that struck us, but
we were in a position to strike Germany,
and it was in time to prevent a great deal

of mischief and disaster that would have been carried out in this country by the large number of German aliens who had infested it for years past. Referring to the present situation he said that he had been put on a job that was new to him, and that was office work. The time came when he had to make way for younger men. His physical fitness was no longer what it was some ten years ago, when he had the honour of commanding the County Regiment for the full period. (Applause) But quite rightly the time came for somebody younger to take it on. He could have only wished he could have knocked five years off, and been where Colonel Huskinson was now. (Applause) He was on the Territorial Force Reserve, and the only thing he could do was apply for such work as came to him, and he was asked to take on this job; it was all new work, and he could hardly find his way about his new office yet, but so far as he could make out the difficulty was that men were anxious to come, but the machinery for taking them was not yet perfected. He was not going to encroach upon this matter, but there would be work for everybody before long. What he wanted at present was for some good fellows to fill up the ranks of the old Territorial Regiment. He had been at the County Association meeting that day and he understood there would be recruiting stations established in Newark, Retford, Mansfield and Worksop, and those wishing to join Lord Kitchener's Army would apply at those depots. That was as far as they had got at present. They hoped the necessary papers would soon be in hand, when they would be able to proceed with the recruiting.

After much further discussion Alderman Knight made a speech:

'Gentlemen, I wish I were 35 instead of nearly 70. (Applause) But although I am about 70 in age I am 35 in spirit.' (Applause) He then went on to say 'that there were two things required in recruits. Candidates must have two special qualifications, they must be able to see well and have good feet, and those matters must not be overlooked. If candidates had not those qualifications then they should not offer themselves, because it would be spending money unnecessarily, besides being disappointing to the men themselves. The War Office were not so particular about teeth as they were ten years ago.'

It was clear that Newark would support its Territorial battalions and that George would be very heavily involved in every aspect of it over the coming months.

Dora's letter to Rachie in India continues:

7th August   *Absolute quiet at Osberton – I hire a car and drive over to Newark to see Father who stays with the Applebys and works at the Drill Hall. Godfrey and Mary come with me. Tea with Mrs Appleby. Mansfield Company, last to come in, arrives while we are there, the 8th Notts Batt. is to move to Derby on Monday and then Father is left at Newark with a company to guard the railway and a bridge over the Trent. He has a bad cold but is content as you may imagine to have definite work.*
9th August   *I encourage Granny to go to London to see Hubert before he starts in the expeditionary force, Godfrey is to go up with her. Italy remains neutral and the [German warships]* Goeben *and* Breslau *have to leave Messina in 24 hours. We saw them at Portofino in attendance on the* Hohenzollern. Goeben *is faster than many of our ships – she can go 32 knots. Shall we catch her?*
10th August   *Uncle Hubert is in the expeditionary force. Granny is anxious to see him before he goes, so Uncle Godfrey takes her to London and they are to stop at the G.N. Hotel. I go with them to the station and then represent Granny at a meeting got up by the Duchess of Newcastle and Lady Robinson to establish some means of working during the war at needlework or relief work of some kind. I send to the Red Cross for patterns of the most necessary garments. General Ruck Keene comes to stay a night which is nice for Grandpapa – Avice and Doris bathe in the lake near the waterfall!*

CHAPTER 3

Mons, Le Cateau and the Retreat

Advance to War, 12–22 August 1914

The original plan of British mobilisation had been for all six infantry divisions and the Cavalry Division to deploy to a concentration area near Maubeuge on the left wing of the French Army. The 1st (with Hubert and Henry) and 2nd Divisions deployed together in I British Corps under the command of General Haig and the 3rd and 5th (with Francis) Divisions formed II Corps under the command of General Grierson (who died during August and was replaced by General Smith-Dorrien) and, with the Cavalry Division and an additional cavalry brigade and some extra infantry battalions, made up the initial deployment. The 4th Division (with Ted) and 6th Division were initially held back.

OPPOSITE *Men of the 2nd Scots Guards and 2nd Gordon Highlanders on the SS Lake Michigan at Dover, en route to France.*

LEFT *Men of the BEF, newly arrived in France, march along a cobbled street. Many of them would be dead before the year was out.*

The Germans also did not know where
the BEF was or its plans. On 20 August
the commander of the German First Army,
General von Kluck, advancing through
Belgium against the French left wing, was
told that 'a landing of British troops is
reported at Boulogne. It is believed that a
disembarkation of British troops on a large
scale has not yet taken place.'

The 2nd Battalion, King's Royal Rifle
Corps, embarked on 12 August on the
SS *Galeka* alongside the 1st Battalion,
Northamptonshire Regiment. Getting the men
aboard was easy – they just walked up the
gangways – but the horses were a different
matter. All the big horses had to be slung on
board by a derrick, and stowed far down in
the interior of the ship. The smaller horses
and cobs were walked on board up a steep
gangway, across a deck and down another
gangway into rather cramped quarters on the
main deck. In all 2,313 officers and men and
140 horses set sail for Le Havre.

They docked the following morning and
disembarked the men. The horses were a
worse problem as there were no stevedores
and the machinery for lifting the horses
and vehicles out of the hold was very ropy.
They left behind a party to get them out
and the battalions marched to a rest camp
that had been set up by the French. They
were the first to arrive and the route was
memorable, as it took them up a cobbled
road (very uncomfortable on the feet) to the
top of an extremely steep hill. Luckily they
marched in the cool of the morning but for
other regiments, which continued to pour in
during the sweltering hot day, the hill was
an enormous challenge to many of the unfit
reservists, and many men dropped out. The
evening was brightened up by the senior
major foraging in the town and returning with
a decent quantity of beer, which the men
drank gratefully but complaining that it was
far too light.

During 14 August a route march was

undertaken. It was oppressively hot and not helped by the guide making a wrong turn, which resulted in a march of 5 miles becoming one of over 7 miles. Many men, and particularly the reservists, gave up near the end and had to be swept up by the transport.

Just after midnight the battalion left the camp during a thunderstorm. One of the travelling kitchens overturned on the road and the whole convoy was held up for 20 minutes whilst it was righted. Everyone got soaked to the skin as they continued the march to the station. They arrived at 1.30 a.m. and got onto the longest train they had ever seen which took the whole battalion plus its transport. It had a carriage with seats for the officers, 8 open wagons for the transport and 30 other carriages labelled 'Hommes 40: Chevaux 8', which was fine for the *chevaux* but awful for the *hommes*. The men scrambled on board to get out of the rain, the horses were led up steep wooden ramps and in 2 hours the train was loaded. The lightning had helped as the lights from the station were so weak. They then waited in their wet boots and kit a further 2 hours for the train to leave.

It was extremely uncomfortable for the men since they could not all either sit or lie at the same time. After daybreak the sun got up so many sat in the open doors and some even ventured onto the roofs, although they had to keep a close eye ahead for low bridges. Every station was thronged with French men, women and children, cheering and shouting. The troops gathered flowers, flags, and more usefully cigarettes, food and sweets handed out as they passed through.

They detrained at Busigny and were bedded down for the night close to the station in the local glass works (fresh straw provided). On the 16th they marched to company areas and were billeted in farms where they were well looked after by the French and fed with fresh bread, butter, milk and cheese. Their abiding memory was the all-pervading smell of ripe cheeses that seemed to be kept in the bedrooms of the farmers.

The following day was again hot and they started to take the possibility of an attack seriously, although they had little idea of the location of the Germans. They washed their clothes (every soldier only had one shirt so it was important that they should dry!) and in the evening blocked the roads leading into their area with farm machines and carts to ensure they were not taken by surprise. The next three days were again boiling hot and they rested and spent most of the time in their billets. On 21 August they were told that German cavalry had reached Brussels, with a very large force moving up behind them. They set off again for Etroeungt at 7.30 a.m. and marched for 3 hours and 9 miles. The road was crowded with other members of the division and with refugees and they had to wait for the village to clear before they could reach their billets.

The following day they were roused at 3.30 a.m. and got sudden orders to march at 4.10 a.m., which was much earlier than they had expected. Consequently no fires had been lit so there was no food before they set off. They marched through Avesnes to 4 miles from Maubeuge, where they halted at 10 a.m. The lack of food, the length of the march (they were to cover 25 miles before the day was done), the heat and the dust had their effect on the men, several of whom were done up. Luckily they managed a long halt, cooked up some food and snatched some sleep by the roadside.

They moved off in the afternoon to billets in St Remy-Mal-Bati and were settled in by 3.15 p.m. An hour and a half later they got orders to march at once and at 5.50 p.m. set off again. They marched through Maubeuge, where the shops were all lit up and the streets crowded with French soldiers and civilians, and reached Villers-Sire-Nicole at 10.30 p.m., where, with difficulty because of the dark, they went into billets.

Francis had also mobilised, starting from Ireland, and his diary takes up the story.

Saturday 15th August   *Marched from Newbridge to a rest camp in Dublin arriving about 6 p.m. Had dinner with the RAMC.*
Sunday 16th August   *Spent morning riding around the docks trying to find our ship.*

Found her at last and returned to camp just in time to pack up and march down. Loaded the guns and horses without trouble on SS Courtfield. *Our shipload consists of ½ our battery, the 119th Battery, some Royal Engineers and Army Service Corps.*

Mrs Alexander and Mrs Congreve [officers' wives] down to see me off. A beautiful day. Woods nearly cut his hand off carrying my sword which slipped out of the scabbard. No cabins and only one small room for everyone to eat in. The room held about 8 people [and was] at once crowded. Bulteel and I made our beds on the upper deck. Sailed about 6 p.m.

Monday 17th August *Still beautiful weather. No one knows where we are all going. Supposed to be Southampton! Spent the day walking round the horses and seeing that everything is in order. The*

horses don't half stink! My watch tonight; this means going round the ship from top to bottom every two hours. A beastly job. Very nearly sick once!

The trouble with the horses was that there were no passages behind them so the men could not get to them to clean up the dung. The smell became very overpowering!

Tuesday 18th August *Same as day before. Hear we are bound for Havre, where we arrived 7 p.m. Spent from 8 p.m. till 5 a.m. unloading.*

Wednesday 19th August *Marched to rest camp. Very sleepy and nearly fell off my horse on the way there. Had a good sleep and moved off in the evening at 9 p.m. Entrained at a small station close to Havre. No trouble with the guns or horses. [Lts] Lindsay, Bulteel and I in one carriage, the major and [Captain] Congreve in another. C. very angry with B. who ate all the biscuits!*

Thursday 20th August *Arrived Landrecies at 5 p.m. Unloaded and bivouacked close to the town. An excellent meal in a farm with the brigade headquarters. Slept in an outhouse.*

Friday 21st August *Marched to Amfroipret and bivouacked. Went to requisition hay and was forced to drink bad beer everywhere. Slept in an orchard. Cows a great nuisance. Got up and drove them into the colonel's part of the field.*

Saturday 22nd August *Marched to Boussu. Thousands of people crowding out to see us and giving away drinks, tobacco, cigars and handkerchiefs all the way. We had to forbid the men taking any more drinks. I had too much but laid in a vast stock of cigars which lasted for a long time. We marched with the advanced guard into Boussu at 4 p.m. Major H. and I rode on and selected a billet. The town was partly deserted and everything very quiet. Found ourselves looking round corners rather nervously. A good meal and slept well on a hard stone floor.*

On 19 August Lord Kitchener decided to send the 4th Division to join the BEF in France. On the 22nd, before daybreak, 1st

Rifle Brigade entrained for Southampton, embarked 24 officers and 964 other ranks and arrived at Le Havre at noon on the 23rd where they marched (up the steep hill) to No. 3 camp on the heights above the town, escorted by French Boy Scouts.

Back in England life went on. George was working hard at Newark but found time to write to Rachie in India:

Here we are installed in the office with an accompaniment of the typewriter's clicking going on without ceasing. I went to spend a few days with the regiment in camp and though I did take the precaution of having some service kit with me I little thought I should have to live in it indefinitely.

We got the order to be ready at an hour's notice to go home and pack up on the 3rd at 8 a.m. Tents were struck. Stores returned and the men were ready to move at 10.30. On the 4th came the order to mobilise, and the regiment marched to Derby on the 10th where the division was assembled. They went to Luton in Beds last Saturday where I believe there is a great concentration of Territorial troops. We have had a guard night and day on the railway bridge on the GER here, it is now taken over by regulars from Doncaster.

There has been a constant stream of troop trains most nights, north and south. Those going north appear to be mostly regulars and it looks as if there was a possibility of a big raid in the mind of the authorities and preparations being made in consequence. The fog of war has been lying very thick over us, and we can only conjecture and endeavour to appreciate the situation as best we can. It looks rather as if the main attack will be delivered by the French through Alsace, holding the Germans in some defensive position up in Belgium until the Russian legions can move up. There will be an awful battle before long, and we are rather anxious to know what is in the mind of the German Admiral.

I believe Ted has gone to Belgium. Francis has left Newbridge but where he is I do not know.

I am thankful that you are in a comparatively peaceful spot, such peace hard to find in the globe just now. I trust that you may not lose the company of your gentleman yet awhile. Keep a stout heart dear. Every one is doing splendidly at home and I am thinking we shall not retire from the contest till peace has been dictated at Berlin.

Dora was also still keeping her diary and sending the pages *en bloc* to Rachie in India:

21st August   *There is a new moon today but it managed to eclipse the sun between 11 and midday, I was walking in the town and got a piece of smoked glass to look at it. Some clouds came up and round a little tiny cloud that came over the sun there was a rainbow just circling round the sun, I*

BELOW *Claud Lindsay, MID, was killed on 31 March 1918 as a major commanding 33rd Battery, RFA. His younger brother Archibald, who was a lieutenant in the Royal Engineers, died in action five days before him.*

ABOVE *Haymaking*
by the tennis court at
Osberton

never saw anything so glorious, then very
shortly after a thunderstorm began and
heavy rain.

The harvest is, I hope, mostly gathered
in; at Osberton it is and Grandpapa was
sending his men to help the tenants to
gather theirs. Today there are services of
intercession for the troops going on all day.
I go to see 31 Castle Gate in which one of
the curates and his mother live; he has a
new post in Nottingham, so has to leave
next month. The house is very clean and
newly done up, quite near here, facing
the castle ruins, there is no garden only a
back yard and a stable but with so narrow
a turn to get to it from the street that a fat
or big horse would not get through and of
course no cart. I think we shall take this
house as it is clean and ready and there
will be room for you and V. and the tiny

with a squeeze, which we shan't mind
for the pleasure of having you all with us
together again. It will do to warehouse all
our extra furniture which otherwise we
should have to sell. Drive with Father to
Farndon to see Mrs Harkenbury but as
Zulu cast a shoe we stop and have tea.
When we start again he goes lame and
a man called Mills who used to live at
Southwell passing by shouts 'Can I lend
you a pony?' He takes us into his back
yard and shows us a basket he has been
lent to copy (he is a basket-maker) usually
made in Germany. He is afraid he cannot
make it at the price – there is a great effort
now being made to get English industries
that have been swamped by Germany to
work again.

22nd August   Go to see 38 Lombard Street,
a horrible house, I was told it had a garden

so thought it worth looking at, but I was met by five black beetles – and there was no garden. Very little news comes in, it is strictly censored. Father hears from Frank Yeats-Brown [Victor's brother, a cavalry officer] wanting to get some work in a cavalry regiment. He recommends him various people to apply to. He is lucky not to have been sent back to India like many others. I hear from Edmond, his battalion is at Harwich, sleeping on the football ground (very hard) but ready to start at any moment. You will realise how anxious we all are; indeed you and Victor must be more than anxious yourselves – so little news comes out. We only know that one of the most tremendous battles ever known is going to take place and your uncles will be in it, and possibly Edmond and Francis. Father has started electricity for his leg which will I trust do him good, Dr Appleby recommends it.

23rd August   Sunday we hear Brussels is in the hands of the Germans; having been evacuated it has no defences. There is a special service today with a procession of the Mayor, Father, Aldermen, Red Cross nurses, etc. and a collection for the Prince of Wales's Fund. Father has sent £50 but as it was given through Worksop by Mr Lister Kaye it is not acknowledged. Grandpapa sent £500. The fund is now over a million and a half; it is to be hoped it will be administered properly. Mr Briarley (whose house we are taking) preaches an excellent sermon on giving. Father and I have a quiet afternoon in the little back garden. I feel as if there is tremendous fighting going on. But no news.

Mons and Le Cateau, 23–26 August

When Francis woke before dawn on the 23rd in the village of Boussu, he had no idea of what was in front of him or of what was to come. He slept well on the stone floor of the billet, wrapped in his 'flea bag', little knowing it would be the last time he would see it. The officers grabbed an early breakfast before moving forward to reconnoitre positions.

To the east lay the town of Mons, which lies a few miles inside the Belgian border between the Rivers Sambre and Escaut/ Scheldt which are connected by the Mons-Condé Canal. It lies at the centre of an industrial and mining area with the canal running through a continuous belt of pit-heads, slag heaps and mining villages. There were no clear fields of fire for either the infantry or the artillery and the ground was quite unlike anything the BEF had trained on before. Their experience had been gained in the outposts of Empire, in South Africa during the Boer War, and on Salisbury Plain or in Ireland. They had never trained in the Black Country or the urban areas of the Midlands, which were the closest in comparison. The lessons learned during foxhunting were hard to apply on this ground.

The Germans to the north were beginning their big hook south, having finally and successfully cleared the Belgian Army out of their way. The Germans were not even aware that the British were in Belgium and, full of confidence, thought they were bearing down on a weak French force that they could brush aside on their relentless march to Paris. Facing them, unknowing of their exact strength and dispositions, the BEF was stumbling into position on the line of the canal.

The cavalry had led the British advance north and, by the morning of 22 August, elements of 2nd Cavalry Brigade had outposts just north of Mons at Casteau. At about 7.00 a.m. they saw movement to the north-east and Corporal Drummer of the 4th Dragoon Guards 'observed some movement to the north-east and fired at a mounted figure' (which he claimed he hit). These were the first British shots of the Great War. Behind the cavalry screen the rest of the BEF continued its march towards Mons and the canal, in sweltering heat, on the terrible cobbled road, laden under their packs and, for the reservists in particular, their feet still raw from chafing boots.

Field Marshal Sir John French, commander of the BEF, was having his own problems. He had thought he was conforming with the French Fifth Army, which he was expecting to attack on his right, and still had no clear idea of German strength, location and intentions. He discovered at 8.00 p.m. that evening that he was in fact in front of the French Fifth Army, that they had started to pull back in order to conform with the French Fourth Army on their right and that the Germans were bearing down on him. He gave the order that there would be no advance the following morning and that he would hold the current position for 24 hours. This came as some relief to the troops, who were aware that the Germans were near and were spoiling to fight them, albeit with sore feet.

The 1st Queen's Own Royal West Kent Regiment were in 13th Infantry Brigade, 5th Division and was the battalion that Francis and 120th Battery RFA were to support. After a tough march north on 21 August, they reached St Ghislain at midday on the

22nd. They were ordered to entrench and take a position on the Mons-Condé canal, so the battalion fell to work, entrenching, barricading roads and bridges, loop-holing houses and garden walls and clearing forecourts. The southern canal bank was 10ft above the general level and commanded the low ground to the north. However, one of the companies had to deploy north of the canal as the houses and other buildings would have masked their fire from the south. They worked until late on their positions and started digging again at dawn on the 23rd and finished preparing their positions both sides of the canal.

Also at dawn Francis and 120th Battery came forward to look for positions to support the West Kents, though good positions were difficult to find on the canal bank. Major Holland, the battery commander, brought two sections with four guns forward. Francis,

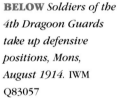

BELOW *Soldiers of the 4th Dragoon Guards take up defensive positions, Mons, August 1914.* IWM Q83057

who was in command of one of the two-gun sections, takes up the story:

Sunday 23rd August   *Up early and spent morning looking for positions which were few and bad. Selected one on the canal in a factory. Put up parapets and protections by the guns. No definite orders but understand the canal must be held at all costs. Rifle fire at about 11 a.m. somewhere in front. This did not surprise us as we had been told to expect some German cavalry and horse artillery. Shortly after a shrapnel [round landed] close to us. 11.30 a.m. heavy rifle fire and thick columns of German infantry advancing within 2,000 yards. Fired hard and Major [Holland] reported afterwards that he had done a lot of damage. Two batteries opened onto us and I had a direct hit on the parapet in front of one of my guns.*

Fortunately I had put up two steel plates with 3 feet of stones between them and this stopped the shell. Things getting very hot so we ran the guns out by hand under cover of buildings. Limbered up and went behind the town hall. Bombardier Cultram was killed and a shrapnel shell swept the road as we were going down it, wounding several. Major Holland rode back for orders.

Lindsay, who had his gun in reserve, went to look for another position. We found one a few hundred yards east of our former one and the two guns were brought into action. The platforms were hopeless and we could only just clear the crest. We opened fire, however, at a German battery in the open at about 2,500 and got effective fire to bear. Observation was dangerous. The front crest was swept with bullets and at 3 p.m. Major Holland was shot through the throat. His last shot a few seconds before blew up

BELOW *Officers, men and horses of the 1st Middlesex are struck by shrapnel and run for cover.*

one of the German ammunition wagons. We took it in turns to observe but fire was very slow owing to the bad platforms. The guns kept on running down the hill. Paige came up but had no orders and didn't know what was happening! The Germans had one battery shooting at us all the time but fortunately were bursting their shells too short. There were several nasty ones, however. One burst between the guns and wounded Ironside. Another burst just above Woods and myself as we were carrying up ammunition. A bullet hit Woods in the chin. Several horses also wounded. At 7 p.m. heavy rifle fire started in our rear – most unpleasant, bullets coming from all sides at once.

Not being able to see any of our infantry and as the section was doing very little good on account of the bad platforms, Congreve decided to withdraw, which we did at 7.15 p.m. arriving at bivouac near Dour at 2.00 a.m., less two guns. The baggage wagon got stuck in a manure pit and we lost all our kit and baggage. We left Major Holland lying on the table of the villa which we were using for shelter for the wagon line. Found BHQ at Boissu le Bois.

Francis had had a torrid time on his first day of war; the noise, the pressure, wounded and dead horses and men, the death of a man he liked and respected, mixed with adrenaline, excitement and exhaustion. At the end of the day his battery had lost two guns in the final battle. The end was most unpleasant with their position being outflanked by the German infantry who were shooting at them from the rear. One gun that had been firing was lost and another that had been brought forward close to the position was surrounded by the enemy infantry and had to be left behind. These were the only two guns lost by the BEF on the first day of battle.

It is difficult to imagine how they might have felt. Captain Congreve took command of the battery; he was a very capable and energetic man who was liked by the officers and soldiers alike. They knew that they had caused serious casualties to the Germans but

they had been pushed back and lost two guns and all their personal kit. They would have moved back on their horses, probably carrying wounded infantry on their gun limbers, and when they arrived at Boissu le Bois they were without changes of clothes or their flea bags, and probably wondering what would happen next. Their first concern would have been to the men, to patch up the lightly wounded, and then to their horses, without which the guns would be useless. They would then have had to reorganise the men as they had two fewer guns to serve.

Francis recorded the items that he lost in the wagon as St Ghislain and their value. He received £28 14s 0d compensation in March 1915:

Blanket	1 00/0
Valise	2 10/0
Flea Bag	3 03/0
Serge	4 00/0
Breeches	3 10/0
Boots	2 00/0
Trousers	1 00/0
Gaiters	1 10/0
Tente d'Abri	1 10/0
Tennis shoes	12/6
Underclothes	4 14/0
Greatcoat	6 00/0
	£31 19/6

Francis continues his story:

Monday 24th August   *2nd Battle at Dour. Up at 4 a.m. and dug emplacements for guns in a field at Champs des Arts. Lindsay's section came into them and I put mine in a field a few hundred yards back. The Germans appeared to be in great strength and drove our infantry back all the time. They got a good number of field batteries into action and late in the day hopelessly outnumbered us in the matter of guns. Congreve and I and the headquarters observed from a house close to my guns. Two shells came through the roof and later in the day bullets came freely through the window. We had a shoot at a German observing party and made it clear out very quick. We fired a good deal of shielding*

*fire in front of our infantry but had few
visible targets. As usual we had no orders.
At 3 p.m. the infantry were practically
back to the line of guns and were holding
on till we got the guns away. We and the
121st Battery on our right limbered up and
walked away under a heavy but inaccurate
fire. All the German shrapnel burst far too
high and I don't think there was a single
casualty. We marched to St Waast les Bavay
where we met the 119th Battery who had
had a very bad time. Preston and Walford
wounded and about 30 men hit.*

Francis has not done full justice to either his
part in this battle or that of his sister batteries,
as Captain Ramsden, the adjutant of 27th
Brigade, reported in a letter home written in
early October:

*Captain Congreve had Mr Foljambe's and
Mr Lindsay's section in pits, and Major
Ballard [121st Battery] had Mr Davidson's
and Staveley's sections also entrenched.
Their field of fire was poor, but they had
carefully concealed their trenches, and for
a time escaped unnoticed. Meanwhile, the
village of Wasmes on our right whence we
had just come was burning, an inferno of
shell and bullets, and the enemy began to
turn their attention to us. About this time it
became obvious that our work was nearly
done, and the infantry were ordered to
retire, and in the early morning General
Headlam [Commander Royal Artillery,
5th Division] had told the colonel to hold
on at all costs. When the colonel heard
that the infantry on both our flanks had
been ordered [not] to go, he refused to
withdraw, and sent me to Colonel James
with a message to that effect. Colonel James
said, not prettily but decidedly, that as
long as we stayed he would stay too, and
so said Colonel Bond of the KOYLI [King's
Own Yorkshire Light Infantry]. Fortunately
for us all, however, the latter had just
received a message to tell us to retire. It
now became a question of getting out the
8 guns entrenched on the open forward
slope. It was a sight for the gods, shell
whistling round and lots of rifle bullets.*

*The colonel led each pair of teams out
himself, and brought the guns back under
cover, the drivers going steadily as on
parade. The last pair, Mr Davidson's, were
the worst, as they were cramped between
houses which were being freely filled
with HE shell, but with the exception of 6
unfortunate gunners we got the guns away
without loss [in fact two gunners were
killed and two wounded]. The Manchesters
supported us most gallantly, and if we
live we shall mutually present each other
with a piece of plate. Certainly the colonel
and Ballard earned the VC over and over
again, as did everyone there. Judged by
the old standard of VCs Ballard deserves 3!
and Alexander [commander 119th Battery]
who I think is certain to get it, an equal
number, but they only did their job, but so
splendidly! That night we withdrew rather
despondently about 8 miles, as we did not
understand what we had been there for,
but we were not downhearted.*

The British troops were hungry and
exhausted as they stumbled into their rest
areas but new orders had already been
received – Operation Order No. 7 from GHQ
stated: 'The Army will move tomorrow, 25th
inst, to a position in the neighbourhood of Le
Cateau, exact positions will be pointed out
on the ground tomorrow.' Francis's diary
reports simply:

*Tuesday 25th August Marched south.
Everyone wondering why we are retiring so
fast. Bivouacked near Le Cateau.*

Whilst Francis had been involved in the
white heat of battle, Hubert and Henry
and 2 KRRC had been having a much quieter
time, and Ted had only recently arrived in
France with the 4th Division, but was finally
moving north.

Hubert, Henry and 2 KRRC were on the
right of the BEF. I Corps under General Haig
had missed the swing south of the Germans,
whose entire attack landed mostly on General
Smith-Dorrien's II Corps. On 23 August, when
Francis was fighting at Mons, there had been
a number of alarms and 2 KRRC had been

on tenterhooks all day expecting to fight and could hear the noise of the guns and the battle to the north. The men had struggled out of their billets in Villers-Sire-Nicole before dawn with great difficulty as the narrow streets were blocked with a seething mass of troops and eventually, at around midday, moved into billets in Rouveroy a short distance to the north-east. At 8.00 p.m. they were ordered to reinforce a battalion of another brigade at Harmignies, about 3 miles away, which was apparently under heavy attack, and they raced to the scene but found it all quiet. They spent the night there with two companies entrenched and two in reserve. They knew there had been a battle that had involved the BEF and knew that the Germans were advancing, but had no idea of the outcome.

They stood to arms at 3.30 a.m. on the 24th and then moved to rejoin their brigade at Bettignes, where they stayed until 4.00 p.m. before carrying on to Feignies, further to the south-west, where they billeted. There were crowds of refugees streaming past them all day which were a pathetic sight. They reported very few men among them, and saw many parties of women with children driving wagons drawn by animals of all sorts, even cows, and mares with foals by their sides. Most of the wagons were piled high with household goods, and now and then they saw a woman wheeling a barrow that she had loaded with her most precious belongings, including a small child or two on top of it all.

On the 25th they marched 15 miles south to Marbaix, which they reached after dark. Their only excitement on the way was when their cyclist scouts spotted a dismounted *Uhlan* at a range of 600yd and potted a few shots at him and two others who rode off together, all unscathed. The cyclists put their bad shooting down to the light, which was fading rapidly as dusk fell.

Ted had had an even quieter time. On 23 August, whilst Francis was fighting for his life at Mons, the 4th Division with 1 RB was still at Le Havre preparing to entrain. On the 24th, at about noon, the battalion was escorted to the station by crowds of cheering civilians

and boarded 'the longest train that any of us had seen (and the slowest) which took the whole battalion and its entire transport'. The train, which rumbled along throughout the night of the 24th, suddenly pulled up at 5.30 a.m. on the 25th. The men put their heads out through the windows and saw the name Le Cateau, which meant nothing to them. An anxious staff officer hurried up to Colonel Biddulph (CO of 1 RB) and gave him orders that were then taken down by dim candlelight. In the bustle of detrainment Ted began to get a hazy idea of the general situation. It seemed that things were not going well at the front. 'The station was full of bustle owing to the packing up and retirement of GHQ. Not a cheery greeting!' When they were clear of the station the map boxes were hurriedly unpacked and the maps issued. It was a foretaste of many similar surprises in the future to discover that the contents of the boxes consisted almost exclusively of maps of Belgium.

Marching through the town, A Company passed Brigadier General Wilson, Deputy Chief of Staff to Sir John French. He had just come from the neighbourhood of Mons but looked cheerful as ever, and called out a greeting to the company as it marched by (Wilson was a Rifle Brigade officer and so known to the battalion). After the gloom and apprehension in Le Cateau station such an encounter was a tonic to the men. The battalion proceeded via Neuvilly to Briastre where it rejoined 11th Brigade. The march had been hot and tiring but there was no time for rest. At once two companies were set to work digging in north of the village, while battalion HQ and the remaining two companies stayed in a farmhouse by the light railway at the road-fork at the northern end of the village.

The day went quietly enough. There was a steady retirement of the troops of 3rd Division through 11th Brigade's position and the distant sounds of guns were the only evidence of war, other than the tragic flow of the civil population with their few moveable possessions heaped upon any available vehicles, and an occasional detachment of French infantry that strayed across the British

front. But the evidence in all conscience was grim enough to the waiting soldiers. The appearance of the 3rd Division troops told eloquently of what they had been through. The newcomers suddenly realised that they were on the threshold of experiences such as none of them had ever before encountered. The few words snatched with friends in other units as they passed gave an idea of the potential of the German artillery. And it seemed that preconceived ideas of trench construction were in need of revision. One party in particular made an unforgettable impression upon an officer of the Rifle Brigade. It consisted of a lieutenant-colonel, a dazed subaltern and some 200 men, 'that's all that's left of my battalion' (in fact more than this number had survived but had become separated from their unit). The speaker was Colonel Hull; the battalion was the 4th Middlesex Regiment which had given so splendid an account of itself at Mons.

At about 10.00 p.m. that evening 4th Division was ordered to move back, once 3rd Division was clear. The march was a nightmare; earlier in the evening a heavy thunderstorm had broken and the rain still continued. The downpour and the heavy volume of traffic had combined to convert the road to a quagmire of such consistency that most of the signallers' bicycles, with their wheels immovably clogged by mud, had to be carried a considerable part of the distance. The mere effort of walking on such a surface was a trial of endurance and the road was still thickly congested with groups of stragglers in addition to vehicles and horses. By 2.00 a.m. on 26 August the main body of 1 RB was bivouacked to the north-west of Fontaine-au-Pire on a track that ran down a forward slope towards Cattenières and Estourmel. They lay down on either side of the track and sought what rest the inclemency of the weather and the exigencies of the situation were disposed to allow them. 'The corn had just been cut, and the sheaves made excellent beds.'

Ted settled down for the night with the rest of 1 RB, having hurried forward earlier in the day to support an operation, the nature of which they were only vaguely if at all aware of. They had hurried back at night, with the enemy on their heels, uncertain whether the next day would bring an advance, a defensive action or a continuation of the retreat. They were composedly awaiting whatever the future might have in store and in the meantime snatching some important sleep.

Back with the main body of the BEF, Francis and the rest of the soldiers who had been in action had all reached Le Cateau and, although tired, hungry and footsore, knew they had bloodied the Germans. Although some units had taken heavy casualties, they were still very much an Army and eager to fight and inflict more damage on the Germans. General Smith-Dorrien had realised that unless he turned and faced the enemy and fought them to a standstill he would be in danger of being overtaken and swamped by the huge German force still bearing down on him. On the morning of the 26th his troops were in position, turned to face the enemy and were determined to inflict further heavy punishment on the advancing Germans.

Francis describes his next battle:

Wednesday 26th August   *3rd Battle at Le Cateau. Up early and ready to move, but later rode out with Congreve to reconnoitre positions. Found a nice one under cover and rode back to bring the battery up. Dug in and concealed the guns. Heavy shelling started on our right. At about 11 a.m. we had orders to go to the assistance of the 3rd Division on the left. Limbered up and proceeded to the headquarters of the division. Told to take up position to draw fire from 6th Battery which was being heavily shelled. Rode out with Congreve past the heavy battery. Lots of bullets and shells all the way. Found a position and returned to battery which was halted under cover of a bank about a yard high.*

Came into action but found we could not clear the crest. Ran the guns up by hand. Opened fire and after some trouble with trees in front got effective fire onto edge of wood occupied by Germans. Fired 550 rounds in two hours from our four guns with considerable effect. A hail of bullets flying just overhead and heavy shelling by some small howitzer firing HE. Their shells landed left and right, twenty yards in front and behind but never hit us. The 6th Battery close on our left were knocked out and lost all their guns and many horses in the wagon line a few hundred yards in rear. The village of Audencourt on our right front was shelled to ruins; the inhabitants were still there and most must have been killed or buried. We lost a few horses in our wagon line. Quite deaf by this time and the orders had to be passed down by signs. At 3 p.m. the infantry had fallen back to the gun line and we stopped shooting. Soon after Colonel Wing rode up and told us to withdraw, which we did in good order. We walked back a few hundred yards and brought two guns into action to cover the retirement. No Germans appeared, however, so we limbered up and followed on behind. An extraordinary state of affairs. Hardly a single formed body of troops and every field full of wagons and transport ready to turn into the column which was already miles long. The inevitable block and I thought we should probably be cut off by the Germans but much too tired to care. An awful march all night and to make matters worse it started to rain. We would go on for 100 yards and halt for a minute then on again only to halt 50 yards further. At a longer halt than usual we all went to sleep and woke up to find the column had moved on. After that we marched steadily till we caught the column up. We remained with 3rd Division till after St Quentin.

It had been another busy battle for Francis, though his phlegmatic account hardly does justice to the occasion. His battery's orders were to 'come into action under cover between 6th and 23rd Batteries with a view to drawing fire away from the 6th Battery which was in the open and suffering severely from the enemy's artillery fire.' During the course of the fight they saw 6th Battery being repeatedly hit and most of its horses died, with more horses killed in their own wagon lines. Their guns were firing at such a rate that the breech blocks jammed repeatedly so that at the end only two guns were in action. Then there was a dignified retreat, with all of them absolutely exhausted.

Meanwhile, on the left of the battlefield, shortly after 4.00 a.m. on the same day, Ted and 1 RB were standing to arms in cultivated fields on a forward slope covering the village of Fontaine-au-Pire. It was a glorious morning and the dawn had revealed to the outpost company a body of German cavalry and artillery advancing upon Cattenières. The outposts fell back steadily upon the main body of the battalion fighting their ground and causing casualties to the advancing patrols.

The attack that now developed during the morning was in its earlier stages confined to artillery, machine-gun and rifle fire. No effort was made by the enemy to advance. However, 1 RB was ordered to retire and they saw the enemy moving forward to their vacant positions. 1 RB moved back, taking advantage of natural cover such as hollow roads and folds in the ground, and fell back in succession of companies at a steady walk – almost, despite the hostile rifle and shell fire, as though on Salisbury Plain. There were a number of casualties, the first to be suffered by the regiment.

The Germans continued to press forward and the whole of 11th Brigade was gradually forced back under tremendous fire. Eventually, the Riflemen held a strong line along a sunken road and at about 2.00 p.m. beat off a determined German effort to advance in force with a withering hail of rifle and machine-gun fire. By about 3.00 p.m. the situation was becoming so tenuous and confused that the battalion was ordered to extract itself to Ligny. This was no easy move. The Germans had crossed the railway embankment on either side of the battalion and, but for a gap of about 400yd behind them, the Riflemen were encircled.

They laid down volley after volley of fire on the advancing Germans, and Ligny church was appointed as the assembly place. Such was the pressure that they were unable to evacuate their wounded. At last the Riflemen fell back upon the Ligny position and 'the German infantry sprang up from their concealed positions and rushed in pursuit'. Three Jäger battalions and a cavalry brigade had been held at bay by three shattered companies of British Riflemen.

For 1 RB their baptism of fire had been intense and their casualties were heavy. Their losses were 8 officers, including Ted, and some 350 other ranks; nearly a third of the battalion. Ted was badly wounded and left behind with a large number of men in the sunken road under the care of the medical officer.

Whilst the fierce fighting was still going on, little news had yet reached England as Dora's continuing letter to Rachie shows:

24th August   *Mrs Briarley calls and takes me again over 31 Castle Gate. We can fit into it quite well, though small. There are two rooms opposite each other and a fairly wide entrance between – study and dining room I expect. Over the study is a drawing room, three of the bedrooms have tiny little dressing rooms like powdering cupboards. I think the Briarleys will be moving out in a month's time, so you will be able to think of us getting all the furniture not wanted in London to fit, probably all too big! I shall now have Mary to help with the two houses which is a great comfort. This afternoon Mrs George Branston, Mrs Huskinson [wife of the CO of 8th Sherwood Foresters] and Mrs Herbert Branston call. On hearing I am going to Southwell to tea with Mrs Starkey, she takes me over in her car with two very pretty daughters. She is going to enquire after Dulcie Warwick who has had a baby three weeks ago. I pick up the Starkey car at the station and arrive at Norwood in a tremendous thunderstorm. Hilda Starkey is working as a nurse in a hospital in Nottingham for a time; she does not like it much. Everyone is now having only two courses for dinner. I started it* when I came here and I find other people are doing the same. I go to see Mrs Becher [an 8th Sherwood Foresters officer's wife] – she is looking very thin. The evening papers bring tidings of the fall of Namur [and] an engagement of our troops all Sunday and into the night.

25th August   *This morning we hear Lord Leven was seriously wounded last Friday. The fighting must be tremendous. One can only hope and pray that all may go well with our dear ones and the allied forces. We must win!*

Drive with Father in the pony cart, Zulu all right again now. Call on Mrs Branston; she very kindly invites us to stay at the Friary. It is most kind – I shall be able to go and see about things, and Father will be well looked after. It is a great comfort until we get our own house ready. Call on Mrs Herbert Branston, there are many nice prosperous people living here.

I hear the Germans have enough men to go on fighting for fifteen years! But I hope we shall put a stop to that!

Father goes to visit the G. N. Bridge Guard and found there a Mr Boyd who knew Edmond well and was at Oxford with him.

The Retreat, 27 August–6 September

The BEF started its march south. At the beginning there was a certain amount of chaos as individuals and units withdrew from the battlefield of Le Cateau and long lines of marching men and wagons stretched down the road heading south. Losses at Le Cateau had been significant and had fallen mostly again on Smith-Dorrien and his II Corps, nearly 8,000 men and 38 guns. The Germans had suffered more but at the end of the day they were in control of the battlefield and many of the British missing turned up in German prisoner of war camps. However, at this early stage, no one knew of Ted's fate and neither Francis nor Hubert even knew that 1 RB had been in action.

For the next ten days the BEF retreated south, as Francis recorded:

Thursday 27th August   *Arrived early at St Quentin and got an excellent cup of tea in the town. No rest here and we pushed straight on to Ollezy. At last a night's sleep.*
Friday 28th August   *Marched early to*

Noyon. Lots of fruit all the way.
Saturday 29th August   *Marched to Attichy. A large field to bivouac in and everyone thought we had reached a rest camp.*
Sunday 30th August   *Marched to Coolisy.*
Monday 31st August   *Marched to Crépy.*
Tuesday 1st September   *Held our own for the first time. Heavy rifle fire as we were having our breakfast. Came into action and covered the ground in front of the right flank of 5th Div. Nothing to shoot at in our zone but the 121st in action on our left got some Uhlans advancing across the open and killed a lot. Rode around to Bulteel several times to find out what was on. A bad bullet-swept road. The Germans only had Uhlans, motor machine guns and Jaegers against us and we easily held our own. The retirement was continued at 3 p.m. and we marched through Crépy to Silly-le-Long. Bivouacked. Found a good cellar of wine and a bottle of brandy cherries.*
Wednesday 2nd September   *Marched to Vinantes and bivouacked.*
Thursday 3rd September   *Marched to Coulommes and bivouacked.*

This was the day that Francis managed to write his first letter home, the first of many. Mail and parcels still seemed to get through, even though the Army was in full retreat.

Dear Father,
   Many thanks for your letters. Keep to the same address – they seem to reach me alright. If you can find time I wonder if you can send me out in small parcels at intervals, a pair of socks, vest, pants, a handkerchief or two, a packet of grape nuts, tin of cocoa, pair of puttees, etc. We got nearly surrounded by Germans on the first day's fighting while we were advance guard battery and had to beat a hasty retreat leaving behind every scrap of clothing. So for the last fortnight we have been rather uncomfortable. Luckily it has been glorious weather, almost too hot in the daytime, but a bit cold at night. When we arrived three weeks ago, they rushed us right up north, where we bumped heavily into about five German army corps and since then have marched across about five sheets of maps fighting rear-guard actions at intervals, most unpleasant as it seems usually to end each day in limbering up the guns under heavy fire. We have lost pretty heavily, I believe, but they say that the Germans have lost in the proportion of about three to one.
   I haven't seen or heard anything of Edmond but the 4th Division I know have had a bit of fighting too. I hope he is still alive and safe.
   Our major was killed the first day.
   Please thank Mother for her letter.

Francis's diary also continued.

Friday 4th September   *Spent day in bivouac. Marched at midnight to Tournan.*
Saturday 5th September   *A rest day. Slept and eat.*
Sunday 6th September   *Marched back to Villeneuve. News that Germans are retiring fast. Marched on to Courtry.*
Monday 7th September   *Marched to Coulombs.*

Francis's diary does not tell the full story of the march south or give a real flavour of the state of the men or the horses, or the hardships they faced. Francis will have ridden for some of the way, leading his horse from time to time to rest it. The other horses in the battery would have been pulling the guns and the wagons. He would have been fairly uncomfortable, having lost all his kit on the first night of the war, and they would have spent most nights either in billets or in fields.

The 2 KRRC war diaries left a fuller account of Hubert's march south and Henry Warre started a notebook on 1 September of his daily activities. Hubert and Henry marched south over the same period. Whilst Francis was again in the thick of battle at Le Cateau on 26 August, 2 KRRC was still on the right of the BEF. On the early morning of the 26th, the battalion was roused early and had to leave the men's packs, with everything in them, except ammunition, food and water, at the church at Marbaix. They also left behind a dozen sick and footsore Riflemen to look after the kit, but heard later that the Germans entered the village a couple of hours after they had left and a staff officer had had petrol poured over the packs and set fire to them to stop the enemy from looting them. Most of the Riflemen left behind were taken prisoner but two managed to evade the Germans and rejoined the battalion later.

The battalion marched to Le Favril and halted for most of the day, hiding under trees to avoid being seen from the air. They could hear heavy firing from Landrecies to their north, and later took up defensive positions but ended the day without seeing the Germans and marched south to billets in Oisy. They continued the march south during the next two days, spending some time in defence and as rear-guard, but apart from seeing the odd *Uhlan*, were not pressed by the enemy. They spent the night of the second day in a 'very dirty field' and took apart two large stacks of straw for the men to sleep on.

They had a rest day on the 29th (as did Francis several miles to their east) and brought up their baggage wagons and spent the day washing, cleaning, issuing kit and compiling returns. They could hear a battle going on all day and assumed that it was the French engaging the German advanced guard. The next day they were up at 3.00 a.m. and continued the march south, the highlights of the morning being given coffee and bread when they passed a large convent and in the afternoon stopping for a bathe in the canal at Anizy-le-Château before finding billets in Anizy. Battalion headquarters was in a very comfortable house owned by a young married couple. They had their mess in the garden and after dinner got their host to drink a large number of toasts in 'fine champagne'. The host then insisted on bringing up some bottles of wine from his own cellar and was rather tiddly by the end of the evening!

There was another early start on the 31st. The weather was again hot and the roads dusty and they bivouacked in the late afternoon near Verte-Feuilles. The artillery appeared with a great number of horses and watered them at the wells of the farm and by early evening the water had run out, so the battalion had a rather dry night. On 1 September they started south at 5.00 a.m. and marched until mid-morning. They then became the rear-guard with the North Lancashire Regiment and both battalions entrenched themselves in a position that would stop the Germans if they should emerge from the forest to their north. They stayed there until 10.00 p.m. to allow the rest of the division to get away and then followed, marching throughout the night with very few halts, until they reached Fulâmes, turned into a field and almost at once fell asleep.

On 1 September Henry Warre's notebook entries start and add to the story. He describes: 'A long day and night march. Took up an outpost line to cover entrenchment and for the night but abandoned it by 10.00 p.m. and marched on and off all night. Bivouacked for about 1½ hours in a field and up to Varreddes at 5.30 p.m.' There was a heavy dew and they all got soaked legs and feet in the early morning as they again took up the rear-guard role around Le-Plessis-Placy. It became a very hot and bright morning and the battalion was very tired after its work and march the previous day. They set to work digging trenches but in the early afternoon were withdrawn and marched to Meaux, where they went into billets. The regimental war diary expands: 'The heat, the work we had done, and the almost unquenchable thirst which had assailed us all, had completely worn us out, and, whilst waiting in the streets to be allotted our billets, both officers and men lay down and slept on the stones. Henry added in his diary: 'Bridge over the river blown up in rear. The 8th Brigade had a hot fight and lost a good many. George Morris wounded. A first class billet and got 2 letters from Gwen.'

On 3 September they started again at 5.00 a.m. for a day of straight marching, with a long rest at midday to avoid the heat of the day. They arrived at Romény at about 5.00 p.m. and were allocated billets in the village. They found the houses and cottages so thoroughly unpleasant and dirty that most of the men preferred to sleep out of doors. Most of the inhabitants had fled and only a few very old people were left, who soon sold out of their small stock of milk, eggs and chickens. Henry added:

3rd September   A filthy village so slept under a tree. A much disturbed night owing to issue of rations about midnight.
4th September   Started at 4 a.m. and marched southward. Stopped in a covert from 11.00 a.m. to 2.00 p.m. then marched on Aulnoy where we had only one house for the men. About 3.20 p.m. when we were washing and cleaning having got our 35-lb kits we were ordered to thin out at once and all luggage was loaded and sent off.
    Our cavalry got into close touch with the enemy apparently heading for us [and] we dug ourselves in in anticipation of an attack. The artillery duel took place but nothing more and we went back into bivouac.
5th September   Shots came from the piquets about 1 a.m. and we paraded at 1.25 and marched southwards. The piquet north of Coulommiers bagged four Uhlans, one an officer. One of my men picked an unwounded man out of the road ditch.

Marched in advance guard and got mixed up with baggage column. Broke away and eventually went into billets at Bernay. Had a very good billet and a delightful hostess.

2 KRRC settled in for the night and received their first reinforcement. An officer and 91 other ranks had been sent out from the depot at Winchester and eventually managed to make their way to the battalion in billets. Those who had been with the battalion throughout the retreat from Mons, 24 August–5 September, worked out they had marched for 12 days and halted for 1 day. In that time they had covered 180 miles of road. By the end of the retreat the men had all toughened up and their feet were harder. Although tired, they had received food and water throughout the retreat, still had all their weapons and ammunition and were ready for anything.

News was now trickling home about the battles that had been fought in Belgium, and the names of the first casualties were being reported in the papers. Dora was watching for anything that might give news of her family. She saw and kept an article in Thursday, 3 September's *Daily Telegraph* in which a Rifleman, by then in a London hospital, gave an account of being wounded in action at Landrecies. However, in the absence of more definite family news, she continued her diary letter to Rachie:

Thursday 3rd September   Mary, Avice and I motor to Newark for the day. Father has been in Nottingham for [a county Territorial] Association meeting and gets back late for luncheon. He says a new battalion for the Sherwood Foresters is to be enlisted. About 250 of the present 8th Battalion will come into it and these have to be sent to fill up. He has to find altogether about 1,000 men and they are to make Newark the headquarters and be billeted in the town so there is plenty to do. After a talk he goes back to the Drill Hall and we go to the Town Hall to the sewing meeting. Clothes are being made for the Belgian refugees. We go back to Castle Gate and have tea in the garden and then Mary goes off to the Town Hall again for her first aid lecture. We start off about 7 to motor home and find supper arranged as I told Granny we should be too late for dinner. The first casualty list comes out today; we are very sorry to see Major Victor Brooke's name amongst the killed and Mr Pennington's name amongst the missing – he was Kitty Beaumont's nephew. The French government has moved to Bordeaux.

4th September   *News of a tremendous victory by the Russians over the Austrians at Lemberg. I got a letter from you, a great surprise, dated 12th August, in which you say Victor has had to mobilise and that two companies are going down next day to Meerut. I am so dreadfully sorry you are to be left alone. It is most unfortunate, but at such a time as this everything is happening like this, all sorts of tiresome things. I only wish more than ever that we were all together, as we are in anxiety, with Ted and Francis and Uncle Harry and Uncle* Hubert and Rudolf and Wilfred Jelf and Victor's brother Alan and Philip Warre and others all fighting.

Also mentioned in the first casualty list was the death of Major Holland. George wrote to Francis on 4 September:

The news which reaches us is quite rightly very meagre as regards details, but I am most grieved to see you have lost your battery commander. I think the service has lost a fine officer and you a good friend. I trust these few lines will reach you sometime and that by the time you get them that the Russian steamroller will have resumed its progress towards Berlin.

Did you ever read Bernhardi's book Germany and the Next War. Everybody jeered at it, and at me for even mentioning it, but what he said has come true to the letter. News has just come in that five German ships had put their ugly snouts out of the Kiel canal and been bust up. No details. We shall probably know in the morning.

People are doing well here, and we are keeping busy from morning to night in the office. We are now busy in raising a reserve battalion for my old regiment which is going for general service. I am afraid you have had a very tough time but, come what may, we are going to pull through this and I trust we shall for good and all smash the German Empire to pieces. It has been the scourge of Europe for the past fifty years. It makes me sick not to be out there, but the days are past when a man could be carried in a sedan chair into action. My old legs won't work properly any more. I am going through a course of galvanisation, but I don't know that it is very much good.

I hope that Rachie will get through this next fortnight all right and that Victor will not have to leave her just yet. Mother is at Osberton again. The accounts from there are not altogether good. If you can, let us know if there is anything in a small way that you want. Shirt, socks or suchlike things.

Dora wrote to Francis the same day:

We are very much concerned to see that Major Holland was killed in action the other day, whether at Mons or Cambrai or Le Cateau we do not know. This shows that you have gone to the front and are not at Ostend. It is a great blow to your battery. Do write when you can, if only a line, and I should be thankful. The 11th Battery seems to have suffered very severely and up to now the artillery losses seem to be heavier than any others. I thank God continuously for him to keep you and Edmond safe.

I have ordered some woolly things from Shetland some time ago and hope soon to send some, although you may have enough with you but a little later on you may be glad of more. In the meanwhile I am sending you some other things which may be useful. I can send you a parcel of 3 lb for 1/- which would take a shirt, drawers, socks etc. If you have any wants a postcard could perhaps be posted from near Paris? I dare say up to now there have not been many chances of posting.

Father is very busy at Newark getting another battalion of the Sherwood Foresters together. It is unfortunate his leg will not allow him to train these. There are a lot of spies about – Granny and I thought we caught one the other day. Everyone well here.

Dora then continued writing to Rachie:

5th September *I have stopped in bed for two days to have a rest; the Germans are quite near Paris; Lord Kitchener said to be perfectly calm. We wonder and wonder if the Russian cossacks are really being brought through England from Archangel – trains are running all night and are full of troops.*

This afternoon a telegram arrives with the exciting news that Arthur is taking a year's leave by doctor's order 'overwork but otherwise well' and has started today! Send for Mary and tell her, she is wild with delight. It is a delightful prospect to be so unexpectedly having him home. I expect he has written to you, so you will know he has started. I do hope the voyage will quite set him up. If only he could have brought you with him! The wedding will be some time after he has had time to see to all the details himself, banns etc. No fearful hurry as there would have been. How I wish you could have been back for it. So many extraordinary and unexpected things are happening that I feel almost as if we might see you back for Christmas! Lovely day, day after day of glorious warm weather this summer, which we have not been really able to enjoy because of our anxieties.

I am collecting money for a pipe fund for the Sherwood Foresters – they were anxious to have a memento of their mobilisation. Now there is to be an extra battalion, it will mean about 2,000 pipes! Go downstairs after luncheon, Gerald and Constance F. come, he is drilling some of these new battalions at Camberley and they have leave to come to Doncaster Races! Very few people will go but I believe he has some horses to sell so is especially interested. He has a very bad cold.

CHAPTER 4

The Allied Counter-offensive

Advance to the Marne, 6–12 September

Francis, Ted and Hubert Foljambe had had no contact with each other during the retreat, nor had they been able to communicate with the rest of the family in England. Francis was still with his battery in 5th Division, and Henry and Hubert still together in 2 KRRC in 2nd Division. Ted was last seen by his battalion at Le Cateau on 27 August and had now been reported missing up the military chain. In England, George was at Newark running the depot for 8th Sherwood Foresters and Dora was at Osberton, carrying on her daily diary for Rachel in India.

Francis continued his account in his diary:

Tuesday 8th September   *Marched north towards Doue. Found German rear-guard holding high ground at St Cyr. A crump battery shelling hard and holding everything up. Walked about with Congreve*

OPPOSITE *J Battery Royal Horse Artillery (RHA) in open positions, 1914.*

BELOW *German infantry advance across open country.*

to find a position. A lot of shrapnel unpleasantly close. Found a position close to where D Battery had been shelled out and came into action there. Observed from a tree. Attacked and turned the Germans out and they retired at 2 p.m. Advanced and finally bivouacked at Noissement in a field. Great trouble with Paige's horse which would graze a foot off my head and keep me awake.

Wednesday 9th September   Another German rear-guard action on high ground on north bank of River Marne. Turned out of the column and shelled transport at long range. A crump battery as usual holding things up. Heavy fighting going on right and left of us. Remained in action all night. Had an awful stomach ache and took large dose of chlorodyne with good results.

I was ordered to turn off one gun of my section and bring it into action. From a position alongside a haystack there was a wonderful view across a valley to the westward. I had just shot at a single Uhlan who was standing looking very nervous in a field when Congreve appeared and insisted on taking charge. Just then a wonderful assortment of German transport and motors and troops appeared on the road on the skyline about 5,000. Congreve missed the lot as he never judged the time of flight. Very angry with him.

Thursday 10th September   Marched to Chezy-en-Orxois. An interesting march. The road littered with dead Germans, a battery and masses of transport which the Germans had abandoned. Batches of prisoners all along the road.

The battery took this opportunity to pick up material on the way, and it is likely that Francis started replacing the kit that had been lost after the first night at Mons.

Friday 11th September   Long march to Hartennes. Rain all day. Signs of a hurried German retreat all the way. Firing ahead of us in evening. Had to ride round close to

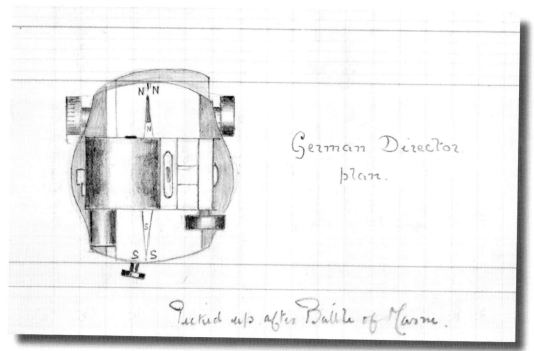

outposts with Davidson to find positions in case we are attacked. A quiet night, however.
Saturday 12th September *Still raining hard. Marched to Serches. A big French battle going on round Soissons.*

Henry and Hubert took a different route on the retreat with 2 KRRC and 2nd Division. Henry takes up the story, which is filled in with detail from the regimental account.

Sunday 6th September *Had a europe [a family expression, meaning obscure!] morning, My knees which had got very tired owing to walking as my pony was lame, recovered well. First heard of the German retirement eastwards and began to move northwards. A good deal of big gunnery to the north and we moved with many and various hesitations to Vaudoy where we bivouacked to the north-east of the village. One whole platoon!! detailed for guard of HQ of division and one platoon on outpost which covered with that of another brigade.*

They had problems finding water for the horses and for the men as they arrived in Vaudoy at 10.15 p.m. to discover that the artillery and transport had been there first and taken all the water. Several parties from the

battalion were sent a long way before they found more and could water the horses and fill the carts ready for the next day.

Monday 7th September *Told that we would move about 4 a.m. so up at 3. Breakfast at 3.20 and our men covered with the straw they had used for bedding, then we were told to move 600 yards at 4.40 a.m. and lay till 7.30 a.m. Good arrangements!!! Then we started north-east and the heat was trying.*
Eventually got up to the cavalry screen and got into Jouy at 7 p.m. The 9th [Lancers] had showed well against the Germans. Jouy-sur-Morin. Good billet, slept in curé's house.

The regimental journal adds that they passed several German bivouacs along the way, crossed the bridge over the River Aubertin at Amillis, which the enemy had left intact, and halted at Choisy from 3.00–5.00 p.m. for rest and food. They found Jouy was one of the few places not abandoned by its inhabitants and the shops were open when they arrived. The bakers were doing a roaring trade with fresh loaves until a supply officer came along and commandeered the lot. They were left with twenty loaves for a thousand hungry men.

Tuesday 8th September   *From Jouy-sur-Morin to Flagny Farm.*

They were ready to move at 6.30 a.m., but such were the numbers of troops, all trying to advance, that they just had to stand in the streets watching a continuous stream of troops passing through for nearly 5 hours, until their turn came to join the column. That evening they dug trenches on the east side of Flagny, facing east. At 10.00 p.m. the second reinforcement joined the battalion, adding another 2 officers and 89 soldiers to its strength.

Wednesday 9th September   *Flagny Farm. Marched 12 miles at 11 a.m. though ordered to move at 6 a.m. and went to La Croisette and bivouacked in the open. Dry and warmer than night before.*

Thursday, 10 September was the day when 2 KRRC finally caught up with the Germans and their real battles were now close ahead.

Tuesday 10th September   *The brigade marched from La Croisette bivouac at 3.50 a.m. via Le Thiolet–Lucy-le-Bocage to Courchamps. The brigade did advance guard for the division. About 1 mile north of Courchamps the advanced troops moving northwards came under shell fire. The advanced troops consisted of 1 Section 25th Brigade (2 guns of the artillery), 1 Section 26 Field Company RE and the Sussex Regiment. The last were directed to the ridge north of Priez on which small parties of the enemy had been seen and were then shelled not only by the enemy but by our own batteries. They came back southwards as did the Northamptonshires and North Lancs who were in immediate support. The enemy artillery were in position east and west of Neuilly and did a certain amount of execution.*

The war diary added some further detail.

The 2nd Division which had been in action about Hautevesnes and St Gengoulph swung round and threatened the enemy's

right and the action which commenced at 9.15 a.m. slackened off about 11.30 a.m. when the enemy's guns retired. An advance was then made to the ridge north of Priez and artillery (howitzer brigade, 25th Brigade and heavy battery) moved forward to this ridge and came into action against the enemy retreating northwards. The Cavalry Division on the right did not move forward till about 3 p.m. and the enemy at 4 p.m. retired all along the line. The brigade moved forward and occupied billets and bivouacs. Sussex Regiment in billets at Rassy. Northamptonshire Regiment on ridge to south-west [in] bivouac. KRRC covering Rassy village [in] bivouac. North Lancs in bivouac south of village. B Company KRRC [which was commanded by Hubert] sent forward to ascertain if Neuilly was clear and the state of the bridge over River Ourcq.
They found some German stragglers and wounded in Neuilly village and took some prisoners.

Friday 11th September   *The brigade marched at 4.15 a.m. in rear of the main column via Sommelans–Grisolles and Rocourt to Coincy and reached the place about 11.30 a.m. Impeded on the way by French supply columns. Went into billet at Coincy. Rain fell in torrents practically the whole afternoon. Colonel Knight [of the] North Lancs died of his wounds.*
Saturday 12th September   *Marched at 7 a.m. and just reached the division starting point at 7.45 a.m. (crossroad Bruyères–Villeneuve). Marched about 16 miles and the roads very greasy and the heavy battery had difficulty. Marched via Fère-en-Tardenois–Loupeigne. The brigade halted before entering Mont-Notre-Dame as our guns were in action on the high ground to the E of that place and also to the north-west. Eventually the brigade went forward into billet at Paars.*

Paars was a very small village, and the battalion had great difficulty getting all the men into billets. The night was spent rather damp and very cramped. A final tally of the

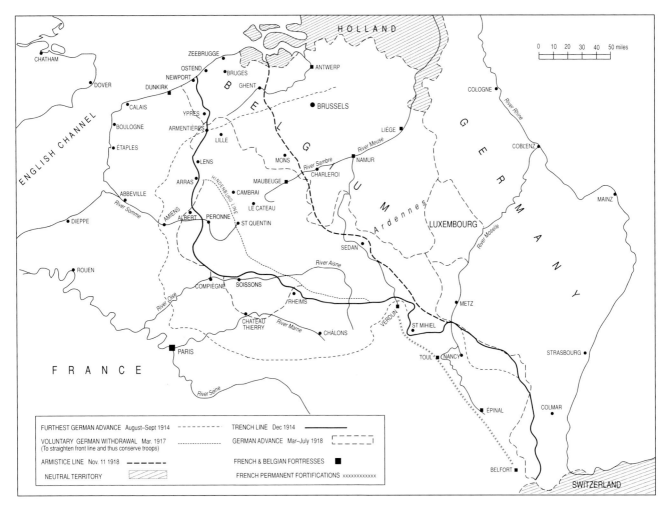

The following text appears on the map:

HOLLAND
CHATHAM
ZEEBRUGGE
OSTEND
NEWPORT • BRUGES
DOVER
DUNKIRK GHENT
ANTWERP
B
CALAIS
YPRES
BRUSSELS
BOULOGNE ARMENTIÈRES
E
LIÈGE
ÉTAPLES LILLE
COLOGNE
River Rhine
LENS
MONS
River Meuse
G
COBLENZ
ARRAS
MAUBEUGE River Sambre NAMUR
CHARLEROI
I
ABBEVILLE CAMBRAI
G E R M A N Y
River Somme
AMIENS LE CATEAU
U
MAINZ
ALBERT PERONNE
M
DIEPPE
ST QUENTIN
Ardennes
LUXEMBOURG
River Moselle
ROUEN
SEDAN
River Aisne
COMPIÈGNE SOISSONS
METZ
River Oise
RHEIMS
VERDUN
STRASBOURG
CHÂTEAU THIERRY River Marne
ST MIHIEL
CHÂLONS
PARIS
TOUL NANCY
F R A N C E
River Seine
COLMAR
ÉPINAL
ENGLISH CHANNEL
HINDENBURG LINE
BELFORT
SWITZERLAND

0 10 20 30 40 50 miles

FURTHEST GERMAN ADVANCE August–Sept 1914 --------
VOLUNTARY GERMAN WITHDRAWAL Mar. 1917 ....
(To straighten front line and thus conserve troops)
ARMISTICE LINE Nov. 11 1918 — — — — —
NEUTRAL TERRITORY
TRENCH LINE Dec 1914 ——————
GERMAN ADVANCE Mar–July 1918 [- - - -]
FRENCH & BELGIAN FORTRESSES ■
FRENCH PERMANENT FORTIFICATIONS xxxxxxxxxxx

distance marched since the battalion had moved to France, taken from 21 August to 12 September was 314 miles.

News was by now beginning to trickle through to England, and Dora continued writing her letters to Rachie:

8th September   *Gerald and Constance go to Doncaster and while they are away a Mr Cecil Walter, who says he is a cousin of Constance's, appears, Granny takes him for a spy – he comes on a motorbicycle from Leicester. We all talk to him and come to the conclusion that he is safe. He stays to lunch and tea and plays Duelo with Mary and Avice but has to go without seeing his cousins. I think he wants to get a commission in Gerald's regiment. I walk with Granny, and a fog comes on. There has been a thunderstorm and much rain. I know that fighting has begun again since Monday. Granny will not allow Grandpapa*

to know there is an evening paper so we have to go upstairs to my bedroom or into the library with a candle to read it. Strong reinforcements have reached the allies and we think it must be the Indian divisions. Is Victor amongst them? And the Russians, no official news of either. The press bureau is so cautious.

I write to Edmond and send him a packet.

On the evening of 8 September George, in Newark, got the first news from the front about Ted, with a telegram from the War Office. Dora continued her letter to Rachie, breaking the news about Ted and mentioning the start of what would be a long search to locate him, find out how he was and how she might help him:

9th September   *Gerald and Constance go off in their motor with their luggage.*

The news in the papers is better: we are advancing and in good positions all down the line from Paris to Verdun. I drive with Grandpapa in the Victoria by Normanton and through the Cabashins. Mrs Kaye and Kathleen come to tea and two little girls have tea with John. After tea I open a letter from Father and find enclosed a telegram from the War Office saying that our dear Edmond is wounded and missing – you will probably see his name, my darling, in the list when it is published. We have no details and can only pray that he may have fallen into good hands and not be a prisoner or badly wounded. Poor dear, it is so unfortunate for him and the uncertainty is very trying. Gladys thinks that, with our troops advancing now, there is a better chance of his being picked up.

Ted has now been reported as missing in the Morning Post, alongside other Rifle Brigade casualties, so the information is now out in the public domain. I write to Miss de Keyser at King Edward VII Hospital as Captain de Moleyns and Mr Coryton, two officers in 1st RB, are there. Possibly if they are well enough they might give us news of Ted. I am going to Newark today, taking Mary and Avice to meet Father at

the Branstons who live at the Friary and shall post this there this afternoon. Goodbye for the present my dear child.

This is the last part of Dora's letters to Rachie that has survived.

The Battle of the Aisne, 12–20 September

The BEF and the French Army followed the retreating Germans from the Marne, with the aim of pushing them out of France and Belgium for good. But the Germans were not content to be driven back for ever. They had already identified that the natural obstacle of the Aisne River and the heights above it would be a good place to defend and to halt the British and French attacks. The battle for the Aisne lasted ten days and was marked by fierce fighting. It marked the start of the very long drawn out stalemate that characterised the rest of the war. The 'mobile' war before the Aisne of armies marching and counter-marching came to an end and the stagnant trench warfare, in a line that eventually stretched for 400 miles, began.

Francis recorded his battle and during this period also was able to send more letters home, and tell his family what he was doing. They must have been so relieved to have heard from him; George in particular would have been proud of his exploits, but his offhand descriptions of the dangers he was facing must have made poor Dora worry even more. With Ted, her eldest, missing, and Francis so close to the front, life cannot have been easy for her. In addition for Dora, there was concern for her favourite brother Henry in France, as well as her brother-in-law Hubert.

Francis fought an artillery battle, guns behind the infantry with observers forward so they could see the targets and bring the guns to bear. The battery was still part of 27th Brigade RFA and was supporting 13th Infantry Brigade in 5th Division. Francis takes up the tale:

Sunday 13th September   *Cold. Saturday about on plateau at Serches. Without any warning a salvo of crumps straight into the wagon line of the heavies, 10 horses killed and the rest stampeded. Soon after the howitzers' horses were hit and 8 killed. Moved on a little further down the road but they kept searching the plateau all day and got some unpleasantly close. I at last persuaded Congreve, who was feeling very ill, to move a few hundred yards back where we remained in peace for the rest of the evening. Bivouacked at Couvrelles.*

Monday 14th September   *Rain. The whole brigade less 121st Battery in line on the plateau commanded by Alexander. Firing at long range. At midday we got the order to move into action at Ciry. The colonel rode down to show the way. An exposed road and the Huns saw us going down and shelled the hollow at Ciry. Came into action on the far side of village up a steep bank. We had to put double teams into the guns to get them up. An extraordinary escape from shells. They put salvo after salvo of shrapnel just over us, most bursting overhead. Only one man and some horses hit. The 121st Battery wagon line, however, which was in the street, was caught by the furthest shells and lost a good many men and about 20 horses. Opened fire on the enemy battery whose flashes could be seen in edge of wood in front of Condé fort. Bivouacked in village.*

BELOW *The 120th Battery's position at Ciry on the Aisne, September 1914.*

ABOVE *The 120th Battery in action at Ciry.*

Tuesday 15th September   *A quiet day. Spent time in digging dug-out and shelters.*
Wednesday 16th September   *Shelled by 5.9-inch howitzers HE. Some very close. A few houses knocked down. One man wounded by splinters.*
Thursday 17th–Saturday 19th September   *Rain. Quiet days for us, but a lot of shelling all round. We are attached to 13th Infantry Brigade. The general (Cuthbert) makes his headquarters close by.*
Sunday 20th September   *Service in morning (Rev Goudge), close to the guns. Fortunately no German aeroplanes up to see us.*

On the 16th Francis wrote to his mother, his second letter home.

Thank you very much for the socks and cigarettes which were most acceptable. My only pair, which have been on for three weeks, were nearly done! Have you heard anything of Edmond – I hope he is still alive and well. At the present moment he ought to be quite close to me, but I never get a chance to look him up.

The most annoying thing at present is a heavy German howitzer which has been lobbing 200-pound shells in all day. Two dropped within 20 yards of me and covered everything with dirt and mud but the majority fell in a volley quite close by – a house goes straight up into the air when it is hit, which must be most uncomfortable for the inhabitants. But the effect is very local – unless one is actually hit by the shell itself, there is not very much danger. I wonder how long this is going on for – I hope we shall get back in time for the hunting season. Up to the last day or two it has been lovely weather but latterly it has been rainy and cold and most unpleasant, especially when one has nothing to change into. But it doesn't seem to hurt anyone. I have never felt better in my life.

Yes, I hope Rachie will be alright – I should have thought it would have been better for her to have come home too. After all this is over, Victor may be stationed at home.

It has been a great loss to us, Major Holland being killed. He was shot by a rifle bullet in the throat the first day up near Mons whilst peering over the crest to observe. The Germans got very close that day and they must have had marksmen specially watching our observing station as a regular hail of lead came along whenever one showed one's nose over the top. Since that I have been at Dour and Le Cateau and we are now having another big battle down here, so we have seen plenty of fighting.

I don't know how long it takes for letters to get to England, but I think at least 3 weeks, so all news we get in papers is not much good.

Please thank Father for his letters and give my love to all.

Your affectionate son,

Francis

Any more contributions* thankfully received. A daring aeroplane has just ventured a bit too close and has got a dozen shells bursting all round him. They don't often get hit!

*Such as, papers, chocolate, soup tablets, handkerchiefs, socks, a shirt, cigarettes, vest, drawers.

At the same time that Francis was writing home from the Battle of the Aisne Ted was able to communicate the first real news of his situation. His letter was written from behind German lines and took between two and three weeks to reach his father in England.

A very quick line as an occasion has appeared, and a post is getting through.

I was wounded about three weeks ago and am still on my back from the result. There is nothing dangerous, but it will take some time. I am in the convent here and being well looked after, and there is no fear of going to Germany at present.

The place where we were all wounded was at Ligny about 12 miles from here. Of course we are all prisoners.

For Henry and Hubert with 2 KRRC the days ahead would be daunting. They would have to cross the River Aisne, opposed by the Germans, and attack uphill to try to clear them from the heights commanding the river.

Their battle would be hard-fought, with the bayonet and even the sword used for the close-quarter battle. Henry takes up the story:

13th September   The 2nd Brigade was in advance and the battalion leading with my company in advance. Was sent to Bazoches by the guard for orders at 6 a.m. and got back at 7.15. Orders to advance to Vendresse and we got [to] the bridge at Bourg. The river bridge had been blown up but we managed to get over by the canal bridge and a tow path and then down the hill to the north. The 2nd Cavalry Brigade out in front and on opening [up] with the horse battery they got a proper shelling and lost several men. They had also had casualties at Bourg amongst others being Rory Grenfell in the 9th Lancers. C Company was eventually relieved by Sussex and North Lancs and went into billet at Moulins. On outpost, a miserable wet night.

About midnight got a message to send an officer on to reconnoitre through Vendresse and Balfour went and saw a German outpost on the top of the hill to the north and got to within 50 yards. Balfour got back about 2 a.m. sending his report direct; a good bit of work.

The battalion war diary reported:

2nd Lieutenant Balfour and eight men were detailed to get in touch with the enemy on the road running across the plateau above Troyen and ascertain their position. The patrol moved straight up the road on to the high ground north of Troyen and succeeded in locating a German picquet at the point where the road turns north-west immediately north of Troyen. Five Germans were seen, and apparently they heard the approach of the patrol, owing to a man slipping down the bank, which caused the mess tin to rattle, but the patrol got away on the grass siding and returned at 2 a.m.

14th September   The battalion less my company left at 3 a.m. and, going through Vendresse, faced the Germans in early morning before daylight. They were then committed to an infantry attack and shortly after the light came the German guns opened on them. General (or Colonel) de Lisle who came past my post told me to occupy a hill to cover a retirement but this was changed. Got up to Vendresse about 7.30 a.m. and joined the Battalion about 8 a.m. The Germans in strength and the whole 2nd Brigade practically in the first line. Took two of my platoons and men collected from various regiments in hand.

The fight went on the entire day and was most obstinate. The firing line on several occasions came back and had to be built up again. The Germans made many counter-attacks, all of which were held. The artillery duel went on till after dark. The battalion was relieved by the Northamptonshires and Loyal North Lancs who took up the line on the hill for the night and the battalion bivouacked on the reverse slope of the roadside. A great relief to get to the end of the day, but it was a rainy night and cold. Our casualties very heavy. Killed: Hubert [i.e. Hubert Foljambe],

Cathcart, Forster, Bond, Thompson. Missing: Jackson, Davison, Barclay. Wounded; Rudolf Jelf [Arthur Jelf's brother], Heseltine, Jackson, Millar, Blake, Ellison, Balfour and 306 NCOs and men.

The war diary reported:

Just before 8 a.m. C Company rejoined the battalion and two platoons were put into the fight at once; the remaining half company was practically the only reserve kept in hand. About the same time the North Lancashire Regiment arrived and pushed straight on to the sugar factory, D and A Companies also progressing on their right, and we succeeded in making good our position and thoroughly establishing ourselves on the plateau, digging in on the reserve slope. The firing line was built up from time to time, and as the men were driven back they were collected and taken up again after a little rest.

During the advance our firing line was pushed right through two German batteries which were in action near the

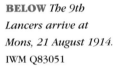

BELOW The 9th Lancers arrive at Mons, 21 August 1914. IWM Q83051

sugar factory, but subsequently had to come back under heavy pressure from the enemy. These guns remained there, but the Germans were unable to use them again that day. However, under cover of a counter-attack about 4 p.m., they succeeded in removing the guns, but left the limbers behind. The fight continued throughout the day, the Germans making several counter-attacks which were repulsed with loss. Towards evening it was recognised that the trenches on the reverse slope would have to be occupied at night. This necessitated a withdrawal, and it was represented that many of our wounded were lying out in front. The stretcher-bearers had done what they could and had been continually shot at, but it appeared useless to communicate with the enemy with a view to collecting the wounded, as they would probably have ignored any message of the sort.

Rain fell heavily all the afternoon, but the artillery fight went on till after dark and it was not till 9 p.m. that the battalion was relieved by the Northants and North Lancashires and went into reserve under the scarp of the hill immediately north of Troyen. Our casualties of the day were 9 officers killed and missing (of whom we could only bury 2), 7 wounded and 306 killed, wounded and missing amongst the rank and file.

Henry Warre was mentioned in despatches for his conduct during the battle. Hubert was dead, and his obituary in the *Regimental Chronicle* of 1914 reported: 'He was killed in action on September 14th during a gallant charge at the Aisne. His body was found riddled with bullets. He was a typical regimental officer and company commander, sincerely attached to his men and by them deeply loved and implicitly trusted. A better man never wore a Rifleman's jacket. His colour-sergeant wrote: 'He was killed instantly. He was a brave man and I miss him. The men all loved him.' Henry continued:

15th September   *Remained in our bivouac. A wet night and some rain during the day.*

A couple of men hit by shrapnel. Several attacks by the Germans but they were all held off. Our guns shot splendidly and kept the German fire down much better.

An alarm took place about 9.30 p.m. but it was really only a few snipers and it soon died away. During the afternoon we could see the French Army up on the right.

The battalion war diary reported:

During the night some wounded men came in. They were all shot in the legs or in such a way as to prevent them walking. They had been hit during the morning of the 14th and had lain out between the two fighting lines all that day and the following

ABOVE *Major Hubert Foljambe wearing his South Africa War medals. He was killed in action on 14 September 1914.*

*night and day. At last in desperation they
determined to try and get in. A German
officer appears to have treated some of them
kindly during the fighting, pulling them
under cover of a haystack. All the men
who could walk had been taken prisoner
and had been marched off after we had
withdrawn to the trenches on the afternoon
of the 14th. The others who had been left
started after nightfall, dragging themselves
along with their hands as best they could
through the turnips in the pouring rain.
Some had one, some both legs broken, but
they helped each other along towards our
trenches. They were shot at as they came
in; one man continued to crawl forward
and fell fainting into a trench, and the
remainder, about 15 in number, then got
in, Sergeant Hinge amongst them.*

16th September   *A filthy night, rain off
and on all the time. Reveille at 3 a.m.
with an idea of an advance which did not
come off. Nothing doing very much. In the
evening the Bosche artillery gave us a lively
time in bivouac and killed one man and
wounded 29.*
17th September   *A shelling morning and
an infantry attack on 3rd Brigade in the
morning. About 12 they started on our
brigade and began to push in about 1 p.m.
Took 2 companies out to support the Sussex
and Northamptonshire. Some enfilade fire
at the start made the situation uneasy but
when the Germans were driven back it
looked better. Priaulx got a nasty wound in
the chest at very close quarters and a good
deal of the shooting was at 40 yards and
some bayonet fighting. About 4.30 p.m.
there were some 30 surrenders and then a
body of German riflemen walking up to our
lines with their rifles but holding up their
hands. They shot an officer who went out
to speak to them and then [tried the same
thing against] the Northampton company
on the road and were driven back by
machine-gun fire with heavy loss. They
attempted twice to get to our lines in this
way. The fight was very stubborn and was
not over until after dark. Showers of rain
and a cold wind added to the discomfort.*

*We had 13 casualties in C Company. Our
shelter had fallen in and we took till past
11 p.m. to put it right. The rain had also
come in through the roof and we passed a
rather cold and damp night.*

The war diary also recorded these events:

*At about 4.30 p.m. a party of Germans
came forward towards C Company with
two officers advancing at a distance of
about 20 or 30 yards in front of their
men, advancing with their hands raised
above their heads, seemingly as a token of
surrender, but with their rifles slung over
their shoulders. Lieutenant Dimmer of
the King's Royal Rifle Corps and Captain
Savage of the Northants Regiment went
forward to meet them. On nearing them,
however, Dimmer heard the bolt of a rifle
being opened and closed and suspected
treachery. He called out to Captain Savage,
and himself dropped down in the turnips.
The Germans immediately opened fire from
their hips and Savage, checked by his sword
as he was in the act of dropping down, was
instantly killed, whist many of the Riflemen
who had been standing up in the trenches
beckoning to the Germans to come in, fell
victims to the same ruse.*

*Immediately after this incident a large
body of about 300 to 400 Germans were
seen advancing in a similar manner (arms
raised and rifles slung) on our left towards
the Chemin des Dames. Our brigade major,
Captain C. F. Watson of the Queen's, came
up and rode out towards the German
troops, ordering our men to cease fire as he
went past them, as he thought the Germans
intended to surrender, but, after speaking
to the enemy, he galloped back, whilst the
Germans continued to advance towards a
company of the Northants, who were dug
in on the south side of the road. They, like
the Riflemen, stood up in their trenches,
expecting the Germans to surrender, but
Lieutenant Purcell, in command of our
machine-gun detachment, trained his
guns on them, as he did not trust them.
The Germans continued their advance,
and when they reached the Chemin des*

Dames, they opened fire on the company of Northants in the same manner. The Northants, taken by surprise, fell back 40 or 50 yards, but our machine guns at once opened fire on the Germans who turned tail and fled, being mown down as they ran across the flat. They were also exposed to rifle fire from our trenches to the north of the road, and very few, if any, of them escaped.

Whilst this was going on, on another part of the line twenty or thirty Germans surrendered, some wounded, some unwounded. One of the unwounded prisoners was approached by Major Warre with a view to his going over to ascertain if others wanted to surrender, but he said that he would have his throat cut if he went back, and there was no intention of surrendering among the enemy as a whole. Our stretcher-bearers meanwhile brought in a Rifleman who had been lying out wounded since the early hours of the 14th. He looked more like a mummy than a man; the skin of his face was drawn and yellow, his limbs limp and powerless. His equipment was still buckled up, and from a wound on his side the blood had stained the webbing of his belt and clothes: one amongst many others who must have been in similar agony, slowly dying from loss of blood and starvation in this so-called civilised warfare. A sip of brandy and water, however, received acknowledgement by his eyes, and he was sent down to the hospital at Troyen.

18th September   A wet day, heavy artillery work and a nasty slice of weather. A report that the enemy were collecting in front of the Gloucesters' line about 10.30 p.m. and went there with two companies as reserve to find it all a cry of wolf. Then about 11.30 heavy rifle fire opened and we turned out again for a time. Next [we were] cursing the report sure that two German columns had attacked each other by mistake. A vile night and our shanty leaked badly.
19th September   Various attacks along the line and in the afternoon the Coldstream Guards had a bad shelling and lost some

men. Squibs Congreve came along in the afternoon. His brigade relieved us. The interchange rather complicated and the Sherwood Foresters who relieved us did not arrive till after midnight.
20th September   Started our march down at 1 a.m. and, although it was only about 6 miles to Pargnan, I felt awfully done as did most people. I suspect it was the relapse after living at high tension for a week. Got in about 4.15 a.m. A very dirty billet and some French signallers in the kitchen. Slept until 11 a.m. Breakfast and round the men and lunch at 2 p.m. Then censored letters. Washed and cleaned. Tea at 4 p.m. and then round to see defences which might have to be constructed. Saw several battles going on and there was no release from shell fire as our batteries were hard at it close by. Chico had a talk with Johnny Gough and Lieutenant General Haig said some nice things about the 2nd Brigade and 2 KRRC in particular. Had to send our kits away by 10 p.m. which was a nuisance.

Also in the family files is the following newspaper cutting:

Mr Francis and Lady Gertrude Foljambe, of Osberton Hall, Nottinghamshire, have lost their youngest son, Major Hubert Foljambe, who was one of five officers of the King's Royal Rifle Corps all killed in action in the same recent engagement. Major Foljambe had served throughout the Boer War and was a very keen soldier, and most popular in his regiment and with hosts of friends. He married a daughter of General Bewicke-Copley, of Sprotborough Hall, Doncaster, and leaves a small son, aged about three years. This is not the only bereavement in the family for Major Foljambe's eldest brother, Mr George Foljambe, heard that his eldest son, Edmond Foljambe, of the Rifle Brigade, was amongst those wounded and missing, and it is now feared that he is not living. After his father, this young officer, aged only twenty-four, was the heir to Osberton, a fine place that has belonged for generations to the family.

Stalemate, 20–30 September

The attacks on the Aisne had essentially failed, and the British forces had been unable to throw the Germans off the heights. The mobile war was now over and both sides settled down for a long hard slog. News started to flow more easily in both directions.

Francis, as usual, was keeping his diary going:

Monday 21st September   A heavy night attack on 3rd Division on our right, otherwise quiet.
Tuesday 22nd September   Saw in papers that Edmond is missing and wounded but don't know any details.
Wednesday 23rd September   Drew panorama of the Chivres Ridge which was forwarded to general. Saturday in the shadow of a walnut tree in front all day.

On the 23rd Francis also managed to send his mother a postcard:

We are taking it in turns to use this special weekly express post to obtain necessaries. Will you please send 'Date' and 'All Well' to: Mrs F. L. Congreve, The Grange, West Felton, Oswestry. Mrs Morgan Lindsay, Ystrad Fawe, Ystrad Mynock, Glamorgan. Mrs Moir-Byres, Dean's Grove, Cranly Road, Guildford (from SDB). Will you also send in a case or cases as soon as possible and charge to me through L. Kaye the following:-
(for 120th Battery)
4 Large tins cocoa (Van Houtens)
1 Set of underclothes (for me)
1 Large bunch raisins
Lots of Cadbury's chocolate
Sugar almonds (sweets)
Salted almonds etc. (you know the sort of thing I like)
Some milk powders
Soup tablets
China tea
A few packets Grape Nuts.
Please fill up any cracks with anything else nice that you can think of.

In the family files there is also a cutting from *The Times* of Thursday, 24 September 1914: 'News has been received that Lieutenant E. W. S. Foljambe, Rifle Brigade, who was reported wounded and missing, is in a convent at Cambrai and well looked after.'

Thursday 24th September   Nothing.
Friday 25th September   Germans shelling aeroplanes hard. Bits falling all round us – very unpleasant.
Saturday 26th September   Nothing.

George Foljambe finally managed to get a letter through to Francis. It was sent on the 20th and seems to have arrived on the 30th. Francis had first learnt that Ted was missing from the newspapers, and was at this stage unaware that his Uncle Hubert had been killed the week before.

So glad to get your letter dated 4th from, I suppose, near Paris. You have indeed had a rough time, and we have been here at home trying to follow as well as we can the very meagre accounts of the movements of troops which are allowed to come through.
One thing is certain, that the country is proud of her sons. They have fought as they fought of old. May you all be given strength to endure to the end. Poor old Ted is wounded and suffering, I think, since 26th August, and we have just heard that my dear brother Hubert is killed. I am going over tomorrow afternoon to Osberton for a night. Those we have lost have fought a good fight and their names will be on England's roll of honour.
The Russians have apparently made mincemeat of the Austrians, who I fancy may soon be removed from the board for all functional purposes, and it seems to me that this might open a back door into Germany.
The new army is going strong, and we have had for the moment to put a bit of a check on recruiting as they were coming in faster than we could deal with them. The 6th Sherwood Foresters goes foreign very soon, and we are well on with a reserve battalion to the 8th Sherwoods here.
Our thoughts are with you day and

ABOVE *Lieutenants Maitland and Hewson take a rest during a lull in activity.*

night and with all your gallant comrades in the tremendous conflict that is now going on. I wish it may end in a German Sedan which it seems may happen if the French drive back the German army at Verdun. My legs are rather groggy, but I can manage my office work which keeps me busy morning till night.

Mother was sending you some things which I hope may arrive safely.

Next in the sequence of correspondence is a letter of the 26th from Francis to his mother:

I received the warm woolly waistcoat last night, for which many thanks. I put it on straight away and kept quite reasonably warm all night. It gets very cold as soon as the sun goes down. In the daytime on the other hand, it is often uncomfortably hot. I have been making enquiries about Ted and sincerely trust he has been well looked after all this time. A great number of missing and wounded people turn up and with any luck he ought to be safe enough. By this time you ought to have got some of

my letters and postcards which I have been sending at every opportunity. I am glad to hear that Rachie is well – I never realised I was so soon going to be an uncle. What does it feel like to be a grandmother! I hope this beastly war will be over soon – at any rate before it gets really cold.

If you follow the doings of II Corps in Sir John French's despatches you will see exactly what we have been doing. I only read the first despatch yesterday in the Weekly Times which arrived safely last night. Thank you! I didn't know till then that we were quite so close to being done for.

Sunday 27th September *At 3 p.m. Bombardier Kelly spotted a dozen Germans in open order making straight for our observing station. The general turned out his HQ with rifles and we fired a round over their heads. (We couldn't hit them because of the crest) They disappeared. An alarm at night. Turned out and shelled Condé bridge.*
Monday 28th September *Gen Smith-Dorrien round on tour of inspection.*

On the 28th, despite the corps commander's visit, Francis again found time to write to his mother and his father:

Dear Mother,

The mails are arriving here well now and I have received a letter most days this week. Many thanks for the papers and parcel No. 3, with khaki shirt and grape nuts and cocoa. At this rate I shall soon have a complete outfit again. I was lucky enough to pick up a Wolseley valise by the roadside the other day which is a great comfort. Things seem to be at a deadlock now; we have been here quite a long time, but we do not mind much as there is plenty to eat and every day the Allies get stronger and the Germans weaker.

Father will be glad to hear that the Sherwood Foresters did very well yesterday. The Germans rushed some of our people out of their trenches. These came rushing back in a great fright into the S.F.'s who were rushing behind. The latter, however, promptly charged up the hill and retook the trenches but lost 16 officers and 200 men doing it.

I wonder when our Indian divisions are coming over and where they are now.

I haven't yet had any answers to my enquiries about Ted. With luck he will be alright I think.

Dear Father,

Many thanks for your two letters. How are you getting on with your new army? You will be pleased to hear that the Sherwood Foresters have been distinguishing themselves.

We have been sitting here for about a fortnight now and it is beginning to get a trifle boring, but there is nothing to complain about really – plenty to eat and mails coming in with great regularity. I know the sound of all the German batteries now in front, from their small field gun to 'Dirty Dick' which only fires very occasionally and is believed to be an 11-inch howitzer. He is very much respected, however, and he makes a hole big enough to hide a house and sends

splinters in all directions up to 600 yards. They found a bit of the base of the shell the other day and its head which has an armour-piercing nose – there is no doubt they meant him to bombard Paris with. It is very dull not knowing at all what is going on, away from the little part of the line where one happens to be. Things seem to be at an absolute deadlock but I hope General Joffre has something up his sleeve for the Germans. At any rate the Russians seem to be pushing on well and should be able soon to get at Germany from a rather unexpected quarter. I imagine that it is on their progress that the length of the war will depend. I hope it won't go on into the winter. There is a touch of frost in the air at night now and the leaves are coming off fast.

It was very interesting to read General French's despatch. I began to realise at Le Cateau that things were beginning to look a bit bad but never knew till I read the despatch how near we were to being wiped out. Half-way through the morning we were sent to assist the 3rd Division on our left and came into action close to the 6th Battery RFA to try and draw fire off them as they were being rapidly knocked to bits. We fired over 600 rounds from our four guns in two hours and a bit, and I am told did considerable damage to the German infantry who were endeavouring to get out of a wood. The guns got nearly red hot and everyone was stone deaf temporarily. I think the Germans thought it was still the 6th Battery shooting as they continued to shell it and practically finished it off. They also spotted their wagon line and planted a few dozen high explosive shell right among the horses, killing most of them and blowing up a wagon full of ammunition. Close on the other side of us was the small village of Audencourt which at 3 p.m. was nothing more than a mass of dust. Of course plenty of stray shell fell amongst us and our wagon line and there were rifle bullets flying about most of the time, but I don't think we were ever spotted all day, which was lucky to say the least of it, considering the state of affairs going on only a few hundred yards either side and behind us. The Germans were using the big howitzer firing lyddite and common shell. They make the most deafening noise. They outnumber our guns by about 4 to 1 at least I should think.

I have put in a claim for £30 for my kit which was lost on 23rd August and I believe there is quite a chance of getting it.

I wonder if this will finish before the hunting season is over, though I am afraid there will be precious few horses left in the country. Have they taken the chestnut mare yet?

Please thank Mother for her parcels which are arriving regularly now and are most acceptable.

I am very well and fear that I am putting on weight rapidly, lots to eat, out of doors all day and nothing to do. My only casualty so far is Mr Northcroft's false tooth which was never designed to stand up to biscuits GS [General Service], especially when they are getting a bit stale, and soon carried away.

Tuesday 29th September   Walked round in evening to see Marten's old position in front of us. He was shelled out of it one day and lost a good many men. The whole place spotted with shell holes.
Wednesday 30th September   A walk in evening.

Also preserved is a letter of the 29th from Lieutenant-Colonel Onslow, commander of 27th Brigade RFA:

Dear Colonel Foljambe,
Very glad indeed to get your letter.
I am very sorry to hear and see in the papers about your eldest son. I hope, now that communication is opened with prisoners, that you will hear good news of him. I am afraid you have also lost a brother in the 60th – I saw this in a paper of the 19th September. I have not told your son yet. Your son is doing very well. He is senior subaltern of his battery, and his captain speaks very highly of him. He is very well in health also, looking as fit as possible.
Yes! Major Holland's death was a great blow. He was the life and soul of the brigade.
I hope you will go and see my sister, Mrs Curtis. She lives at Langford Hall, about 2 miles north of Newark.
Many thanks for all the kind wishes and that 27th Brigade will march into Berlin.

It seems that it was only at this point that Francis heard of Hubert's death, as he wrote to his father on the 30th:

Many thanks for your letter of the 20th. Mails are coming in pretty well these days. I saw in the paper this morning that Uncle H. had been killed – war is certainly a dreadful thing. I am wondering how the old Squire will bear the news.
You must let me know if you hear anything else about Ted. I have been trying to get news of him but it is difficult. I feel pretty sure, however, that he is alright. At that period of the war the Germans could look after prisoners and wounded, and I trust that Ted is at present in a hospital somewhere in Belgium.
These Germans in front of us have fairly wired themselves in, just like a birdcage. I suppose after we have left this, we will go and sit for a month in front of some other fortress or other. They deliver an attack on some part of the line most nights which is rather annoying of them. The Guards seem to have dropped in for a bad time of it. I see that Granville Vernon has been wounded.
I wonder if you could send me a pair of breeches – mine will very soon be on their last legs. Provided they are large enough and very strong, I am not particular about shape, fit or anything else. The bottom half of your breeches I think would about fit me, the waist a good bit smaller. I was an idiot not to send you a few pairs ready to send out as a first reinforcement instead of warehousing them all, but I didn't calculate on losing my second pair on the first day. I expect you are kept pretty hard at work. The colonel showed me your letter.

Henry's diary also continued its narrative during this period:

21st September *Started off entrenching a back position and worked at it on and off all day. Nothing doing except the usual artillery bombardments and light infantry efforts.*

22nd September *Digging in in the morning and fixing stakes for wire entanglements. Spent some time at the observation post. The men went down by platoons to bathe. Black Maria [a generic name for German heavy guns] put up several shells and one hit Kaye's billet which fairly knocked the house down, killed Rudolf [Jelf's] horse 'Sheila' and damaged several men. Sir John French came along and spoke very nicely to some of the men of my company and he was much appreciated. Duke of Connaught, Bonham and Hankey came along about 2 p.m. and had a taste of the shelling and they afterwards came to tea. Hankey took three of my letters as he was going to London so that they would arrive before mine to Gwen written 2 days ago. A French aeroplane reconnaissance disclosed position of German Black Maria and the French guns had a try.*

23rd September *Marched at 4.30 a.m.*

for Paissy which we found full of men so went on to Moulins and then to some caves under the hill where we spent a very uninteresting day. Black Maria tried for our guns throughout the day and put in shot after shot without damage. The brigade or rather 3 battalions marched back after dark. The North Lancs lost a few men from shrapnel going up in the morning. Back to our own billets and had a good sleep.

24th September *A general wash and brush up. Went to see the 1st Battalion in the afternoon who [have] lost 15 officers wounded, but not one killed.*

25th September *A day of preparation. Bathing, cleaning, etc. Marched at 5.45 p.m. to the tune of Black Marias who were shelling Pargnan and the valley and took our trenches in the Troyen Hill by 9.30 p.m.*

26th September *A dark night and in the early morning the Germans came on and attacked in several places. The Queen's next door got 15 with machine gun. Our own shell falling short. I had two men hurt, the Queen's lost 1 officer and 12 men in a few minutes. Sent messages back but our shell went on coming short all day. The last two shots of the day came into the back of*

our trenches. We had worked at these and defended ourselves as much against the Germans as our own fire. Put up some new barbed wire entanglement. Expected an attack which did not come. The Germans entrenching.

27th September   A certain amount of sniping. The morning dull and the usual artillery duel did not begin till about 10 a.m. Sniping on and off and our forward trench got quite a few. About 4.15 p.m. the enemy began to shell heavily and at 5.30 p.m. they began to advance and attacked our line chiefly C Company but they faded away in about ¼ hr and then attacked 3rd Brigade but drew off. Between 7.30 p.m. and 8 the Northamptons came up and relieved the battalion which went into reserve in the old spot. About 11.15 the French on our left were attacked and terrific firing, gun and rifle and star shell, took place and lasted at least ½ hr. We stood to arms but did not go out and shortly went to bed again.

28th September   Heard French held their own. A dull day and not so much shelling. My headache gradually disappearing.

29th September   Nothing doing except the usual shelling. Relieved the North Lancs in the trenches in the Chaussée. My company only. Went into the trenches at 6.45 p.m. A terrific battle to our front between German and French which began at 10 p.m. and went on till daybreak on 30th. The French held their own.

On this day Henry also wrote to his sister Dora, who was affectionately known by him as 'Vorzes', with some news of her son Ted.

My dear old Vorzes,

Very many thanks to you for the present of woollies, etc., packed by Avice, to whom send my love please, and also for your letter.

Poor old Hubert – it is a dreadful tragedy. I asked Gwen to offer my deepest sympathy with Mr Foljambe and Lady Gertrude as I had no time to write. I do hope that you will get news of Edmond and hear that he is alright.

Chico Phillips says that it was reported that Geoffrey Lane was in the hands of German doctors and possibly Ted may be too. Have not had a chance of seeing Francis yet – if I hear of their whereabouts I shall go and hunt him up.

This battalion has done very good work and is now in fine fettle and strength despite losses, as reinforcements have come well to time. The lengthy battle spoken of in the papers still continues and we all hope that things are going well and that there will be success in the not too far future. It must be most trying for all of you at home. Sitting still must be very difficult and I hope you find lots to occupy you.

We had a burst of wet weather a week ago – now it is better, but the clouds are lowering, and if these horrible guns will go on pumping lead into the air I'm afraid the rain will fall again and make things uncomfy.

I am so glad to hear Father is better. I wrote to him and got my letter taken home by a fellow who was motoring that night. It seems so funny to be about 24 hours off London with such a remote chance of getting there for a longish time.

I am longing to hear about the 3rd Battalion – poor dear Rachie would be upset if the Rat had to leave at such a juncture. I trust all goes well with her. My love Vorzes and to George and all.

Chico Phillips was a Rifle Brigade officer who had been in the battalion with Ted, and Geoffrey Lane had also been taken prisoner of war. The 'Rat' was Henry's affectionate term for Victor Yeats-Brown, who was still with Rachie in India with the 3rd Battalion KRRC.

30th September   Left the trenches at 4.50 a.m. and got away alright. Wrote letters, slept etc. and went off to the trenches again at 6.30 p.m. The general gave orders we were not to leave till 5 a.m. next morning. I remonstrated, as the actual time for Germans' truce varies, fog etc. A quiet night. Sniping continued throughout, all at the French.

CHAPTER 5

Flanders and Ypres

Whilst the British and German armies had been slugging it out on the heights above the River Aisne, the staffs had been planning a move north as there was a gap in the line between the Oise and the Dutch frontier and the northern coast of France, and the control of part of the English Channel coast was at risk. Both sides started to leapfrog their forces to stretch north, thinning them out and stretching them in an unbroken line from the Belgians at Antwerp to the Swiss border. The British were to take position in Flanders, which would shorten their supply lines and enable them to defend the northern French coast and the English Channel.

On 1 October Francis heard that the battery was to move and for the next ten days was mostly on the move at night, hiding up during the day so that the Germans would not suspect that they were shifting north. His diary just recorded the route, but with the occasional acerbic comment:

Wednesday 7th October   Train to Amiens and Rue (past Abbeville). A 35-kilometre march back to Bellancourt. Arrived 4 a.m. Fine staff work!!

But mail was still getting through, as Francis acknowledged in a letter to his mother on 8 October:

I have just received a splendid parcel of eatables and some knitted things from a relative I have never met – Mrs Florence Warre who writes from Renfrewshire. Will you please thank her most awfully for sending them. Warm things are now becoming a necessity at night, and thanks to your woolly bear and these things that have just come I have now a very fair winter outfit. There is absolutely no news that I can let out at present.

I hope the news of poor Uncle H.'s death has not been too much for the Squire. I thought Ted would be alright. I expect I shall find him at Berlin!

Your letters and parcels are arriving splendidly.

Finally, the battery joined the battle again at Richebourg l'Avoué, near La Bassée on the Béthune front. The 5th Division started the operation by trying to break through the German lines on the right, but the attack was very spread out, and the Germans resisted. The village of Givenchy changed hands several times but in the middle of the month the city of Antwerp, to the north in Belgium, fell and the Germans were able to redirect troops to reinforce their lines. At the end of the month 5th Division was relieved by the Lahore Division from India and was then moved up to Ypres.

Monday 12th October   Marched with advanced guard to Rue de l'Epinette. In action all day. Shelled by German 15-pounder field guns.

OPPOSITE *Two infantrymen take cover behind a hedge in Belgium on 13 October.* IWM Q53319.

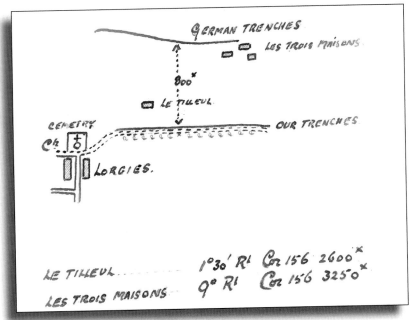

GERMAN TRENCHES
LES TROIS MAISONS
800ˣ
LE TILLEUL
CEMETRY
Ch
OUR TRENCHES
LORGIES.
LE TILLEUL . . . . 1°30' R¹ Cₒᵣ 156 2600ˣ
LES TROIS MAISONS . . . . . 9° R¹ Cₒᵣ 156 3250ˣ

ABOVE *Sketch map showing the relative positions of German and British trenches at Tilleul and Lorgies, October 1914. All the sketches that follow were made by Francis during his time at the Front.*

For the rest of the month 27th Brigade RFA was grouped with the 14th Infantry Brigade for the operations around La Bassée. The 27th Brigade war diary described the operation:

The whole country is absolutely flat and intersected by ditches and canals. There are a great many high trees and many villages and houses. It was impossible to obtain covered positions for batteries, only positions concealed from view could be taken up. Observation stations had to be placed in lofty buildings and every battery, as a rule, had to send a forward observing officer with a telephone.

During the first part of the operations when the infantry were advancing, sections of guns were attached to each battalion, but when the infantry began to stop and entrench, the batteries were reformed and brought into action about 1,000 to 1,500 yards behind the infantry trenches with observing officers pushed well to the front. The brigade fired very successfully at night, the lines of fire being laid out during the day. The fire of the batteries at night kept down the rifle fire from the enemies trenches and frequently repelled the advance of the enemy's infantry to attack our trenches. Two of the batteries remained in action night and day. The horses remained harnessed up at night and the harness was only removed in the day time.

120th Battery, which still had only four guns as the ones lost at Mons had not yet been replaced, was not left in position, as Francis later commented:

At this period the battery was withdrawn at night. Thus, at about 6.30, the teams used to arrive and we would limber up and march some 4 miles to the rear. This moving out was always most unpleasant for the reason that nearly every night at dusk rifle fire would break out and increase to a regular roll of musketry. Spent bullets came humming over by the score and why more horses and men were not hit, I don't know. It was usually 9.30 before we got settled down in bivouac and we had to [be] up at about 3.30 next morning to be in action and concealed by daylight. Altogether a rather senseless waste of energy.

Tuesday 13th October   *In action all day. Made dug-outs and improved the position. Returned at night.*
Wednesday 14th October   *Heavy night attack on 13th and 15th Infantry brigades. Repulsed.*

14th October 1914
Dear Mother,
Sorry I haven't written before this week but we have been very busy lately and not had much time. By this time I hope you are quite well and strong again. Everybody seems to be overworked except the actual troops. We all get fatter every day. I suppose it is from eating a lot and living always in the open air. The parcel post of Harrods' provisions arrived safely last night for which many thanks. The underclothes especially were most acceptable – as a matter of fact I managed to buy some dreadfully coloured pants in a village the other day, but they are much too coarse to be comfortable.
We had some of your China tea today. The worst of it is I shall dislike the soldiers' stewed stuff all the worse.
You won't forget to thank – Houston House, Renfrewshire N.B. for her parcel of knitted things, and provisions. It is getting a trifle chilly at night certainly, and to make

matters worse, there is generally a thick fog in the mornings which soaks everything. What I should really like now is a pair of waterproof overalls down to the knees for riding in, and a pair of warm lined leather gloves.

How is the rest of the army getting on? Hurry up and send them out to help finish this beastly war off. Please thank Father for the Observer and letter.

Thursday 15th October   *A quiet day. Slept in house close to guns.*
Friday 16th October   *A foggy day. Germans retiring. Walked out in evening to look at their trenches.*
Saturday 17th October   *Marched to Auberge de la Bombi the other side of Richebourg l'Avoué. Billeted in the village.*
Sunday 18th October   *Came into action and dug in a mile down the La Barre Road. Shelled out by 4.2-inch howitzers (Black Marias) at 4 p.m. They could see us I think. Ordered up the teams and got the guns away without any casualties, which was lucky as the shells were landing right among the guns, but on soft ground so their effect is very local.*
Monday 19th October   *In reserve. Remained in billets. Infantry attacking without success. Reported heavy losses.*

19th October 1914
Dear Mother,
Will you please communicate as before 'All well in 120th' to the other three addresses.
Chief wants now are:-
Sago, rice and tapioca and other stuff for milk puddings.
Coffee chocolate was very good.
Cigarettes (50 a week).
Some more China tea.
Riding overalls.
Another deadlock now it seems. The Germans were rude enough to shell the battery out of our position yesterday with 'Dirty Dick' 5-inch howitzer. No casualties for a wonder. Just saw an old London Growler pass, Red Cross. They have got beautiful new motor ambulance teams now.

I've seen very few German wounded – they carry them off in the most marvellous way in country carts on mattresses etc. One finds no mattresses or rugs left in the houses. They burn their dead so that we shall not find out their lines.

Tuesday 20th October   *In reserve. Reconnoitred position.*
Wednesday 21st October   *Detached section to take over from Davidson who has been wounded the day before. Marched out before light and chose a position (1,800) from trenches. Went up and ran a telephone to Lorgies church. Dug in behind cemetery wall. I think this place must have been given away, because as soon as it was light the Germans started shooting at it like anything and also shelled it hard. They got 12 direct hits out of about 20 on the church which caught fire and nearly roasted me out. Several other houses also burning. At last a shell about a yard over my head and I got out and ran to other side of cemetery and finally crept out and went behind a house in the village. Full of dead horses. Made my way back to the guns as line was cut and found an OP further away on a haystack. Observed fire on Les Trois Maisons and knocked them to bits. Returned in evening to billet. Find Major Wilson joined us. Graham leaves us for the 119th Battery.*
Thursday 22nd October   *Detached section again. Moved guns back a bit to near X roads. Registered Les Trois Maisons and fired at different targets all day. Walked up to infantry trenches to observe fire. Returned to billet in evening. (On the 2 days detached section; first day fired 320 rounds, 2nd day fired 200 rounds. Destroyed Les Trois Maisons.)*
Friday 23rd October   *Orders to retire back to Rue de l'Epinette. Moved at 2 a.m. Slept on haystack. Retirement successfully carried out. Hardly a shot fired. In action and shooting at distillery. Germans plastering village of Festubert with big howitzers. Moved in afternoon to a new position found by Wilson at Rue des Chavattes. An excellent farm house. Registered.*

Saturday 24th October *Relieved by 121st. In billets near Le Touret. Indian troops arriving all afternoon. News that Germans were knocked badly by I Corps at Ypres. French said to be attacking all along the line. Pollard (119th Battery) killed.*

Sunday 25th October *Relieved 119th in forward position on the left of 121st Battery. A lot of night shooting. Changed the observing station to a house further back, as the 119th's observing station had been spotted. Put a cap looking over the top of the house and had the satisfaction of seeing the Germans shell it all day. A hole clean through the cap when we fetched it in! Planted trees to conceal guns. Fired late at night.*

Monday 26th October *A quiet day but some heavy night attacks. Germans broke through in many places but were counter-attacked and driven back. A lot of shooting to be done. Slept in little school close to guns. A piano and music!*

26th October

Dear Father,

Very many thanks for the breeches which arrived in the nick of time. My only pair were about done, although they were new at the beginning of the war – whipcord doesn't wear at all well. Everybody's have

gone in the same way. I was sorry to move away from the centre of the line where we spent a very happy three weeks in front of Fort Condé, a French fortress close to Soissons. The Germans were wired in like a birdcage and there was no chance of turning them out by a frontal attack. One got to know the noise of all the guns round about. The country round here is horrible – flat and mostly plough which in the rain becomes a sort of morass. I have been having a very interesting, if exciting time with a detached section right up in front and observing, sometimes from our front trenches. The first day I was out I was observing from the wall of a church. Luckily I dug myself a deep hole in case of accidents, because they shelled the church so hard that I couldn't move. The tenth direct hit finished the old place off and next day the whole place was a heap of ashes. I was very glad to get out. There were some Indian reinforcements up here the other day – just like a pageant. I hope they will stand the cold alright.

A rumour today of a big Russian success on the Vistula – I hope it is true. There is also some talk of the Second Army getting a bit of rest soon, but I don't put any faith now in 'rests'. They have never come off yet

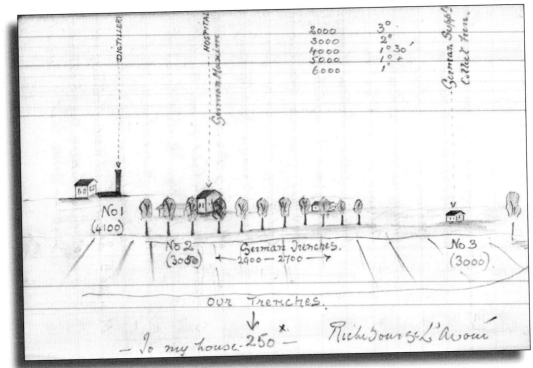

RIGHT *Richebourg l'Avoui, October 1914.*

– still it is about time. I can only remember one day when I didn't hear a gun, and except when we have been in action we have never stayed in the same place for 24 hours for the whole months we have been out. This sort of life (without the shells and the bullets) suits me and I am afraid I am putting on weight badly. I can't see the end of the war at all with these enormous battles; it becomes siege warfare, and progress is too slow for anything. I wonder what this new German advance along the coast will result in. Have you had any bombs yet in England?

We have got a new major and have joined up with the brigade again. Nearly all the war we have been attached to some infantry brigade or other and out by ourselves. Two more of us gone this past week – one killed and one wounded.

Tuesday 27th October *Relieved at 9 a.m. by the 121st Battery. Back in billets all day. Alarm at night and got all harnessed up ready to move, but nothing happened.*

Wednesday 28th October *Relieved the 119th in rear position at 9 a.m. Forward observing officer in Richebourg. Registered German trenches and drew panorama from hole in roof of one of the houses. Shelled from 9 a.m. onwards by big howitzer (11-inch). Sheltered in cellar of house, but most unpleasant. Many houses knocked flat all round and the trenches in front were blown in. Returned to battery at 4 p.m. and very nearly got caught by a German field gun on the way back. Another disturbed night. Attack on right front. Shooting at intervals during the night.*

Thursday 29th October *Took Lindsay down to forward observing station. Went down to KOSB [King's Own Scottish Borderers] in morning. New battalion of Seaforths (from India) arrived. They were shelled out of their billet in Richebourg St Vaast in afternoon. A disturbed night with several night attacks. Kitty wounded by a spent bullet.*

Friday 30th October *Relieved by 121st. In billets at Le Touret.*

Saturday 31st October *Marched at 10 a.m. via Béthune, Merville and Vieux Boquin to Rouge-Croix.*

31 October 1914
Dear Mother,

Thanks for your letter and the woolly waistcoat which I always wear now, and which is quite the warmest thing in the way of waistcoats I have ever seen. It is getting quite chilly these days and frosty at night.

We have got a short reprieve now. Yesterday we were relieved by the Indian divisions. It is quite a relief to only hear distant guns after three weeks solid in action, that is since we moved up from the Aisne. It is about time the infantry of the Second Army had a rest. They haven't had 24 hours' rest hardly since August yet they have been driving back the most violent attacks day and night for the last three weeks and would go on for a long time yet if necessary, but I don't think they would have had enough energy to have pushed on themselves. I think it looks very well for the general situation that they have been able to give us an 'easy'. I am glad you are better now and able to get about.

I wish I could hear more about Edmond – I am beginning to get uneasy again about him as he ought to have been able to communicate before this. I had a letter from the Squire last night – his writing is getting very shaky I am sorry to see – I hope he is still bearing up.

My best horse got a bullet in her the other day which is still somewhere inside. I am afraid it is going to kill her.
Chief wants now:
  A warm blanket.
  A good map case.
  Riding apron.
  A small compass on a wrist strap.
  Cuticura soap.
  Coffee chocolate at intervals.
  1 khaki tie.
  Gloves.
  Puttees.
  Magazines & papers.
  Kolynos tooth paste.

Continued next day:

No rest for the wicked! Pulled out as usual at 4 a.m. and pushed up to the front again. I suppose somebody got the jumps. Anyhow this is far pleasanter country after our last place and I don't think the German has more than one battery of Black Marias here – at any rate I haven't heard them yet.

Please thank Mary for her letter. The last lot of provisions arrived safely but not the overalls. What nonsense all this mentioning in despatches is! Practically all the artillery and the whole staff I think. Some battery commanders sent in everyone's name, some did not. All the battery commanders are mentioned ex officio. Of course there are a few deserving ones (one on this brigade), but otherwise everyone has done more or less the same and had an equally unpleasant time. The ones to pity, however, are the infantry – they have the most awful time – shelled all day and attacked nearly every night. I can't understand how they can stand it.

A rumour just come in that there has been a big naval battle – 40 German ships sunk at the expense of 20 of ours. I hope it may be true. It will stop all hope of an invasion of England.

It has been quiet most of today and I hope we shall have a peaceful night. Just lately I have had as much excitement as I want as forward observing officer. One day we had Dirty Dick on us for five hours on end – he makes a hole big enough to comfortably hide a gun in.

The Kaiser is supposed to be in these parts. An airman said yesterday that they had located him. Today they sallied out and dropped 500 bombs in various places in the hope of getting him! The Kaiser goes about with a regiment of cavalry in full dress so they say.

In Belgium again now.

For the first two weeks of October Henry and 2 KRRC remained in the old line around

BELOW *Kaiser Wilhelm II of Germany (centre) with Field Marshal Prince Rupprecht of Bavaria (left).*

Troyen, above the Aisne, carrying out reliefs around every four days. The time was spent in improving the trenches and making better shelters for officers and men. They were constantly shelled and lost many officers and men both from the shelling and from sniping in the trenches. There were frequent alarms and warnings of German attacks but no serious ones developed. During the period the battalion was filled up with drafts from England, and by the middle of the month was nearly up to strength (over 1,000). Henry takes up the story:

1st October   *Came away at 5 a.m. and was shelled at once. It was a very clear morning. My company not extended but one lot went off with the W Yorks. I had one man killed and four wounded. Digging fatigue at night.*

2nd October   *An easy day and slept a good deal. An attack on the Arras road which failed. Liny Percal got busy on a cross trench with his machine gun. Got the Paris Daily Mail of October 1st and 2nd.*

3rd October   *Just after breakfast German field howitzer shelled our lines and shot very accurately. They killed our orderly sergeant with a shell which pitched about 10 feet from our mess. None of us damaged by it. Another pitched in the fence just above our bivouac. If Bouverie, Crossman and self had moved another yard it would have caught us. We moved at 7.30 p.m. and took up the trenches as before from the fork road. A quiet night except for digging.*

4th October   *Got letters from Gwen. A terrific bombardment in the afternoon to which the Germans hardly replied. Reggie Seymour and 6 officers arrived and I got Bury and Liddle posted to my company. At 7.45 p.m. a platoon of Coldstream went out to fill up the sniper's trench 80 yards to our front. They found 5 or 6 dead enemy in it and went on to the next trench which was occupied by quite a few. These they killed but were fired on by another lot and in coming back had their officer and 8 men hit and 2 missing. Found a lot of parcels from Gwen when I went to Lumer at 9 p.m. A good deal of sniping but no harm.*

5th October   *In the trenches all day, a certain amount of sniping and a good deal of shelling. Several men of the Sussex lost over by the black howitzers. Relieved by the Northamptonshire at 8.30 p.m., a little sniping but not much. Men rather inclined to rush under cover as my riflemen got out. A quiet night.*

6th October   *Some shelling in the morning. Kay hit in the shoulder, a flesh wound. Several men hit in the morning and also in the afternoon.*

7th October   *Very severe German shelling. A field battery, heavy howitzers and ballista throwing an enormous bomb used. The latter did a lot of damage. Liny Percal had his leg badly broken. Two officers North Lancs killed and a good many men. Several of them fell quite close to our headquarters and were quite deafening. Took over trenches from the North Lancs and Northamptons at 7 p.m. No sniping in front of my company but about 10 bombs thrown along the reserve trenches about midnight.*

8th October   *No excitement at dawn. A lot of aeroplanes about, mostly German. Heard heavy gun fire to north-west. The usual fight with the French and Germans took place and lasted for some time but bulk of the firing was French.*

9th October   *Sniping at the French went on all night. Just after dawn the Germans enfiladed our trenches with machine guns but we had no casualties. About 5.45 p.m. there was another attack on the French. We heard the enemy singing Der Wacht am Rhine and then go in but the attack soon died away. Were relieved by the Northamptons at 6.30 p.m. and got to Lisnes at 8 p.m. Got several parcels.*

10th October   *Improved my dug-out and made it very snug. Had a shave, bath and haircut. A great joy getting a new and clean shirt on. Got a parcel from Gwen and a letter. About 8.20 p.m. the Germans attacked our trenches all along the line but they were driven off. The attack lasted some time and they covered it with a lot of artillery. Our guns fired well too. Got to bed about 11 p.m.*

11th October *Wrote letters etc. Changed over to the village end at 6.30 p.m. and went to second row of fence. The mess in the old house again. A certain amount of shelling but no damage.*

12th October *The French advanced to the Chemin des Dames just before daylight. We started the ball at 4.30 a.m. by shelling and rifle fire and the French had no opposition at first. Then they got shelled but as far as we could hear maintained their position. The Germans shelled us hard in the evening and then made a feeble attack. All quiet by 7 p.m. and only a few shells afterwards. To bed at 10 p.m.*

13th October *A certain amount of shelling. Poor young Laurence killed by a sniper and 2 other men. Took out my company and improved communication trenches 8.00–10.45 p.m. List had started stories about the enemy putting up shell which had clockwork arrangement to make them flare during the night and the North Lancs stood to arms expecting attack. The enemy did throw up lights and were hideously jumpy but we had a quiet night.*

14th October *A little rain but not much and the sun was out by 11 a.m. A considerable amount of shelling in the afternoon and evening especially on the road to Vendresse and further out into the valley of the Aisne. An attack began about 9.30 p.m. and we stood to arms but it fizzled out in ½ hour. Packed new blankets and sent them off with some of the officers' kits.*

15th October *A lot of firing on our right and I got the men dressed but we did not fall in and we slept till 7 a.m. Orders that the French would take over from us and a staff officer and some colonels arrived to look at the trenches about 5 p.m. just after we had had tea. I was talking with Eric [Lieutenant-Colonel Eric Serecold, commanding officer of 2 KRRC] and the general and all the officers nearly were outside the mess house when a light was shown in the wood opposite and directly after the battery of high explosive put in 4 and nearly caught us. The French began to arrive about 9.30 p.m. and, as the head of*

the column arrived in the village, the lamp in the wood showed again and the battery opened killing 18 and wounding 40. This delayed them and checked the advance in the narrow lane. The second battalion halted down the road and the third battalion still further behind. Eventually the relief was completed by 1.30 a.m. in a fog.*

The battalion spent the next four days travelling towards Ypres where it was to support the British forces already there and then a further two days at rest before being ordered back into the attack. The First Battle of Ypres was the defining battle of 1914 for the British Army. If the Germans were able to batter their way through the British lines at Ypres, the route would be open to Calais and Dunkirk, the British supply lines would be threatened, and German success could even knock Britain out of the war. Henry was right in the thick of it.

16th October *We started to march down at 2.15 a.m. via Doury reaching Vauxcére about 6.30 a.m. Filthy billets. Slept 4 hours. Knee rather full of rheumatics. Marched at 4.30 p.m. to Fismes and entrained. Left at 9.30 p.m.*

17th October *Slept fairly well as far as 6 in one compartment would allow. No washing place or lavatory. The men like sardines, about 40 in each closed truck. A very slow journey. Owing to an accident we stopped practically all night in one place. And we crawled into Wimereux about 6 a.m.*

18th October *There was another accident in which 30 people were killed and 80 wounded and we stayed where we were until 11 a.m. Walked into the village with Eric, Bouverie and Crossman and bought eggs and butter and had some coffee. Through St Omer and got to our destination about 5 p.m. Marched about 2½ miles to Cassel and went into billets. Quite good.*

19th October *Though the men had had a bad time in the train and we the officers had six in a carriage we were ordered to route march and drill 5 miles. Various* work refitting, pay etc. in the afternoon and a horrible owner of the house we shared came along and made himself very objectionable and hunted through our servants' kits for things they might have stolen. Worth a report on the subject. Got a mail and were told we should move tomorrow and have a short march. Went to bed at 11 p.m.

20th October   At 3.30 a.m. got orders to prepare to move at 5.30 a.m. At 4 a.m. to move at 5.15 a.m. The brigade in advance and the battalion did advanced guard. The road slippery, all pavé, via Steenvoorde crossing the Belgium frontier at Abele through Poperinghe to Elverdinghe where we billeted. Rain at intervals and heard guns firing to the north-east. An excellent night in a small château in which we had the men.

21st October   Breakfast at 7 a.m. and hung about till 10.30 when we marched to the north exit of Ypres. Was sent off with others on a reconnaissance to the south of that town and got back about 2.30 p.m. After reporting slept on some hay in a barn. We marched at 5 p.m. to Boesinghe, which we reached about 7.30 p.m., and luckily got billets as there were a lot of French troops about. Eric, Chris and Reggie came and dined at our billet (Bury, Bouverie, Crossman and self) as the mess was very full. We were on our own and had pork and potatoes and excellent coffee.

22nd October   A europe morning, breakfast at 7.30 a.m. Got some Belgian boots, 9 pairs, for men of my company who were practically through theirs and had several pairs mended. Had a general clean up but no bath. Wrote to Gwen and told her we were in comparative peace, with the usual result. Had arranged a little birthday dinner in my house at 7.30 p.m. and at that moment we got orders to fall in at once. Had just time to eat a little and we moved at 7.45 p.m. and marched to Pilkem. Marched again at 11.15 p.m. having drawn 50 rounds a man and tools. Fight at Het-Sas (Canal lock north of Boesinghe).

23rd October   The Germans had broken in our line held by Cameron Highlanders at the inn at the cross roads about ¼ mile south-east of Bixschoote and had come through. We had dug in all night and at 6 a.m. we advanced D and C Companies in attack and got held up by heavy fire and obstacles. About midday the general started an infantry attack in the wrong direction and it had to be reorganised and this time came in well and drove the Germans right away with loss over the Bixschoote–Kaufemarck [Langemarck?] road. (Took about 130 minutes among shrapnel.) We were sent to take up the original trenches but there was no one, not even a staff officer, to show us where they were and digging had been going on all over the place both our own and German. Eventually got into line with the North Lancs. An officer of the Cameron Highlanders came up while a heavy German counter-attack was taking place and went into some badly dug and sited trenches. The North Lancs and two of my platoons stayed to help him. Spottiswood and Crossman stayed with the platoons and Bouverie and I went into the trenches we originally dug the night before. Could not find out my exact losses but had 25 killed and wounded in the two leading platoons. No chance of relief at all for at least 24 hrs. Very tired and a splitting head from shell and rifle fire.

The battalion war diary adds:

At about 3.30 p.m. the North Lancashires advanced on our right and to the east of the road, and although they lost heavily during their advance, succeeded in driving the Germans out of their trenches. They bolted across the open and gave a splendid target to our leading platoons and machine guns. The Germans all made for a gateway in a fence about 400 yards behind their line. It is impossible to say how many they lost, but they must have left 300 or 400 killed and wounded on the ground. D Company alone took 130 prisoners.

   About 10.30 p.m. Major Warre, as he was on his way back up to the front

BELOW *Lieutenant General Sir Douglas Haig, Commander of the British 1 Corps, confers with Major General Sir Charles Monro, commander of the 2nd Division in a street in France. Second from right is Brigadier General Johnny Gough, Haig's Chief of Staff, talking to Brigadier General E. M. Perceval of the 2nd Division.* IWM Q54992

trenches, heard his name called in the darkness. He found a wounded Rifleman who had recognised him by his walk, and on searching the ground found five or six other wounded men, whom he was able to send in.

24th October   *Improved trenches at early dawn. Sent parties out to get the wounded and after that the dead. Dug a trench for the latter and buried 31 riflemen. A little service at 5.30 p.m. The Germans were more or less quiet during the day except for shell fire. At 9 p.m. the French arrived to take over. Attacks along the line delayed them but eventually they got into the trenches and we moved off about*

11 p.m. Got shelled going away and one man of mine was killed in the outpost line. Marched through the night and had tea near Pilkem.

25th October   *. . . and then on to Ypres where we billeted at 5.30 a.m. Had a hostel with RAMC, the men in tents. Evening service at 6 p.m.*

26th October   *Went to early service with Eric at 6 a.m. Orders received to march at 7.50 a.m. altered to 8.25 a.m. and we marched out about 1½ miles east of Ypres and then halted in a field having a barn ss HQ. March on at 2 p.m. a few yards and back again. Chico arrived in the evening practically all right. Slept in a barn but it was very noisy and my cold was a nuisance.*

27th October   *Breakfast at 6 a.m. quite a europe morning we moved at 7 about 2½ miles along the road and went into some dug-outs a mile or so behind the front line. Nothing much doing but I was glad of an easy as my cold had gone to my chest. Saw [General] Johnny Gough who was with Douglas Haig. Also Prince Arthur [of Connaught, a staff officer in 1914] who kindly took letters and one to Gwen to send by special messenger home. A French attack to our left which lasted 7.30 to 8 p.m.*

28th October   *Joined Battle of Ypres.*

   An early morning again but moved at 10.30 a.m. into a low wood near a race course. We dug ourselves in and some bullets fired from the front line came into the wood, one man hit by a shell. Attacks were made on the German line but they were found to be heavily wired in and had lots of machine guns. Reported attack by enemy in the morning.

29th October   *At 5.30 a.m. the attack began. The Germans broke through 21st Brigade but were beaten back. They then had a go further north. The Berkshires and the North Lancs were withdrawn to the château again and were lucky to escape shelling. We got there about 11 a.m. The 3rd Brigade was sent out to counter-attack astride the main Ypres–Menin road and as I write [at] 11.30 p.m. this counter-attack is in progress. Our other brigade was left up in the low plantation. We have 200 guns in action. Attack successful and we established ourselves in Gheluvelt. As usual a bad salient in our part of the line of trenches and a weak left as well. Several guns at night were driven back.*

30th October   A harassing day of shell fire. Rearranged trenches and units in them. Did not feel at all sure as to our strength.

The British official history of the war says:

Saturday the 31st October 1914 was to prove one of the most critical days in the history of the British Expeditionary Force, if not of the British Empire. The initiative still lay with the enemy. General von Fabeck, we are told, recognised from the outset that the occupation of the Messines–Wytschaete ridge was of decisive importance. The 31st October will always be remembered for the dramatic fighting near Gheluvelt. Orders were given by the Germans for this village to be attacked, as the capture of Zandvoorde on the 30th had made it possible to operate against it from the south-east as well as from the east, and to enfilade, with good observation, much of the British line in the vicinity. A decisive victory seemed assured: for everything pointed to the British being completely exhausted. And they may well have appeared so to the enemy. The line

BELOW *French troops in the main street of Ypres on 29 October 1914.*

that stood between the British Empire and ruin was composed of tired, haggard and unshaven men, unwashed, plastered with mud, many in little more than rags. But they had their guns, rifles and bayonets, and, at any rate, plenty of rifle ammunition, whilst the artillerymen always managed to have rounds available at the right place at critical moments.

Henry and 2 KRRC were in Gheluvelt:

31st October *Enemy attacked just before dawn and were more than held but got to a covered position. They could have enfiladed B Company trench and a company of North Lancs was sent out but failed to get home and came back up into trenches. The enemy had moved a gun to about 800 yards from our front trenches and fairly blew some of them up and the enemy then came forward.*

The Queen's and ourselves stuck it for some time and B Company longer than any of the firing line. Left with rear-guard. Eric went off to HQ and was wounded on the way. Tipton shot in the thigh by shrapnel outside our dug-out. Held my trenches for 40 minutes and then saw the Germans bringing up a machine gun to flank; we got first one platoon away and then the remainder. Had a certain amount of loss but was lucky as the Germans were only 40 yards off when we went off.

The losses in the brigade heavy. We collected after fighting on the way back to the château and found we had about 163 men. The shelling was perfectly fiendish during retirement and had been all day and our guns hardly replied at all. Formed on our front line in conjunction with 21st Brigade and 2nd Division and got to bed at 1.45 a.m.

Henry's version is typically modest. The regimental account takes up the story:

The enemy made a furious attack on the line Poezelhoek–Gheluvelt just before dawn. About the same time our line was heavily attacked south of the main road. At first our men were easily able to hold them, but immediately east of Gheluvelt the enemy managed to get cover, from which, with a machine gun, they were able to enfilade the trench held by B Company and the Queen's.

The enemy's attack was now pressed with extreme vigour, and at one point they drew up a gun to within 800 yards of the trenches on our left, determined to demolish them. The Germans were in very great force at this point; a prisoner afterwards said there were no less than twenty-four battalions opposed to our small force. In any case, the remnants of the 21st Brigade on our right were forced to retire, fighting stubbornly foot by foot.

The battalion was now in a very awkward situation, part of A and B Companies were practically surrounded. Losses in officers and men had been very heavy, and part of these companies were taken prisoners, very few of them unwounded. Captain Currie, with five or six men, had literally to fight his way back through the enemy, but got through with only two men unwounded.

Colonel Serocold [the CO] now decided to retire to a second position on the high ground east of Herenthage Château. He accordingly gave orders to Major Warre to hold on with the remnant of the force left at his disposal for half an hour, and on withdrawal to rejoin him on the position selected.

Colonel Serocold himself, with battalion headquarters, started back to report to the 3rd Brigade headquarters. Several of his men were hit on the way. The colonel himself was severely wounded by a shell in the château grounds, and the command of the battalion devolved on Major Philips.

A desperate situation now presented itself to the little force, composed of the remains

of the 2nd Battalion, one company of the Queen's Regiment, and a handful of the North Lancashires. The furious onsets of the Germans in overwhelming numbers formed a torrent which it was impossible to stem, and it was only by dint of the greatest personal courage and intrepidity on the part of every man that sufficient opposition was made to enable the retreat to be effected. There was fierce hand-to-hand fighting all the time, especially in the village, the Germans bringing up a machine gun into a side street, from which a portion of our reserve trenches could be enfiladed. Orders were given for the troops holding these trenches to clear. Half of the trenches, however, being behind a rise south of the village did not come under this fire, and were held by two platoons of D Company until the Germans got within 40 yards of them. Then, after a burst of rapid fire, the retirement was ordered, and the troops fell back, coming under heavy machine-gun and artillery fire as they went. The position had been held for 40 minutes. The battalion lost very heavily, but eventually formed a second line mixed up with the details of other regiments, on the position which had been pointed out by Colonel Serocold. A good many men drifted back through the woods towards Hooge. Here they were rallied and brought back again to reinforce the fighting line.

The battalion reformed in the trenches east and south of Herenthage Château, which they held for that night and the following day, their losses being very heavy, 9 officers and about 300 NCOs and men being all that was eventually left of the battalion. On the other hand the losses to the enemy were enormous.

October was also a busy month for the Foljambes in England. Dora was not well, George was busy at the depot at Newark recruiting and training soldiers for the reinforcement battalion for the Sherwood Foresters. The 1st/8th Battalion was still training in the south and the 2nd/8th was slowly being formed from a cadre of soldiers from the 1st/8th but with a large number of

new recruits. Hubert was dead and Henry
was engaged in the fiercest fighting of the
war so far.

George meanwhile wrote to Rachie in
India on 6 October:

*I am afraid it is ages since I wrote and I
have hardly heard how it is with you and
your young man, my grandson – nor what
he is like or anything about him. May he
be a great joy to you dear in all the years
to come. We are all very quiet and hard
at work here. It is most remarkable how
quietly determined the country is. We
have about 800–1,000 men here, some
600 or 700 sappers belonging to the new
11th Division now training at Grantham,
besides the recruits for our 8th Reserve
Battalion. We still require about 400 to
complete and I want them badly as until
they are got the regiment will not be able to
go to France and they are spoiling to be off.
I fear they will be rather hard to get as our
area has been drawn upon by nearly every
conceivable recruiter.*

*I am in a somewhat strange position
there having been some error in my
appointment to the depot which seems to
have been irregular, but I am officially a
recruiting officer for this district. However, it
has resulted in my having at least 5 masters
who quite impartially use me to wipe the
floor with! However, it is all in a day's work.*

*My dear brother has died a soldier's
death. Poor Gladys keeps up with great
pluck, but poor little thing I fear she is very
lonely and miserable.*

*I was over at Osberton for an hour or
two the other day while going round on
recruiting business and found the old
people wonderfully well, considering what a
blow it has been to them. You will probably
have heard that I had a letter from Edmond
written from a convent in Cambrai where
he is lying wounded and a prisoner, along
with some others whom he does not name.
Francis I have had several letters from, he
is very fit and well after the rough handling
they had in the first week of fighting. His
battery was in the thick of the stew from
the very start. I am wondering what has
happened to Victor, whether he has come
to Europe or whether he is still with you.
For your sake I hope his services will be
required in India at all events for the
present. It is of course impossible to make
any plans now, but if things turned out
favourably I should think the best thing you
could do would be to come home on leave
before another hot weather and if it could
be swayed stop in Italy on your way till the
cold east winds here are a bit tempered.*

*Mother has been (as usual) overworking
and has had to go into dock for a rest for a
week or 10 days. She and Arthur Jelf, who
has come home rather a wreck, are in the
same place (Dorset Square). I had to go to
the War Office last Saturday and I saw her
for an hour and she looked much better
than I suspected.*

*I hope you are by now getting quite
strong again, don't be too venturesome and
that you find everything comfortable and
are well looked after generally.*

Now, as Pepys says, to bed.

Love to Victor, and yourself.

Ted was alive, but wounded – no one knew to what extent – and in a convent in Cambrai. Dora was determined to track him down and started her campaign to locate him and try to get him repatriated at the earliest opportunity. She asked one of her other brothers, Edmond Warre, to get in touch with the Red Cross, to see if they could help in finding and repatriating Ted. Lord Cecil replied on behalf of the Red Cross from Paris:

7th October 1914
Dear Mr Warre,
Many thanks for your letter of the 1st inst. I note what you say about your nephew, Lieutenant E. W. S. Foljambe, lying in a convent at Le Cambrai. I will do my best, as soon as the Allies regain possession of Le Cambrai, to have him sought for but I am afraid it is not possible at the moment.

Finally, at the end of the month, a postcard arrived from Germany from a Captain Lane of the Rifle Brigade who had been taken prisoner at the same time as Ted. 'In case you have no news of your son, he was wounded 26th August. He is I hear now in hospital at Cambrai and going on well. I expect you have already heard this but I write in case you have not.'

November 1914

27th Brigade RFA had been ordered to the Ypres area with the rest of the 5th Division artillery and was ordered into action in support of the British and French cavalry holding the Messines–Wytschaete ridge under General Allenby. The 27th Brigade took up position between Neuve-Église and Hill 63 and its positions were practically unchanged for the rest of the year. The batteries relieved each other every second or third night, so 'shared' each others' positions. Francis, of course, maintained his diary:

Sunday 1st November *Marched at 2 p.m. to 1 mile north of Bailleul. Bivouacked.*
Monday 2nd November *Marched at 5.30 a.m. Rode on at daylight with the major to meet Headlam. Rode on to Neuve-Église and Wulverghem. A lot of heavy rifle fire in front. In reserve. The 121st and 119th in action south of Wulverghem. We waited on road for some time then returned to Neuve-*

Église and came into action at noon east of the village. *Quiet day, did not fire.*

The next five days were very foggy and visibility was very low. Apart from two children killed by German artillery in the village on the 4th, there was little to report but Francis did manage to write to his father on the 6th:

Many thanks for your letter and for your good wishes. I am afraid I never wished you many happy returns of your birthday the other day, though I did not forget it and drank your good health in some very bitter white wine. This is the land of fogs and the inhabitants tell me that very often one can't see for more than a hundred yards ahead for a month on end. We came round here the other day from near La Bassée, where the Germans made some desperate efforts to get through. It is appalling to think of the numbers they must have lost. Our casualties were far lighter than theirs and as far as I can understand we lost nearly 5,000 from our division alone. We had the ground in front of our trenches covered by our guns and after the first few days it only needed a few rounds to stop their attacks. I wonder how things are going there since we left. We were relieved at that point by some Indian troops. I think the Germans had some of their best remaining troops against us there. Here the enemy have been fairly quiet for the last day or two, but occasionally fire off their scatter guns into the blue. One of their shells killed two little girls here yesterday. That's about all the damage done. One of my horses stopped a spent bullet with her stomach the other day. I thought it was going to kill her but she has picked up again and now seems none the worse. I hope no complications will come. Continued later:
Interrupted by French attack. The French gunners go nearly mad and fairly blaze away with their little guns. They are marvellously good – official telegram from Petrograd just come in announcing a great Russian victory, which is cheering. I hope they will have to reinforce on the

eastern side and fall back here. I believe the Indians are pretty good now but at first they were a bit unsteady and one night the Gurkhas did a bolt. They are at any rate a fine-looking lot of men.*
The Kaiser is in these parts now. The French airmen dropped 500 bombs on various likely places to cheer him up. If the Germans fall back here, it seems to me that they will leave some of their guns behind them – I hope so. The infantry loathe them more than anything.
I wonder how long all this is going to last. I think that if we clear Belgium, there will be a stagnation and a long talk over the situation. Things can't go on at this rate for much longer, the losses are too great. We have been in close touch now for fully three months. Much love to all.

Sunday 8th November   *The German howitzers searched for us nearly all day. They got the observation party in the trenches. Sergeant Ironside killed. An unpleasant day.*
Monday 9th November   *In reserve. Moved into billets down the Bailleul road.*
Tuesday 10th November   *In action again. A few shells over us.*

10th November 1914
Dear Mother,
The parcel containing the overalls arrived safely yesterday, for which many thanks. After the war is over, I expect there will be a large sale of German uniforms, arms, etc., when I shall make up a small collection. I could have picked up a lot of stuff after the battle of Marne but one can't carry anything easily. I also received the parcel from Eton. I expect you will be writing them. Will you thank Grandmama very much from me, and also Aunt Foll for a very warm muffler. I believe Aunt F goes abroad shortly – this may just catch her before she leaves. Haven't you had any further news of Edmond? He ought to have been able to get a letter through before now, one would have thought.
We are living now in a little house with a Flemish family – the kindest people in the

world. They give up everything they have to make us comfortable. Fortunately they speak French as well as Flemish – so one can talk to them tolerably well.

The weekly Times and all the papers have ceased to arrive for some time. Could you rouse Smith and Sons up a bit – tell them to send lots of papers out – say one a day and occasionally a picture paper. The evenings get a bit dull now that winter is setting in. It is quite dark by a quarter to five. The last two days have been foggy – thick white stuff so that one can't see a hundred yards. Above there is brilliant sunshine but it can't get through. I wonder when it will begin to rain. It must come soon. We have only had one week's wet since we came out. Goodness knows what this country will get like in winter. Twice as deep and heavy as the Grove clays. It will be bad for the Germans and their heavy guns on these roads.

Much love to all and many thanks for your good wishes for my birthday.

I think I had better wish you many happy returns of your birthday in case I don't have a chance of writing. I hope you burnt the Kaiser on November 5th.

Please thank Mary for the flint and steel very much – extremely useful. I should love some large silk coloured handkerchiefs.

Forgot to post this and just found it in my packet.

November 11th. Getting very wintry and cold now. Bad day on Sunday when they planted a shell among our observing party, killing one, wounding two, and two more deafened. Luckily the major was not there for the moment. I wish we could leave this place as I am pretty certain that all our positions have been given away by spies. I wish I could catch one – I should enjoy shooting him thoroughly. Our poor sergeant-major who was killed Sunday had been recommended for a commission that very morning. The shell burst within a few feet of him and burnt and shattered his whole side.

Did you see the news that Ted was alright at Cambrai still on 5th November? Our host and hostess didn't like a shell which fell about 30 yards from their door and fled, so we have changed our home to a pub, belonging to a bad-tempered old woman.

Love to all and don't forget the papers please.

Saturday 14th November Set off at 3 a.m. with the major to find a position further forward. Paddled about in the mud for a long time and at last settled on one at L'Alouette. Got the guns down before daylight with great difficulty owing to the mud. Dug in and registered.
Sunday 15th November In reserve. Very cold. Rain and snow.

15th November 1914
Dear Mother,
Just a line to say that we are all well still. Horrible weather – rain and a little snow mixed. The roads are getting bad to move guns about on. I am very glad of your woolly waistcoat now.

Could you send me out a weekly pot of Cleeve's rich preserved cream (tinned). I am going to write to Granny to ask her to send me out a weekly Osberton ginger cake too.

No news at all, but I think the general situation is very good – at any rate the line is a good bit stronger now and we have got quite a few fat guns of sorts. We picked up a German shell 12½ inches across the other day.

17th November 1914
Dear Mother,
Your parcel of gloves, blankets etc. just arrived for which very many thanks. The blanket is worth its weight in gold to me just now. It's getting horribly cold at nights.

Yes – I got the puttees that you sent some time ago, but when one walks in mud half way up to one's knees all day, they do not last long. I thanked you for them long ago.

The Russians seem to be getting on well. I hear that it is unlikely that the Germans will try and hold Cracow but will fall back to Breslau. This will at any rate give the Russians a rich country to live in. There is also a rumour of discontent in Germany *and a feeling rising against the Prussian military party.*

We are not far off Ypres here, which must be a very unhealthy spot just now. There is continuous fighting going on day and night without a pause. I don't think they have broken through at all and have lost a lot of men. At this rate there won't be anyone left in the world soon!

Many thanks again for the gloves and for your letter.

P.S. I saw Bertram last night. He's only been out here a short time and hasn't got sick of it yet!

Wednesday 18th – Friday 20th November *In reserve at Petch Pont.*
Saturday 21st November *Forward observing officer in front of Messines. Fired off a few rounds on register.*

The rest of the month was very quiet with Francis either in reserve or rotating with the other batteries in the line. Again he later expanded his original diary entry with an explanation of the 'routine'.

Wednesday 25th November *Forward observing officer. Combined with the 6-inch siege battery in a bombardment on Petit Doue Farm.*

The brigade maintained an FOO [Forward Observation Officer] permanently at some haystacks some hundred yards east of the farm [the Battery HQ]. There was very little liaison with the infantry, probably on account of the inactivity on the front, the shortage of ammo and the absence of targets. A few rounds would be fired at the German trenches to test that all was in working order and occasional

bombardments in conjunction with the 6-inch siege battery. The infantry desired nothing more than to be left in peace and quiet to deal with the appalling state of the trenches which were mostly half full of water. FOO used to relieve before daylight and it was rather unpleasant going down with 2 signallers through the then totally unoccupied zone between guns and trenches. Several signallers were killed when out on the wire; it is said by Germans living in Armentières.

Whilst Francis was having a fairly quiet time in his sector, Henry was still very much in the thick of the terrible and fierce fighting at Ypres, where the Germans were determined to break through. The battalion had a traumatic day on 31 October and Henry had withdrawn his men, under ferocious German attacks from Gervault. Henry had reported the battalion at about 160 strong at the end of the battle but more straggled in during the night and it was now over 300 strong, but 70 per cent losses overall had taken their toll. The soldiers were exhausted but did not even consider defeat, as he recorded:

1st November   *The Germans came along in the morning and attacked our line and it seemed as if they would break through. The shelling was terrific and they brought up a field gun quite close and fairly shot the trenches out of the ground. The line, however, was kept by help of counter-attacks and by evening all was fairly comfortable.*

At about midnight Captain Hawley arrived with a draft of around 200 men, which almost doubled the size of the battalion. This draft, composed of regulars and reservists, was joining in the middle of the most ferocious fighting of the war, an organisation that was exhausted, had marched hundreds of miles, had fought almost solidly since the Marne and had taken serious losses. Its spirit, however, was still intact and it was fighting for its very existence.

2nd November   *Marched at 5 a.m. about 1½ miles down the road towards Ypres*

and then spent most of our time digging in. Aeroplanes a great nuisance. About 10 o'clock got an urgent message from 1st Battalion for assistance. Went up and a large encounter followed. Three companies of 1st Battalion captured. Hawley, Bingham, Turner and Crossman killed and Currie wounded. Had to go back to get regiment together and then to brigade office as guard. General Capper gave the order. Reported to 3rd Brigade office and on my way back found that the battalions had not started so went round and hurried them up. On the way up I saw our cavalry under heavy shrapnel fire which did not do them much harm. The Germans had broken through by the main Ypres–Menin road and the line fell back. We held on to the woods at the east edge of the château grounds and continually put out outposts on that line. Not a good one but without such a bad salient. Went round about midnight.

Yet again, Henry fails to tell the whole story, as is shown by the regimental account:

The battalion had fallen in and advanced in open order across the ground intervening between their bivouac and the Herenthage Château grounds. There had been no time to tell off the draft to companies, so they were sent in as one company under Captain Hawley.

The draft and A and B Companies crossed the main road west of the château and pushed through the woods in the direction of Veldhoek. They pushed the enemy back and occupied a line just east of the village. Unfortunately Captain Hawley was killed during the operation. After a short consultation it was decided that more troops were required if the Germans were to be met successfully. The other battalions in the brigade had bivouacked in the same wood as we had and Major Warre undertook to go back and bring them up. On his way he met General Capper, reported on the situation, and told him he was going back to get more troops. General Capper agreed. Major Warre then went to the battalions in the wood and told them what was going on, and that they were wanted at the front at once. He then reported to the 3rd Brigade headquarters and started back to rejoin the battalion. On passing through the wood, he found that the battalions had not yet started. He informed the commanding officers of the urgency of the case and then hurried on to join the battalion.

Very great credit is due to Major Warre for his behaviour on this occasion. In order to bring up these reinforcements he had to cover some four or five miles on foot under heavy shell and rifle fire. It was entirely his own suggestion that he should undertake this difficult mission, and there is no doubt that by his energy and resource on this occasion he saved the situation to the south of the road.

A word of praise is due to Hawley and his draft, who only arrived the night before but behaved as if they had been out the whole campaign, although this was their first experience of such desperate fighting and heavy shell fire.

Meanwhile the 1st Battalion had been in great difficulties and was reduced to one company. Captain Willen was in command, but no one was able to give any accurate information as regards the fate which had befallen the other three companies. Two riflemen who had escaped were very much shaken by their experiences and could give no coherent account of the situation. There were nine officers and 437 other ranks reported missing.

3rd November *A tremendous day of shelling and the noise of both hostile and our own shells made my head feel quite weak. I think all our nerves rather shaken by being so continually under it. Various reports of gatherings of the enemy etc. and our guns denied ground to the enemy by their fire. At night there was the usual rattle of musketry along the line, chiefly French. Carter, a parson, had joined with the last batch and we buried Hawley, Bingham, Turner and Crossman, poor dears, at midnight in the piece of park in front of the château.*

4th November *Various alarms during the night but nothing came of them and with exception of messages we had a quiet night and till 5 a.m. instead of 3.30 a.m. A thickish morning and there was a good deal of sniping at fairly close quarters. Terrific shelling went on all day. Was told to take over our 1st Battalion and joined it about 1 p.m. Only 86 men and 4 officers besides myself. A high dug-out for the men but not very comfortable and the mess not as good as the 2nd Battalion. It began raining about 3 p.m. and later in the evening there were attacks in many places after severe shelling. The Germans had a gun which they used at point blank into the trenches but it did not seem to stop the men.*

Henry was now in command of 1st KRRC, but this was rather a misnomer. The battalion only consisted of a very weak company, commanded by 'Dolly' Denison, and battalion headquarters.

5th November *The rain stopped a bit during the night. A fairly clear morning and guns began at 6 a.m. on both sides. A regular inferno followed by a sort of feeling attack by the Germans all along the line. The French were attacking on the south and their guns went on all day. Got orders at 10 a.m. to report to Colonel Westmacott, 6th Brigade, at north-west corner of Polygon plantation but an attack was going on when I got the message. Saw General R. Fitz'Clarence when it was over and got orders to move at 6 p.m. About 4 p.m. the Germans shelled hard again and we had news of them massing in certain places. Our guns got on to them and probably put them off, anyhow the attack fizzled out by 5 p.m. and we moved soon after 6 p.m. The shrapnel came into the mess dug-out and killed one man, wounding another. Found Robin Grant as brigade major and he got us a house to live in which was used by the Coldstream Guards who gave us an excellent dinner. Very little sniping or gun fire up to 10.15 p.m. One other man was wounded by shell during the day and we were lucky to get off with one killed and two wounded.*

6th November *Got busy with our dug-outs about 6.30 a.m. after an excellent breakfast and at 9.30 a.m. got orders to join the 6th Brigade before the mist lifted. Marched past before 10 a.m. and after a little trouble found the HQ about 1 mile south of Zonnebeke. Were given a set of dug-outs and a house for a mess but were told to turn out for the Berkshires [so] about 3.30 p.m. went out to find a place in [another] house for a mess. Got a cottage and cleaned it and got a certain amount of dug-outs for the men by 9 p.m. The company on reserve and visited the alarm post. Several parcels came along but of course no letters for me. A thick foggy evening.*

7th November *Went up to the company about 5 a.m. and we made dug-outs for those who had not got them and for ourselves. About 7.15 a.m. got a message to say we were wanted in the HLI [Highland Light Infantry] section as the Germans had got into a part of their trench. After a hurried breakfast went off there. Dolly Denison after a reconnaissance was starting to drive them out when he was recalled by an order from the general and his company remained there. Went to see the general on return about midday. About 2 p.m. some Black Marias appeared near our little house [and] we went up to our funk holes. About 4 p.m. there was a fearful hustle. The Germans had shelled a portion of the Connaught line and driven the men out. The signalling people of the brigade and cyclists and everyone dashed up and Dolly had to get his company across. Intention to drive the enemy out with the company and the Berkshires but it did not come off and the line was readjusted with one of our platoons in the firing line, three in support. Got back about 7.30 p.m. and had dinner about 8.30 p.m. Fearfully sleepy. Went to sleep at dinner over my food. Had a large wash in a bucket at midnight and slept very well.*

8th November *A thick mist in the morning which only partially cleared during the day but quite sufficiently for some shelling. The Germans had a 'row' with the next section of the line southwards about Polygon Wood and were at it for a couple of hours or more. Went up to see Dolly Denison at his post in the evening. Had a splash of firing about 9 p.m. but it worked off and left the snipers in possession. Wrote several letters. Supplies came up about 10.30 p.m. Heard the enemy had shelled the village in our rear during the day and that Ypres was on fire. No letters. A Company found a platoon [for duty] in the trenches and three in the little forts. The former was withdrawn at night to its dug-outs and the whole were in reserve.*

9th November *Very hazy in the morning. Breakfast at 7.30 a.m. Orders to change HQ to a house about 250 yards up the road. Remonstrated as we had no carts and crowds of things stored for the men etc. but with no avail. Furious shelling of the French to the north during the afternoon and some of the shells came our way. A Company took over some HLI trenches at night. The relief took ages and Knox Gore and I got dinner at 1 a.m.*

10th November *Dolly Denison went sick and Eva Willan had to take his place. On arrival found heaps of parcels which had come overnight, many really for D Company, 2nd Battalion. Up at 5 a.m. after dining at 1.45 a.m. and shaved with my own razors from my kit which I repacked and forgot to take any drawers. Some very good parcels from Gwen and others: a cake, sweets, etc. and cigars from Phennick. Went up to dig funk holes near our new HQ and also designed some excellent ones. The French to the north started an attack and artillery fire on both sides was very heavy. The Germans paid us considerable attention and put in a good many Black Marias and small shrapnels. Some of the HLI wounded. Went to sleep in the new dug-out during 6 a.m. shelling and the side fell in pinning me to the ground. Lunched in our old house and gave out clothing for brigade HQ men. Pardoe came to tea and we went up to our trenches which I took over while Eva Willan gave assistance on*

a court of inquiry over the 1st Battalion's
three companies being taken prisoner. He
did not get back till 9.30 p.m. and I had
dinner about 10.15 p.m. A very dark night
and a few snipers about. Trenches occupied
by our men in an absurd position and the
whole line disjointed and so placed as to
occupy more men than necessary.

11th November *Turned out of bed at*
6.30 a.m. by a shrapnel bursting over the
roof. A considerable amount of shell fire,
the Germans trying chiefly for a French
battery in the direction of Zonnebeke. Then
they attacked south of the Polygon Wood
and broke through the Black Watch and
Camerons who had been heavily shelled.
The 5th Brigade sent for assistance and
the HLI went. There were also the 2nd
Battalion, Coldstream, and the 52nd. These
turned the enemy out and re-established
the trenches taking some prisoners behind
our line. In the evening had a report that
about 1,200 Germans were about Veldhoek
and prisoners reported a corps in the
neighbourhood. A certain amount of
firing among the French to the north
about 10 p.m.

12th November *The Germans broke in the*
French lines on our left and we could see
the enemy about 1,200 yards. We shot at
them from our window and roof at 1,200
yards and got a field gun on them, driving
them back. Hung on like this all day sending
out patrols for protection. The French came
along in the evening but only made a half-
hearted attack and did not re-establish the
line. Ours is consequently much in the air.

The regimental account adds:

At about 6.30 a.m. I looked out of the
window of our headquarter house and saw
about fifty Germans, 1,200 yards away,
in front of and among some houses near
the cross roads north of 6th kilometre on
the Becelaere road. Apparently they had
broken through the French line near that
point, and had just taken up a position
just west of the road. Sergeant O'Leary,
the servants and headquarters signallers
manned the windows and some holes
in the roof and opened fire. We kept
the headquarters [personnel] with their
equipment on all day.

13th November   *Excitement began early. The Germans shelled hard and our line broke back on the left HLI about midday. The German support, however, did not follow up in strength. Then opposite our trench they pushed forward firing in the Berkshire forward posts and they collected in a wood to our front. Met the general at 12.45 a.m. with other COs and the outpost line was readjusted at 3 a.m., taking rather a back line with posts forward in certain places for information and delay. All the same the salients were not good.*

Rainstorms and wind and a vile day. At midday our forward post (the NCO killed and two wounded out of five) came away to the supporting trench. The Germans had got into the old trenches of the forward line and sniped our men out. Report of this arrived about 3 p.m. and I went to see the general again. Proposed new line which was eventually put out of court owing to the necessity of demolition of houses and the RE could not carry this out. Went to see the Worcesters' left company in the outpost line and then across to our own and got 180 sandbags to improve revetments. The earth was always falling in (the trenches knee deep in mud).

Went down about 5 p.m. to see the situation. A Company of Staffords put in as a backing and the Berkshires to join hands with our left digging in. It was a vile day: wind and rain and cold. Changed to the back room of our house and put the men in the big room. To the brigade office at 6.30 p.m. News unfavourable. We had five killed (all shot in the head by snipers) and five wounded during the day.

A reinforcement of 170 and Captain Tate arrived about 11 p.m. Told off 40 men for trenches, 40 men close at hand for reinforcements, the remainder into dug-outs in a wood near Polygon. Rations etc. rather a business. A regular battle going on to the south. A very dark night and a late one.

14th November   *The men near HQ dug in. A filthy day, rain and wind. The Germans attacked but just did not push hard. Went down with Maxwell Scott and Prudoe to see the OC of the left company of Worcesters piquets and confer with him and as to blowing the salient and blowing up more houses but the RE had too much to do so gave it up. Very wet and cold and the men miserable in the trenches. Rheumatic and could not sleep well.*

15th November   *A very rough morning again. The enemy brought up a machine gun and guns and shelled our trenches making them very dangerous. They killed two and wounded ten. They collected in the wood in front of our post but we got the guns on to them. Got news we were to be relieved by the French. They began to come along about 6.30 p.m., having said they would come at 3 p.m. Heavy fighting in Polygon Wood and they had a certain amount of fire on our point but we managed to get the relief completed by 1.15 a.m.*

The regimental account takes up the story:

One of the most unpleasant days I have ever spent. Rain and a little snow in the morning. Our hut leaked continuously, and the trenches a sea of mud and water, in addition to which the Germans, having apparently spotted some new loop-holes I had made during the night, gave us a really nasty shelling with 'Fluffies' [big howitzer shells]. These completely enfiladed the part of our trenches in which our headquarters was. Two burst right inside our trenches, one right above, and only a few feet from the top of the headquarters dug-out, in which six of us, Second Lieutenant Birkett, Company Sergeant-Major Tedder, three others, and myself, were. Six pieces of shell came through the wooden roof, one piece hitting the bank within a foot of my head, another going through Birkett's burberry, and another piece through a book someone was reading, but no one was touched – great luck.

The above two shells killed two and wounded nine men in the trench near our dug-out. We were feeling rather depressed, but were much cheered by a message that we were to be relieved by the French in the evening. Soon after dark a party of about thirty Germans crawled up to the wire about twenty yards in front of the left of our trenches. We opened fire, but before I could fire a shot from my pistol they had gone. About 11.30 p.m. 150 men of the 9th French Corps [sic – Regiment?] arrived to relieve us. The relief passed off all right. The Germans sniped at us all the time, but we did not have a man hit, which was lucky, as we had to move along the top of the trenches behind the French to get out.

16th November   *Got out at 1.15 a.m. and then marched by the railway to a wood near Hooge. A vile place with dug-outs full of water. It rained a good deal, the roads half way up one's leg in mud and the whole arrangements scandalous. We found a heavy battery mess and they allowed us to feed there. Hear at midday from the GOC, who came to see us, that we were going on that evening. Marched at 6 p.m. to a place north-west of Ypres and went into billets. Shelling going on. Major Shakerley arrived with a draft of 88 Riflemen.*
17th November   *Shelling all day. Ordered to march at 4 p.m. but cancelled at 2 p.m. with orders to be ready to move to assist in the firing line; the Guards Brigade heavily attacked. Ready to move at a moment's notice up to 7 p.m. and then the situation cleared and we dined and went to bed. A furious flash of rifle fire and gun fire at 11 p.m. which woke me up but it died down. Rheumatic knee.*
18th November   *Marched at 4 a.m. and got along a very bad road somehow. Met the 2nd Brigade on the way and did 2 marches in one getting into Ca'stre about 3 p.m. Met Newman on the way. Reggie Otley came to tea. We were almost out of shell fire or rather the sound of it which was something.*
19th November   *A morning round the billets and a bath. Then heard we had leave and Ure and I got into Hazebrouck and left by 9 p.m. for home. Bobby Bower there.*

This was the end of Henry's fighting in the trenches. He left the 1st Battalion physically exhausted – he was after all 48 – and during his short leave in England was seen by a doctor. During his time in the trenches he was mentioned in despatches twice, once for his actions in the battle around Troyen in September when Hubert had been killed, and once for his actions around Ypres with the 1st and 2nd Battalions.

Victor Yeats-Brown was still commanding D Company, 3rd King's Royal Rifle Corps, at Meerut in India at the outbreak of war. In October the battalion had gathered together and embarked in Bombay on the SS *Ionian* on 13 October. Two days later they set sail and, taking over a month for the journey, arrived in Plymouth on 18 November where they entrained to Winchester. They camped there for a month to mobilise properly, bringing the battalion up to war strength, and to train, learning the early lessons already emerging from France. Rachie also returned but we do not know if she was allowed on the same ship or had to travel separately.

There had been no more news direct from Ted, but George and Dora were determined to try and find their eldest son and to see what they could do to get him back from the Germans. They started writing in an effort to obtain more information. George had the following reply on 9 November from the adjutant of 1st Rifle Brigade (still in Belgium):

Dear Colonel Foljambe,
    I am so sorry I can't give you any news of your son at present. If I hear anything I'll let you know at once. I only heard that he was being well looked after in a French convent, and that probably got to me through you originally. Who the 'we' includes I don't know, probably Lane may be one of them. It's more than probable that he hasn't a Cox's cheque book with him, as he certainly had no kit at all, but he could of course write a cheque on a piece of ordinary paper if he could secure a stamp.
    I really don't know how badly he was hit, but he wasn't quite helpless as I know he walked back about a mile with us when we retired, and then went into a hospital

established in a church. All the wounded in that church were afterwards captured as far as we know.

I do hope things will turn out all right: perhaps you'd drop one of us a line if you have news of him before we do. We live a pretty strenuous life here, apparently making little progress all along the line, but one knows very little, probably no more that you do at home.

Meanwhile, Dora had a reply from Martin Hammond, a friend of Ted's who had wanted to get a letter to him in Cambrai:

Imperial Hotel, Hull
Dear Mrs Foljambe,
I got your letter today, it having been forwarded on from home. I quite see that it might be very unwise to try and get a letter to Ted, and I feel sure he is looking after himself very well – a thing Ted could do in almost any circumstances, I think! As he was only wounded in the leg I expect you will either hear of him among the Allies or see him home soon.
I have a commission in the 13th

Lancashire Fusiliers and joined here last Monday. At present we are doing duty in another battalion while the 13th is being formed. We are living in almost unbelievable luxury in this hotel, commercial though it be. I imagine there is no hope of my getting out to France, or rather Germany if we go on as we are now, within six months or so, but we live and hope of seeing something of the real thing before we are done.

Thank you very much for asking me to come and see you and I hope I shall be able to some day and find Ted there too.

She also continued to write to the Red Cross in Paris, and received another reassuring response:

Your letter of the 11th inst has just reached me about your boy. We have had his name on our enquiry list ever since he was reported 'wounded and missing' and had already noted that he was at Cambrai 'doing well'.

You may be sure that we will keep our eye upon him and the others who are probably with him; but of course one can't expect, except by the merest chance, to hear from our prisoner friends and relations until that part of France is cleared of these Prussian fiends.

At the same time it is something of a consolation to know that, on the whole, our men are being well treated by the enemy.

Dora was still reading the newspapers avidly and came across the following:

MISSING OFFICER FOUND
A FATHER'S PERSEVERENCE REWARDED
Mr Irvine, of Drumgoon Manor, Maquire's Bridge, Ireland, received on Friday a letter from his son, Lieutenant C. G. S. Irvine, of the King's Own (Royal Lancaster) Regiment, who has been 'missing' since August last. The young officer, who was then a second lieutenant, was wounded in the retreat from Mons, and although his father twice visited France in search of news of his son, and took other steps, with the aid of the The Times,

to ascertain the officer's fate, no definite intelligence could be got. On at least two occasions Mr Irvine was assured that his son was dead, but the evidence was never satisfactory to his mind, and he persevered in search. Nearly three months passed between the date of the report that his son was 'missing' and the receipt of the letter on Friday which set at rest all doubts as to the young officer's fate, and in the meantime Mr C. G. S. Irvine had been promoted to the rank of lieutenant in his regiment.

Lieutenant Irvine, it appears, after being wounded in the field, was taken to a neighbouring village, and the last heard of him until the other day was that he was seen lying grievously wounded in the parish church. The Germans, he says in his letter, took him to Cambrai, and when he was fit to be moved they slung a stretcher by chains from the roof of the carriage, put him on it, and took him to Würzburg, in Bavaria. The journey took three days (it is usually an 11 hours' run), so careful

BELOW *An Army chaplain ministers to wounded soldiers later in the war.* IWM Q2854

were the German doctors and officers of their patient. Mr Irvine can now walk 100 yards a day with the aid of two sticks; he is still very thin and weak, but his hosts give him good food and every care. When he is strong enough, he believes, he will be interned as a prisoner of war in a fortress. Professor Mendelssohn-Bartholdy sees Mr Irvine daily and shows him every kindness and attention, as indeed do all the German officials. Mr Irvine had, of course, written to his father as soon as his wounds enabled him to do so, but presumably all his earlier letters had gone astray or had been stopped in the German Post Office. It should be added that one of the letters sent to Mr Irvine at the front was returned to his home in Ireland marked 'Killed 26th August'.

Dora wrote to Mr Irvine to see if she could find out any more details, and to congratulate him on finding his son. His reply was as follows:

I have your letter and certainly do not think it any trouble to give any assistance I can, and thoroughly sympathise with you. You should not on any account despair unless you have definite information. When abroad I got a graphic description of how my son was shot through the chest while being carried in wounded from the battlefield, and was informed that he was left in a mangel field. I also got a graphic description how he was killed in a beet field and left there and a letter written to him at the front returned officially marked 'Lieutenant Irvine was killed in action on 26th August 1914'. Soldiers sometimes are confused and their stories are not always reliable and they very often mistake the persons they are talking about. In the retreat as a rule no ambulance was available and any that were wounded and could not walk had to be left behind. I will ask my son if he heard of Lieutenant E. W. S. Foljambe when he was in Cambrai.

Behind the German lines there are several English officers in hospital and in châteaux and no communication can be got with the hospitals and the owners of the châteaux dare not give information, but you may rest assured that if he fell into the hands of German doctors he is very well cared for. They do their very best and look after the wounded British with the same care as their own.

Owing to the serious nature of my son's wounds they brought him to Würzburg in order that he might be under the care of the best specialists probably the world can produce. The University is famed for its medical facility. Professor Mendelssohn-Bartholdy who is considered to be the shining light of his profession, sees my son every day, and he is getting every care that science can suggest.

There are hundreds and I might almost say thousands of officers in places where, up to this, it has been impossible to communicate with them, but on the back I give you addresses of those who are specially looking after the missing and other means of communication. Our Foreign Office is doing its best to get the names of all prisoners, but naturally it will take a long time, and these lists will require careful revision.

I need scarcely to tell you that if I get any information I will be only too happy to let you know at once.

My son said he sent me a postcard from Cambrai but it never reached me and I know several officers detained there and in other hospitals behind the German lines and all attempts to communicate with them have failed.

Thanks for your kind congratulations. I only wish I could be more use.

On the back were the address of the British Red Cross in Paris, with whom Dora was already corresponding, and the suggestion of asking the United States Embassy in London to forward a letter. In addition Mr Irvine wrote:

There is a Mr H. M. A. J. Van Asch Van Wyck, Weestallen, Utrecht. He was recently stopping in the Premier Hotel, Southampton Row, London WC. I do not know anything about him, but I understand that for a fee he searches for missing relations in

Germany, France, Belgium & Holland. I am informed the Cecils [Lord Cecil was with the Red Cross in Paris] employ him.

Dora also wrote a last letter to Rachie, whom she knew was leaving India:

I am wondering if by the time this reaches India you will have started! It is possible by now you even may have left. Of course it would not be possible to cable. I don't suppose we shall know until we hear from Southampton that we are to expect you. I long for that day and I trust you and the babe will be able to travel with Victor on the trooper – it will be much less trouble and expense. I do hope the 3rd Battalion will not be wanted to stop in Egypt, but anyhow I understand from Victor's last letter to Father that you will come back all the same. If Victor is still with you, Father wanted me to thank him for his letter. He is still very busy recruiting, outfitting, taking chairs at meetings and lectures. I have just got a letter from him saying that just before starting for a meeting yesterday rumours came of a naval battle off Yarmouth. When I got to Retford rumours that Germans were landing at Cromer, that Colonel Bingham who was hunting was urgently wanted back at Doncaster. And his wife was hunting him in a motor car. Today we see the cause of the reports – but I think something is brewing and we shall see things 'ere long. The uncomfortable thing is that there are so many spies still about and the Home Office are being so apathetic. Cousin Gemma is leading a crusade about it and wrote to Lord Charles Beresford and Lady Jellicoe; the great thing is to raise public opinion which seems to be the thing that most affects Mr McKenna [the Home Secretary]! It is dreadful to think that lives should be lost owing to his incompetence. We are still mystified about the Russians – a stream of motor lorries have come from the north and are now standing outside the WO [War Office]. Rudolf Jelf saw Archangel written on it. Captain Lane has most kindly written to Father on a postcard from Torgau where he is prisoner of war to say that he hears Edmond is at Cambrai

and going on well. We think that he has had this news since he got to Germany and that all the time he has not been with Edmond as we thought. I have today written him a postcard to forward. We have not been able to hear from Ted as we were afraid of drawing attention to his whereabouts, but I suppose now it is known. I wonder his not being taken off to Germany before now, I should imagine Cambrai would be almost in sight and hearing of the guns.

We heard from Francis. They have moved further north and joined up with the battery and got a new major (Wilson). Up to now they have been alone with an infantry brigade. He was in a flat country with tall chimneys and spires and ploughed fields, very awkward for observing. I trust the dear boy will come safe out of this terrible fighting – he seems to keep well and has put on weight. I send him out boxes of stores and clothes, Father sent him some breeches. His were just done for when the new ones arrived on the 26th and they were new when he started! He had a French house in which they had cleaned out a room, the whole being filthy from the Germans' occupation and he had found a piano and a book of French songs and played 'Gai gai il faut passer l'eau' all day. Which reminded him of Mme Manuel – did you see that she had lately died at Sand Hall from paralysis?

I hope baby is not crying so much and that he will be good on the journey. Poor darling he is having a varied existence to start with! How I long to see the tiny. I am wondering about his clothes, but of course three months is quite enough time to change into shorts.

Now my darling I must post this and wonder if you will ever get it. You may be on the sea or at Ranikhet or at Bombay? I wonder if Mrs Wyndham has gone home. It was good news to hear that you are well enough to travel and to hear baby Alan had been christened on the 7th.

My blessing and many kisses to you and the wee one and love to Victor. Grandpapa is certainly better but still leading an invalid life.

George was fully established running the depot at Newark and recruiting men for the Sherwood Foresters, although his legs were giving him trouble – he had gout at the very least. The 1st/8th was still in the south of England training hard and waiting for news of deployment to France and Belgium. The battalion was sent to Essex in November to prepare defences against any possible German invasion on the east coast. The men dug trenches, redoubts, gun positions and other defensive works in the clay of Essex. They shot on ranges, and practised all the skills they would need when they eventually got to the front. George kept in touch with the battalion and was responsible for keeping it filled with recruits and officers.

In addition, the 2nd/8th was now filling up but was having a more torrid time. Most of the experienced Territorials were with the 1st/8th but a cadre of 'the unfit' had been weeded out from the 1st/8th when it was deployed in September, and these became the nucleus of the 2nd/8th and Lieutenant-Colonel Coape Oates was selected as the commanding officer.

The 2nd/8th started training with route marching, drill and physical training at the fore, but it all had to be carried out in civilian clothes for a considerable time as supply of uniforms had not kept up with demand as the Army expanded. The men were all placed in billets locally, as there was no barrack accommodation in Newark. This caused problems for the CO who reported: 'Discipline under such circumstances always suffers, and much time is wasted by the company officers in paying landladies. During the early days a sort of mothers' meeting used to be held for this purpose, but the babel of sound which issued on such occasions from the room used soon resulted in the ladies being paid at home.' Billeting payments were an important source of income for many homes, particularly those where the men had enlisted to go to war.

At the end of October the battalion marched to Collingham by invitation, and had lunch in one of the fields next to the main road. The men were afterwards given an hour's leave in the village, being on their honour not to enter a public house. The privilege was not abused, and the march gave an opportunity for the people outside Newark to judge the strength and discipline of the battalion, and gave a much-needed change of routine for the men.

In early November a draft of 100 men was sent to join the 1st/8th. They were a fine lot of men, and their officers were very

ABOVE *Officers of the 1st/8th Sherwood Foresters pictured in formal pose at Harpenden in November 1914, shortly before they went to the Front.*

RIGHT Looking east from battery forward position at Kemmel, December 1914.

MESSINES

RUINED CHÂTEAU

NEUVE EGLISE

LA HUTTE

PLOEGSTERT
ARMENTIERES

LOOKING. E. FROM FORWARD POSITION

BELOW The Belgian town of Neuve Eglise lies close to the Franco-Belgian border and is seen here under a blanket of snow in December 1914.

sorry to lose them. Recruits were now coming in well, the battalion was popular and good clothing was available, a very important point. In one week in November 170 men were attested, and the standard for a time was raised to 5ft 7in, as the battalion was up to strength.

December 1914

For Francis, December was the quietest month of the war so far. The battery had settled down into a routine, with either guns from the section resting, or the whole battery rotating with the other batteries in the

LEFT *Officers and men of the battery wrapped up against the cold, outside Neuve Eglise.*

BELOW *Gun pit design drawn by Francis, which was used by the Royal Artillery in their* Notes on Artillery in the Field *produced in early 1915.*

brigade. Francis was either in an observation position – he spent some time in this way with the Duke of Cornwall's Light Infantry – or he was in reserve. The trenches in front of the guns were filled with mud, as were the dug-outs of the guns themselves and much time was spent in improving conditions to make them liveable. Digging was the theme of the month with positions being continually improved and reserve positions prepared. The weather was miserable and it either rained, or the area was covered by fog, or it was so cold that the mud froze and made life even more miserable. The

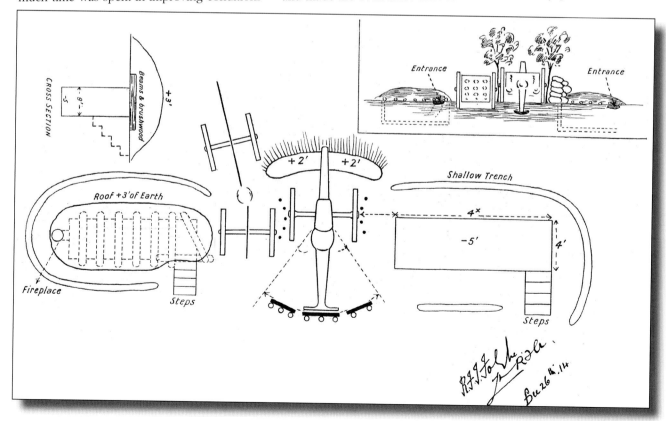

Army was trying to work out how it could break through the German lines, and if it did so, how it could exploit any success. Francis takes up the tale:

Thursday 3rd December   *Marched down with a party to be inspected by the King at St-Jans-Cappel. Very cold. A large shell fell close to us in the morning.*
Sunday 6th December   *Rear position. 3 large shells into observing station at Alexanders' farm. Smashed all the windows. 11.2-inch howitzer. Circumference of crater 21 yards, 5–6 ft deep.*
Sunday 13th December   *Moved over to Kemmel position to assist in attack. Dug new pits and improved position. Guns got into position in evening.*
Monday 14th December   *Started firing early. A great bombardment all day.*
Fired off about 900 rounds. The Germans hardly replied at all. Infantry made a little progress.
Tuesday 15th December   *Renewed bombardment. Fired about 600 rounds.*
Wednesday 16th December   *Quiet day. Got a hare and two cock pheasants roosting with Congreve's gun.*
Thursday 17th December   *Quiet day. Another hare.*
Friday 18th December   *Fired a good deal.*
Thursday 24th December   *Forward observing officer Norfolks. Shot at Petit Douve.*
Friday 25th December   *Foggy. Still FOO. A semi-armistice – Germans came out of trenches and talked and exchanged cigarettes and things with our men. Altogether a most curious Xmas!*
Saturday 26th December   *Forward position. Finished new gun pits.*

BELOW *German soldiers of the 134th Saxon Regiment fraternise with men of the Royal Warwickshire Regiment in no-man's-land during the Christmas Truce in 1914.*
IWM HU35801

At the end of the year Francis was posted to G Battery, Royal Horse Artillery. The RHA supported the cavalry brigades and was equipped with a smaller gun than the Royal Field Artillery (a 13-pounder as opposed to an 18-pounder).

Francis wrote in his diary a note of what had happened to the officers of 27th Brigade, RFA, who had set out to war those few months before in August 1914.

119 Battery
Major Alexander, promoted Lieutenant Colonel, VC
Captain Walford, wounded 24th August, DSO
Lieutenant Preston, wounded 24th August, DSO
Lieutenant Pollard, killed Richebourg
Lieutenant Davidson, wounded Lorgies, DSO

120 Battery
Major Holland, killed 23rd August
Captain Congreve, wounded, DSO, MC
Lieutenant Foljambe
Lieutenant Lindsay [killed 24 June 1915]
Lieutenant Bulteel [killed 5 April 1917]

121 Battery
Major Ballard, died
Captain Masters, DSO, MC
Lieutenant Davidson, sick, DSO
Lieutenant Stavely (RHA), DSO
Lieutenant Chapman, killed, MC

Victor and the 3rd Battalion, King's Royal Rifle Corps, had arrived in Winchester from India in November and spent the next month preparing for deployment to Belgium. Rachie had arrived back in England and was living in Winchester in lodgings with Victor and Alan, their baby. Victor was commanding D Company and was very busy with the

BELOW A page from Francis' diary explaining what happened to the original officers from 27th Brigade, RFA. Out of 15 officers 5 were killed, 1 died and 4 were wounded; between them they were awarded 1 Victoria Cross, 7 Distinguished Service Orders and 4 Military Crosses (Francis got an MC in 1917).

arrangements. Finally, their orders arrived and on Sunday, 20 December the battalion marched from Winchester to Southampton, embarked on the *City of Edinburgh* and arrived the next day at Le Havre.

According to the 3 KRRC war diary the battalion arrived at Aire-sur-la-Lys by train on 23 December and marched to billets at Blaringhem, where it remained for the rest of the month. The men spent time practising trench digging and the company commanders, Victor amongst them, spent some time visiting the forward trenches to gain experience of actual conditions. He had a miserable Christmas. The weather was foul, he was separated from Rachie and the soldiers were finding the weather and conditions very tough work after such a long time in India.

George had finally managed to sort out the administrative problems that had left him with so many masters at Newark. He had been officially appointed as commander of the depot at Newark (even though he had been running it since the start of the war) and Colonel of the 8th Sherwood Foresters, and was also trying to recruit at full throttle to keep the 1st/8th up to strength. The men of the battalion were very pleased that their old commanding officer had been officially appointed to look after them and Captain E. T. Collins, the adjutant, wrote to George:

My dear Colonel,

I was so pleased to see your name in the paper this morning, and just as it should be. I had a look in at the War Office last Thursday, and had a hint given me that it would be alright, and at last they have done what they should have done months ago. Now that you are our senior colonel, and will be able to give orders, we shall be able to get in proper order. If at any time there is anything I can do for you, I hope you will let me know, but I am afraid you will always find me a nuisance, as we always seem to have men going sick, and requiring more. Now of course all correspondence will go through you, and you will give the orders. Hoping you are well. We are doing

a great deal of digging, and I think the men are fit, but they now want some drill again.

Major Fowler, the battalion second-in-command, also wrote:

I am writing for Clarke as well as for myself, to say, as being the seniors who have had the privilege of serving under you, how delighted we are that you are officially in harness again. Even red tape has its virtues, and now that you are securely bound up with it, all must needs go well. May you long continue to hold the position which you held so long, and which you have now so honourably re-occupied.

The 1st/8th spent the rest of the month in Essex, continuing to prepare positions against invasion from Germany. Their Christmas leave was cancelled. Scarborough had been bombed on 23 December and the government were a bit rattled. Christmas Day was opened with a church parade and 'dinners were issued on a sumptuous scale' and in the evening the officers were entertained at the White Hart in Braintree by Colonel Huskinson and Major Fowler.

The 2nd/8th was successfully building its strength and by early December was up to complement in men, although still short of officers. The men were thrilled with the arrival of '200 charger-loading rifles and 243 non-charger-loading' which made it much easier to train. There was now nearly one rifle to every two men! But with the clothing coming in and the equipment taking shape, the battalion was able to do more tactical training, although most of the work involved digging and the construction of trenches.

Dora was still in London, now recovering from influenza, but was still trying every avenue to find out more details of where her beloved Ted was being held, and what state he was in. She had written to the Red Cross in Geneva at the beginning of December. Their reply gave details of procedures for sending money or parcels to prisoners, if their location was known, but there was no news of Ted. The family had also tracked down a man who was reportedly specialising in trying to find out more about missing personnel and had a letter from him:

17 December 1914
Dear Lieutenant-Colonel Foljambe,
    It will be a pleasure indeed to me to do everything I can for the relief of your son, and it is probable that I shall be sending a special courier into the Cambrai district in the near future; I would therefore recommend that you place a sufficient sum of money in my hands for meeting his requirements, and also perhaps for the purpose of making a contribution to the convent or other place where he may be under treatment, as these things would naturally contribute to his welfare.
    There is no charge for my services, but I should be grateful for any contribution which you or your friends might see fit to make for relief work among the British prisoners of war which I am carrying on in Germany. I expect to leave this week for my fourth expedition into that country.

Dora had been trying to get letters to Ted, but did not know if they had been getting through. She tried again on 15 December:

I hope and trust this may reach you and that we may soon hear of you, I have written postcards to you to Germany but have had no answer from you. We have all been very anxious and long for news.
    Rachel and her baby are back. He is a darling little thing, of the Bellingham type I think – so far I have not discovered any likeness to his mother. They are just now at Winchester. Francis is well; we hoped he might have had leave by now. Avice has come from school today. Mary and Arthur's wedding was on 28th November at Holy Trinity Church, quite quietly. They have taken a tiny house in London, in 3 Alfred Place West, not far from South Kensington Station. They will be in London for Xmas and so shall we as the
doctor will not let me travel to Osberton. My heart is still rather bad from influenza effects. Father is at Newark and comes up for Xmas. And Rachel and the tiny Alan come here too. We can just get in. Gladys and John go to Osberton – the Squire and Granny are well. How everyone would send love if they knew I was writing and thought it might reach you! I hope your wound (in the leg?) is quite healed and that you have clothing and food sufficient. God bless you and keep you, is the constant prayer of your loving Mother.
    Write a line if you can!

Henry had been seen by a doctor and wrote to George at the end of December:

I was waiting to write to you in case I heard what was likely to happen to me. A medical board at Bristol passed me for light duty recommending me for indoor work, and I went to the War Office yesterday afternoon. My name had gone up two or three days ago but General Braithwaite, whom I wanted to see, was engaged so that I got no further. They will let me know. This uncertainty prevents me from accepting your invitation to come and talk to your people at Newark. I have told them at the WO that I have been asked to lecture, and that I would do so if it was considered worthwhile. I have now eight requests for the lecture, so it must have got about, and I can see that the fact of its having been given here [Eton] is quoted in today's Times. I will let you know as soon as I can. Best wishes to you and Dora and all for 1915, and may we soon have peace, after teaching the Germans that they cannot be top dogs. I think things are going well but the discomforts and difficulties of fighting in this weather must be fearful.

Henry in fact was promoted to lieutenant-colonel and posted to the Royal Military Academy at Sandhurst, where he would spend the next two years.

The year 1914 changed the family for ever.

CHAPTER 6

New Battles and the Search for Ted

January 1915

The long cold winter carried on and both sides continued to develop their trenches opposite each other, and occasionally attack each other, often with artillery and sometimes by patrols at night, and occasionally more elaborate attacks. Casualties continued to mount up, many from the cold and the mud and disease. No-man's-land and the trench area were littered with human bodies that could not safely be recovered for burial, and dead horses in various stages of decomposition also lined the routes into the trenches.

At the beginning of the year Francis was posted to G Battery, Royal Horse Artillery, and Colonel Onslow of 27th Brigade RFA wrote to George:

Your son left us today [3rd January 1915] to join the RHA in the 3rd Cavalry Division.
I recommended him for it about a month ago. I also sent in his name for Despatches, in which his name should appear in due course. He has developed

OPPOSITE *Francis as OC trench mortars. McIlwaine is on the left of this photograph taken in Sanctuary Wood near Ypres.*

BELOW *Royal Horse Artillery Battery moving through a village near Amiens en route to Ypres.*
IWM Q56310

into an excellent soldier, and we are all very sorry to lose him.

It took some time before he found himself, but during the last eighteen months, he has done admirably. Being left as senior subaltern of the battery did him more good than anything. I hope he will do well in the future, in fact I am sure he will.

I hope you have good news of your son in the Rifle Brigade. We are all well here.

The Royal Horse Artillery supported the cavalry brigades and considered themselves the cream of the artillery, with a touch of dash and flair. They were armed with the smaller 13-pounders and were fanatical horsemen. G Battery was a Regular Army battery which had been stationed in England at the outbreak of war, but had initially been stripped of most of its men and horses to reinforce the BEF when it had deployed in mid-August 1914. The battery had been built back up with reservists and remount horses and had eventually deployed to France at the beginning of November, reaching the front line in mid-November. It had not seen very much action and was moved back in December to join the 8th Cavalry Brigade near Morbecque and then Hazebrouck, a little further north. They had lived in the thick mud of Flanders and had had to learn to cope with the cold and the wet, but had not suffered any casualties.

Francis joined the battery having fought three tough battles at the beginning of the

war, seen his battery commander and other members of the battery killed, had nearly been killed himself on at least four occasions, and had been fighting without a break for nearly four months. He was an experienced and hardened soldier, had lived through some of the worst weather he had ever seen and had survived.

He took an instant dislike to his battery commander, Major Dawson, who had been commanding the battery for over two years, but otherwise settled in well. They were based in a farm at Borre just to the east of Hazebrouck. Like all Belgian farms it was rather smelly, with a huge midden in the middle of the yard. Practically all the horses had to be kept in the open and the soldiers built straw windbreaks with thatched roofs to protect them from the worst of the elements.

For the next three weeks, the weather remained foul and most of the time was spent training. Francis was particularly irritated that Major Dawson did not seek to draw on his experiences, so he could only pass on what he had learned to his own section of guns. The cavalry had imported some hounds from England and taken up drag hunting to keep themselves fit. Each regiment took it in turns to lay out a line and become hosts for a meet. It was the battery's turn to host a meet in early January and Francis walked a prospective course on the 6th. However, the sight of cavalry officers riding across the countryside had upset the locals, who

BELOW *Battery position at Neuve Eglise, January 1915.*

believed that the British were being trivial whilst their country was invaded and their relatives were being killed. They had quite missed the point of what it was for. The cavalry commanders realised the sensibilities of the locals and cancelled the meets before Francis managed to take part. It did not stop them hare hunting, and Francis rode out twice, but with little success. Finally, on Friday, 22 January, he left Hazebrouck at 3.53 a.m. and arrived in London at 2.00 p.m. for a week's leave, his first break since the outbreak of war.

His mother and sisters, Dora, Rachie and Avice, were in London. He took Avice to the Hippodrome, went shopping for all the things he knew he would need in the trenches and caught up on family gossip and sleep. He went to church on Sunday morning and the Albert Hall in the afternoon and took the train up early the following morning to stay at Osberton with his grandfather and to see his father at Newark. He tried to go hunting, but it was too foggy, and he met with Arthur Jelf, who was also on leave from 2 KRRC and found out exactly how and where his Uncle Hubert Foljambe had been killed, and heard of how well his Uncle Henry Warre had done. He walked down the river with his grandfather's gamekeeper and shot three duck and a snipe and, mentally refreshed, took the train back to London on Thursday and went to a show *Potash and Parlmultes* in the evening with the family.

He returned to France, laden with all his shopping, clothes and delicacies for the mess, on the Friday and discovered his battery had moved to Morbecque.

Victor Yeats-Brown and his battalion were now ready to go to the front. 3 KRRC was part of 27th Division and had finished its practice trenches at the beginning of the year and marched up on 6 January to take over real trenches in the front line east of St Eloi from a French unit. The trenches were in a terrible state. The French had not put much effort into maintaining them and the terrible weather and conditions – the mud was thick and treacly – made it almost impossible to improve them. The battalion was to spend the next three months in this area, rotating

LEFT *Major Dawson, Officer Commanding 'G' Battery, Royal Horse Artillery (RHA). Francis, who didn't like him, thought he was only interested in everything 'in front of the wheel' (the horses). Francis was particularly annoyed that he wasn't asked to share his experiences of warfare to date with the Battery.*

between the trenches in the front line and the billets further back. They suffered from continual sniping and shelling and lost a steady trickle of casualties. The battalion war diary takes up the tale:

5th January   *Continuous digging in wet ground has had a very ruinous effect on the men's boots, some being completely worn out though only three weeks old.*
6th January   *Dispatched men with worn-out boots to Méteren in advance but only succeeded in getting 60 pairs instead of the 290 indented for.*
11th January   *Battalion parade at 7 p.m. for march to billets in West Outre which we reached at 11.50 p.m. 110 men in the battalion were unable to march as their feet had become so swollen from immersion in mud and water that they could not get on their boots. These men were brought to billets on GS wagons.*
12th January   *144 men of the battalion rendered hors de combat due to swollen feet. These were sent to Boeschepe under Captain Brady and Lieutenant French where they joined the rest of the sick of the brigade.*

Victor's correspondence with Rachie now features in the family record.

In Billets
12th January 1915
My very own Sweetheart,

You must have thought I had forgotten you entirely, darling, for it must be four days since I have written to you, but indeed at times you have seemed very close to me, and I longed to write and let you know just what I was feeling at the moment.

Well, we have had our first forty-eight hours at a stretch in the trenches. By the way the reason some people write and say they are quite comfortable can only be that they are not describing the fire trenches, but support trenches in second line some long way behind, which is a totally different thing. Some of my trenches were only twenty-five yards from the Germans – you can't exactly expect your tea brought you in the morning I can assure you. It is the second time I personally have been there, and in a totally different part of the line, and in neither case was there any question of the unpleasantness of them and what Francis (our F) said in his letter is in a great measure true. I don't mean in the least that we are as miserable as he says, but they certainly represent the acme of discomfort for the period during which one holds them.*

Since last writing, my Tiny, we marched into the trenches. I can't explain how one does this by letter as it is not right to do so. Forty-eight hours there, relief which takes a long time and then we marched off to some rotten billets yesterday where I was busy the whole time looking after our men, some of whom were very done up by the exposure, cramp, swollen feet, etc. Yesterday evening we came on here having to go a roundabout way as the direct way was being used by other troops, a distance of some six miles which was too much for some of the men. We got into bed about 2

p.m. Sleep most of today, look after men, orderly room at 4 p.m. and conference of officers afterwards till 5.45 p.m., when I rushed off to write this, and am on a court martial tomorrow, and we move from these billets again tomorrow evening. Rather strenuous, my darling child, and you must write to Mother and tell her I don't mean to neglect writing to her, but that at present when the men are strange to the work, there is so much to see and do oneself that one can hardly find any spare time.

Two lovely letters, my own, I found waiting here for me and now another has just come dated 7th. My darling, I can't thank you enough for them or tell you how I love hearing from my sweetheart. It makes one so lovely and warm all over reading them. I do long to see you and so, please God, I shall see you again before so very long after all.

Masses of parcels have come for me these last two mails. The second lot I have not had time to open, yet I see one is from Garmage, and that must be the boots – they are sure to be very good – and I was just going to write and ask you to send me some really big ones instead of the others, and am delighted to have them now. Now I want quite one refill for my torch a week. I use it sometimes for a long stretch at a time and it is much better to have one or two in reserve than to run short.

I don't know if in all these parcels you have sent me another woolly, if not please do so because the trenches are not exactly warm. Also one pair Shetland wool drawers to wear over my other ones. Everyone says they are invaluable.

We were quite severely shelled and of course sniped at etc., but had no casualties in D Company. Generally shell fire when you are in the trenches is very ineffective, though it is rather alarming without a doubt, and the noise from the continual bombardment (ours and theirs) most unpleasant and makes one rather deaf. I wish I could tell you all about it but this must do for when I see you my darling. In the meantime Francis (ours) will have given you a fair idea of it all probably.

* Victor's brother, Francis Yeats-Brown, was in the cavalry and after the war became a noted author with such works as *The Lives of a Bengal Lancer* (on which a well-known Hollywood movie was later based). He is referred to by Victor as 'our F'. Rachie's brother, Francis Foljambe, is referred to as 'your F'.

One's feet are the worst part I think.

I had a letter from Father about the £100 for Captain O. Please thank him for it and tell him I will answer it very soon.

Goodbye my own sweetheart, don't spoil the baby! In spite of what you say I am sure you do so and Mum aids and abets you instead of backing me up. Love to all at No. 12. Very sorry your F. has not managed to get back.

My whole love to you and wee Alan and God bless you all and every day.

Your own husband

Again, from the battalion war diary:

13th January *Weather greatly improved. No rain for 12 hours.*
18th January *Day of complete rest.*
19th January *Parties of fifty men were sent every ½ hour to the brewery at Boeschepe where they obtained hot baths.*
22nd January *Battalion strength since Blaringhem reduced by 500 men due to frostbite. Battalion total 20 officers and 441 men.*
26th January *B Company heavily shelled with high explosive (howitzer). One killed; one officer and one Rifleman wounded. Casualties chiefly due to parapet. Ground drier but still very foul from unburied Frenchmen, dead stock of all sorts and excreta, resulting in most offensive smells.*

On the 26th there is another letter from Victor to Rachie:

Well my own darling child here we are again. No mail was sent up to me from the battalion so I'm afraid none can have come up to them.

I saw a paper of the 25th with a description of the fight in the North Sea. I only wish we had collared them all, but they seem to have turned and fled pretty sharply. I suppose the Germans will say it was only done to draw our fleet on, so as to have a real battle. In any case we sunk one of their ships and seem to have had but little damage done to ours.

My silly old insides still give trouble, I have eaten no meat now for about a week, practically have not smoked during this time and have touched no spirituous liquor, so that the insides should have nothing at all to complain of, and yet they go on teasing me quite a lot. The doctors have a theory that the way this is started is that when eating in the trenches, one eats a certain amount of mud too perforce, as mud is everywhere, on ones hands etc., etc. That this mud contains many germs must be a fact considering the state of all the ground about and the trenches themselves, and they say that it gives one various forms of internal troubles of which mine I suppose is one. I wish anyhow they would find a cure as I am sick of it.

The more I think of this war, and the more I see of war, the more it seems to me that war as waged nowadays is retrograde, does not bring out the finer side of human beings, or a nation either on the whole, and the less I feel disposed for our wee son to enter either the Army or Navy. I don't mean that he should shirk fitting himself for personal service in case of national necessity, but that he should choose some more productive form of occupation unless, when he comes of age to choose for himself, he should very strongly want to go to either of the services. There could be no finer services, I am firmly convinced from a military point of view, but they are not themselves constructive, but primarily destructive, though I admit to build on solid foundations often must be proceeded by demolition. Still what we admire is not the work of pulling down the old houses, but the new houses when they are built. At the end of this war you may be quite sure people will realise this even more acutely than ever before, and though our Army from the very diversity of its duties is a fine schooling and has produced many fine administrators, yet their advent as such has in many cases been rather fortuitous, had they remained in the Army they would perhaps have made excellent generals, but would not thereby have benefited the world at large. Personally I would prefer an architect or engineer to be his [Alan's] choice as a profession, or the church.

Anyway you might think these things over and tell me what you think. Looking on here at what is going on certainly makes me wonder whether all this is not God's punishment for all the time, money and productive brains wasted in Europe during certainly the last twenty years in piling up armament upon armament. Of course one can quite well say we had to follow suit, as a nation we could not get left behind, and this to my mind is quite true. At the same time the waste seems to me there, very apparent here, and to become infinitely more apparent to the whole world during the next few months.

Well I must read now, my own darling child, and then to bed to dream, I hope, of you. Good night sweetheart. My whole love to you both and God rest and keep you always.

Same letter continued on the 27th
My own Tiny one, your dear long letter of the 23rd was brought over to me this morning in time for me to write in answer. I simply loved having it. Very much amused about your opening your own letters first. You must have had a shock, as you say serves you right for greed! My Poora and instead you only found nasty scratchy little letters from me.

I don't at all like to hear of your having a cold and being in bed, though, having the cold, of course bed is the place for you and you are forgiven this part of the business.

Of course if there were any sense at all in this show, they would mark down a big chalk mark where the various troops were say on 1st October, on both sides, and then everyone would go away until 1st April (appropriate day) when they would come and sit on their chalk lines again and start afresh. In the olden days they always did something of the kind, until stupid Napoleon I came along and made war winter as well as summer.

I am glad Francis turned up and looked well, I suppose he must have got over the frostbite. It is good of him to go out and get me things, at least I take it it is your F. and not ours, though matters get a bit confusing if they insist on being at home at the same

time. I think we shall have to call the wee Geoffrey for a bit, though I like Alan ever so much better and don't want him to grow up called Geoff at all.

I don't think Harrogate a good place for Alan at present. You never know when the Germans might not come and drop bombs or something there, and although I don't think Mum would care a button about the bombs, the noise they make is most unpleasant and bound to give one a nasty start if it comes unexpectedly, so I should chose some place the other side of England if I were Dr Beauchamp.

Very glad to hear the paper etc. is on its way as I have only two envelopes besides this one left and hardly any paper. I shall be very thankful for waterproof puttees, breeches, etc. I hope all these things are not costing untold gold, anyhow I should think except for socks and eatables and candles I really shan't want anything more for some time.

Rifleman Dowden who brought me over your letter told me Mr Lees and his servant were both wounded by a shell which came into their trench. The former rather badly as he has his arm broken, and was hit on head and in leg besides, but Dowden says he is going on well, he hears.

I had two men killed and one wounded that Dowden knew of in my company. One of the killed was a Sergeant Wilkins and apparently he had done just exactly what I particularly warned them not to do, that is expose themselves by day for no purpose. Of course it is madness to get out of your trench by day with Germans within 100 yards. The worst fool could hardly miss you. I am very sorry indeed about it as, though not very bright, he was a good hard-working little fellow.

My new medicine has just come up and smells beastly; lets hope it does some good. Goodbye my own own darling. God bless and keep you both. All my love to you.

Your own husband

Yes, Mother's map case came all right. I thought I had acknowledged it but I know I have been very stupid about that kind of thing. Sometimes when one gets things just before moving and does not write for some

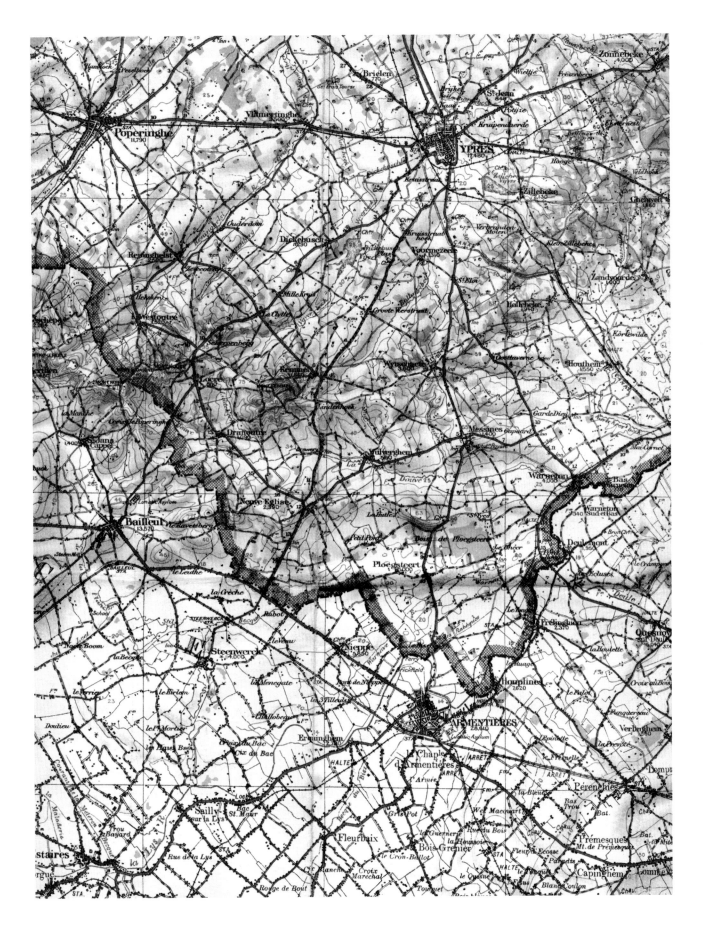

days one thinks one has already thanked people for things.

I never re-read my letters so you must forgive many errors.

In Billets
28th January 1915
My own darling sweetheart no mail of any kind arrived up here today which is very sad. However, really it does come almost every day so I don't think we have much to complain of considering it is wartime. Parcels seem to come so quickly and so regularly too, which is even more wonderful. They must have a very large staff of people on the PO work I should think.

This is the French ink. Rather poor in the way of colour, but I wonder if it won't soon get thick in the pen. Anyhow, the little bottle cost but a penny and a pleasant chat with the old lady in the small 'épicerie' where I bought it, so when I throw it away, or better give it away, it won't be a fortune lost.

I walked to a convent on a hill not far off, about two miles I suppose. They are white monks, Cistercians I think that is; a kind of under-monk in brown showed me round. The actual buildings are quite modern, 1892 they were rebuilt, and are very clean and tidy. The chapel is really very much more like an English one than an RC one. I mean there is almost a total absence of tawdry decoration. The pews, and all the wood work, which is moderately well carved, is modern too, and I thought the whole balanced rather well, though of course it lacked age to make it mellow or appeal much to me. The glass, such as there was, was poor. The outbuildings are all used as billets, 1½ squadrons of the 5th Dragoon Guards being there.

I was feeling simply rotten at lunch time and only managed a bowl of soup, no toast or butter, but the walk did me good I think in spite of one rather bad go of colic on the way back.

I have sent you rather a long letter for the Aunts in a separate envelope. I think it better to go from England because I rather think they open letters and mess about with them, sent from the front here to addresses abroad, and they will probably get it quicker sent from England than direct from here, also I have no stamps, not that there would be any difficulty getting them in the village just by.

I don't think I ever duly acknowledged the fact that you told me baby had been promoted to ordinary milk and cream. That is a tremendous thing and I only hope he duly appreciates the fact! I'm beastly jealous of him you know, my own Tiny. He is seeing far too much of you and his father far too little to suit him. He better come over and take my place for a bit – he would certainly be about as much use as I am just at present.

I tried the waterproof breeches on this morning, and they are grand worn outside my ordinary coat, so that they come most of the way up to my chest. Outside that will come my British Warm coat and the mackintosh over that again, so that one is about three feet thick in every direction and most unwieldy, as you can imagine. As I mention no names there can be no harm in giving you a little diagram showing how my own particular lot of trenches run and it may amuse you. I won't put in where the supports are or how far off exactly because if the letter were to fall into wrong hands this information might conceivably be of use to the enemy, nor will I say anything about any trenches except those so far allotted to my company.

Wood with ‍aaaaaa
German trenches ‍aaaaaa
aaaa
aaaaa
aaaaaaa
X   Z
Y

The left-hand corner of the trench I call here X is about twenty-five yards from them. Y trench is the one I make my headquarters in and is about fifty yards further back. Z is in line with Y but not so near the Germans as their trenches lie further back here.

Between X and Y there is a very slight rise in the ground, so that only snipers from the trees can actually fire into my trench except from the flanks. At night, therefore, my trench is almost safe from rifle fire, though their trench mortars can reach it, and have gone well beyond it, though luckily none have come inside so far. Into Z trench they dropped six of the brutes the time they wounded those two men, but this shows you how little harm these noisy, nasty things do. From what I hear this last time no one was hit by them so their bark is very much worse than their bite.

My own trench has a very snug 'dug-out', that is a position that is roofed over. It was very wet when we got there first, but has been since bailed out, had brush wood put in it, and is now quite snug.

Where I get so wet and beastly is wandering to my other trenches, and going about (at night of course) to get to know my way about, to the supports, and the people to my right and left. At first I wandered alone but since then I take the precaution of having one or two men with me, in case one met someone trying to creep into our lines, or were hit by some shot for, as I told you, the Germans keep up a more or less incessant rifle fire, none of which is aimed at anything much I think, but one might be hit and then alone one might not be able to get back etc., so it is as well to have someone by.

It is slightly eerie work as you can imagine, because when they send up their flare lights one has to crouch down and remain still for the ten or twenty seconds the thing burns for. At first it seems to light up the whole place so vividly one imagines one must be seen and immediately picked off, but really the lights help but little I think, except where there are fairly large bodies of men on the move, and I don't think the light would be steady enough to enable a man to aim by decently in any case.

Now I must pack off to bed as my store of coke in the stove is nearly finished and unless I am in bed before that is gone I should just about freeze, my own Tiny. So goodnight sweetheart and God bless you both now and always.

Same letter, 29 January 1915
Well, my own Tiny Child, the medical officer is putting me to bed for a couple of days on nothing but milk once more and some medicine. I do hope that may do the trick as it is really ridiculous my stupid old insides going on as they have been, and this should just give me a chance of getting really all right again before going into the trenches again.

I shall be able to write in bed just as well as out of it, and I hope with all my heart that there are two fat mails during the two days to keep me going as it will be a great bore spending forty-eight hours in bed, far worse in fact than forty-eight in the trenches.

I think ½ dozen large elastic bands might be rather useful three about 8 inches long and three about 6 inches. At present I only know of one thing I want them for but they are useful to have by one, so some time or another you might send them me – there is no hurry at all about this.

It is a lovely sunny day today, rather cold as it froze last night, but brilliant sun and hardly any clouds. Of course this means a good day for aeroplanes and for the artillery and one can hear them shooting away like anything.

I expect Osberton has been tremendously cold these last few days. Probably you have had quite a lot of snow, because some of these last days it tried hard here. I hope you may not have made your cold worse my own Tiny, also I hope you don't try and save money by going those fairly long journeys 3rd class in icy carriages? It does not pay because it simply means you pay twice what you save to the doctor instead of to the railway company, and have a much less comfortable journey into the bargain. I don't mind you doing it in the summer, sweetheart, if it makes you feel virtuous, but in the winter it should only make you feel very naughty and I object strongly to it from every point of view. So there.

Well my usual budget of letters to read and censor has just come in and I must wade through them, worst luck, and finish this afterwards.

Finished my letters, just as the doctor came in and brought me the pills I am to take, so now I am off to bed my own. Please

*don't think there is anything much the
matter, there is not, it is only to enable me
to get quite right and much better to make
a job of it than to hang on as I have been
doing half ill and half well, in fact I feel
better already having taken one of the pills
½ a minute!*

*Goodbye sweetheart mine. My whole love
to you two and God bless you always.*

Dora and George were still dreadfully
worried about Ted and were trying to get
every snippet of information about him.
January was a good month for news as the
war had now settled down into its stalemate,
and this allowed all the various agencies to
concentrate on finding 'missing' personnel.
The first news they had was a letter of 13
January from the mother of Captain Lane, who
had been captured at the same time as Ted:

*I have been wondering so often what you
have heard of your son. I had a letter from
mine today and he says 'Tell Mrs Foljambe
I have seen the French doctor who was with
her son and he says he was doing splendidly
the end of September', but I hope you may
have heard some better and later news.*

Shortly after this Dora got a postcard from
the Red Cross in Switzerland.

*At present, we are not able to communicate
to you any precise indication concerning
the person you are in search of. However, we
might point out to you that on the German
lists of the 30th September there is a:*
    Name: *Foljambe, Lieutenant, Rifle Brigade*
    Christian name: *Edward. Wounded arm
and back*
    Reported: *at Etp. Lazarett. Et. Imp. 6
Cambrai (Nord). France*
    *Lacking sufficient information, we
are unable to undertake the necessary
verification. For this purpose, kindly apply
to the English military authorities.*
    *You may also write to the prisoner
in question to the above address, in
order to make sure of his identity. Direct
interchange of letters between prisoners and
their families is now allowed.*

Dora's family were still helping where they
could and Amryas Warre, one of her brothers,
wrote on 21 January:

Dearest Vorzes,
    *Miss Foster of 70 Church St, Chelsea,
very kindly came round here today to say
that she had heard from a Rifleman, I don't
know who, that your Edmonds' address
was: E. Foljambe Esq., Rifle Brigade,
Prisoners of War, Kriegslazarett, Institution
Notre Dame, Cambrai.*
    *I believe Francis telephoned this to you.
There was also a message to say that a
certain Mr Pager, an American, who took
out messages and parcels to prisoners, was
not to be trusted.*
    *One of Miss Foster's brothers, an officer
in the Fusiliers, has been missing ever since
the retreat from Mons – and this, as they
have never given up hope, is no doubt
why she gets news of others in that part
of France.*

Dora was now much relieved to have so
much confirmation that Ted was definitely
alive and recovering in a convent in Cambrai.
She was also relieved to hear that he was
still in France and had not yet been taken
back to Germany and hoped that it would be
possible to get him repatriated at the earliest
opportunity. Her next wish was to get news
to him and try to send him either money or
anything else he might need in his hospital.
The American Express Company had links
everywhere and Dora wrote to them, with the
following result:

22nd January 1915
Dear Mrs Foljambe,
    *We duly received your favour of the 21st
instant, and we have instructed our Berlin
House to deliver your letter to your son,
Mr E. W. S. Foljambe, at Cambrai. We are
sending same through to destination, and
if it is possible to obtain any message from
this source we shall do so.*

The letter also included the printed
statement: 'The American Express Co can
make limited payments for maintenance

purposes to prisoners of war detained in Germany, Austria-Hungary, or interned in Holland. Also forward packages and institute general enquiries.'

In early February Dora also heard from Captain Lane himself, who had been captured at the same time as Ted:

Just a line to say that I got a postcard from your son yesterday from Cambrai. The card was undated, but he wished me a Merry Xmas in it, so he must have written it some time in December. I'm writing as I thought perhaps you might not have heard from him as letters from people in hospital in France don't appear to be getting through. He says that he is still on his back, but can turn about a bit without help or pain. He must have had a very bad time of it, poor chap. The French doctor who looked after him is here, and says that in the middle of October he was going on really well. If you have not heard lately I hope this letter will be a relief. Hôpital Notre Dâme, Cambrai, he writes from.

And finally Dora heard again from the Red Cross in Geneva: 'The Commandant of the Prisoners' Camp at Mainz reports concerning the above-named officer (whose name appears in your list of missing) that, though wounded, he was 'going on well' in hospital at Cambrai (Nord, France). The date of this information (which is supplied by R. F. G. Burrows, Manchester Regt, now at Mainz) being October 20th.'

Dora also continued her correspondence with Ted's friend, Martin Hammond:

The Industrial Schools, Chesterfield
31st January 1915
Dear Mrs Foljambe,
I was so pleased to hear about Ted. I can just imagine him having the time of his life at Cambrai, making allowance for his wounds. I'm sure he'd be just as popular with the Germans as he was with everyone here. If you are sending him a letter and have not yet done so, I wish you would give him my love and just tell him what I am doing. We may meet out there, but I hope

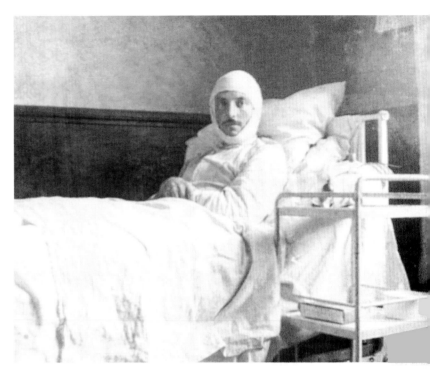

he'll be back before I get out there, and I'm afraid we can't hope to go before August.
We are really in clover here. The schools [are] a perfect barracks. They only hold 400 men but the officers have a house apart for themselves – the old 'Master's House' I suppose, and we are really quite comfortable. We only came in yesterday, but it seems perfect. Recruiting around here has fallen off for the present, so we only have about 750 men all told.
Thank you so much for your letter and I do hope you will let me know any more news you have of Ted.
Martin Hammond, 13th Battalion Lancs Fusiliers.

George was still hard at work at Newark, gathering recruits and running the depot. He had seen Francis when he had come up on leave but had been unable to join the family in London.

The 1st/8th Sherwood Foresters was still in Bocking, with the men carrying out final preparations and training before their deployment to France. More equipment arrived and much of their time was spent in putting it all together and inspecting it. This was not too easy a job for the young company or section commanders, as the men by this time were up to all the old soldier tricks, and were very clever at making one article appear almost simultaneously in half a dozen different kits. Drill included a certain amount of the new bayonet fighting and other exercises. Mules arrived and the collection of transport and floats that had come with the battalion from Newark was replaced by new Ordnance Pattern issues and the ladies of Nottinghamshire presented the battalion with two Lune Valley cookers.

Their chief 'relaxation' was searching for elusive spies at night, who were supposed to carry on lamp signalling; more often than not, when these were tracked down, they turned out to be innocent stable guards doing their nightly rounds. At other times they picketed the roads to hold up motor cars which were supposed to be acting as guides to Zeppelins!

The 2nd/8th was still at Newark building up its strength and training. Drill was at the fore of the training and they were inspected twice by senior officers. On the second inspection, 'The men were very steady on parade, and favourable comment was made on the fact that when one of the men fainted, no one moved until ordered to do so, a detail of which the company officers were very proud.'

George was also receiving letters from friends at the front, so had a good idea what was going on. Lieutenant Hugh Hole, his former adjutant from his days in the Nottinghamshire Volunteers, was in France attached to the Indian Lahore Division, and wrote to him on 21 January:

Dear George,

I have been out here since mid-September as interpreter with the Indian Army. I hope your boy is going on all right and over his wound. It is a sad time for people at home, who have to wait, but we're all right out here. I got home on leave a fortnight back and was appalled to hear the lies in London that people were giving out about the Indians who have done very well indeed. We stood off a three to one attack in October and had 5,000 casualties, and held the line intact. We were reduced to under 40 per cent of our effective, and had another bad cut-up before Xmas, when the Guards Brigade took over, and had to quit a trench which the Indians had been previously holding, so everyone is much shocked at this gossip.

I like my column and the Gunners: time slips away, and I shall soon have done five months of active service in this war. We hardly ever see any other troops but French, as we are next to them. A colonel of artillery has just been to see me who tells me of the death of young Pat Musters. Tony was his favourite subaltern, and we hear that he is in a bad way. I am very sorry to hear about Patrick, but what family has escaped. My son-in-law comes out this week to the Irish Guards, and my boy is, I believe, a captain in the Kitchener Army, and will shortly be out.

February 1915

Francis returned from leave to find the battery had transferred to Morbecque, with the officers moving into a small white house close to the village. It was devoid of furniture but they made themselves as comfortable as they could under the circumstances. At least they were dry and warm.

BELOW *McIlwaine, who, with Francis, was involved with the trench mortars.*

ABOVE *Requisitioned London buses were shipped over to the Continent to help with the movement of Allied troops on the Western Front.*

Early in February all the batteries were asked to provide volunteers to set up trench mortars. These mortars were in their infancy and were little more than a tube that blew a shell more or less straight up in the air on a high trajectory so that it could be landed directly inside an enemy trench. Francis volunteered like a shot, picked some men and prepared to deploy. A Lieutenant A. H. McIlwain had also volunteered, but from a different battery. After the war he wrote this letter to *The Gunner* magazine:

I was very interested to see the pictures of the 2-inch trench howitzer in your issue of the December Gunner, as it reminded me very much of February 1915 when the Field Troop RE of the 7th Cavalry Brigade, which was then resting in billets in Hazebrouck, produced something very similar. The 7th Cavalry Brigade was to go up to Klein

Zillebeke in the Ypres sector, in the good old London bus, to relieve the French, for a matter of a month and volunteers were called from the RHA of 7th Cavalry Brigade to man the first battery of trench mortars. Lt R. F. T. Foljambe and I were given a couple of day's training in how to handle the mortars.

The mortar was a very primitive affair, consisting of 2 feet of 'drain-pipe', a field clino[meter], a few shells made up from black powder and a roll of toilet paper! We made our own range table, a combination of charge and elevation. We measured the black powder in thimblefuls and screwed the powder up in pieces of toilet-paper.

The 'charge' was then dropped down the pipe. At the bottom end of the pipe was a touch-hole through which was inserted a length of fuse, which we screwed around until it pierced the 'charge'.

The 'shell' was then dropped down the drain-pipe until it sat on the 'charge' at the bottom. We then lit the fuse, and ran.

The trenches were only eighty yards apart and we had good fun to start with until the Germans got a bit fed-up and sent away down the line for their only (at that time) Minenwerfer. This was a huge affair but the 'thud' when it was fired, and the burning fuse when on its way, gave the show away.

This performance led, in June 1915, to the introduction of the Stokes Mortar, and apparently to the 2-inch trench howitzer, which must have been a great improvement on the above!

Francis's diary described what happened:

Tuesday 2nd February   *Experimented with bomb guns at Hazebrouck.*
Wednesday 3rd February   *Continued experiments and preparing range tables, etc.*
Thursday 4th February   *Left Hazebrouck, thoroughly oiled all over by MO [Medical Officer], by bus at 2 p.m. Arrived market square Ypres 5.30 p.m. Reported at headquarters of the Cavalry Division on the Hooge Road and proceeded to trenches with three guns and detachments. A pitch dark night and difficult way though Sanctuary Wood. Slept with Major Stanley and Captain Wyndham (1st Life Guards).*
Friday 5th February   *Reconnoitred for*

position for the mortars but trees make it difficult. Quiet except for sniping.
Saturday 6th February   *Got guns into positions but not satisfactory. Walked a long way up and down the trenches which are not good. Bad traverses and thin parapets.*
Sunday 7th February   *Found and moved guns to a new place behind Leicester Yeomanry. Satisfactory position. McIlwain arrived with four new guns. Started a mess with McIlwain.*
Monday 8th February   *Sniping and some small shell. The French 75s [75mm guns] are behind us here. An officer comes down every morning at 10 and knocks down the German parapet.*
Tuesday 9th February   *Quiet day. Walked out with McIlwain to see Zillebeke. Everything in ruins and the cemetery a disgusting sight with coffins unearthed by shells.*
Wednesday 10th February   *Quiet day.*
Thursday 11th February   *McIlwain bombed a sniper in morning. The Germans replied with five large bombs and spoiled our luncheon. The first one fell ten yards off us and nearly on top of one gun. The French shelled their trenches in reply.*
Friday 12th February   *Germans started early with small shell and bombs. First one fell by our dug-out again and landed on a sleeping man who was blown to bits. They sent altogether about fifty bombs. We soon got all our guns going onto the spot where the German mortar seemed to be and the latter soon stopped. The French gave them a really good shelling in the afternoon.*
Saturday 13th February   *Rain all day. Feeling rather miserable after nine days in a wet trench. Stores nearly run out. Handed over with pleasure to Barry, in the evening. Marched my party back to Ypres and embussed on market square. Slept soundly till we got back to Hazebrouck.*
Sunday 14th February   *Slept most of the day. Got clothes off for the first time for ten days. Perfectly filthy dirty!*

BELOW *Francis made this simple sketch of a trench mortar, with a cutaway to show the detonator, fuze, bullets and gun cord contained inside the casing.*

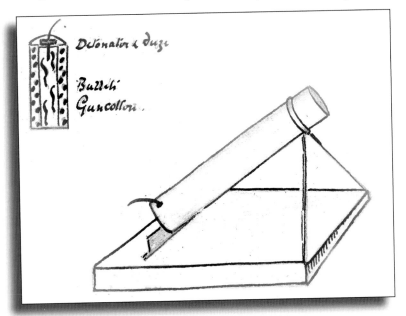

Detonator & fuze
Bullets
Guncotton.

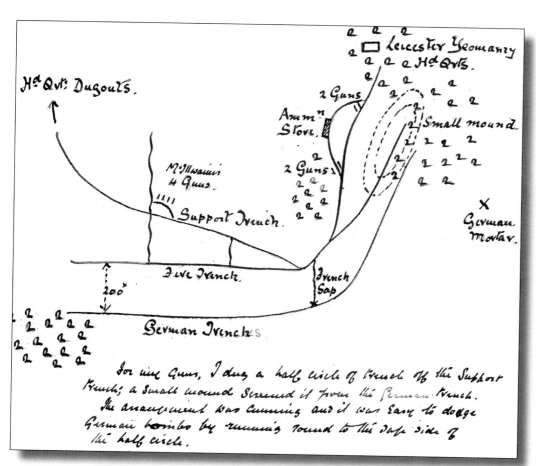

LEFT *'For my guns I dug a half-circle of trench off the support trench; a small mound screened it from the German trench. The arrangement was cunning and it was easy to dodge German bombs by running round to the safe side of the half-circle.'*

For nine Guns, I dug a half circle of trench off the Support Trench; a small mound screened it from the German Trench. The arrangement was cunning and it was easy to dodge German bombs by running round to the safe side of the half circle.

G Battery, RHA
16th February 1915
Dear Father,

A hurried line before the post tonight. Thank you very much for your telegram which arrived in a letter from Mother just as I was starting for Ypres where I have been living an uncomfortable life for the past ten days in mud up to the knees and thirty yards off the Germans. I have been OC trench mortars and had on the whole a very interesting time and more narrow escapes packed into ten days than I have had during the whole of the last five months. But ten days on a stretch is a bit too long and continuously dodging snipers and bombs and shells gets on one's nerves a bit towards the end. We had a great duel with the Germans' mortar on Friday which was rash enough to start throwing bombs – as we had nine mortars to reply with the result was rather a foregone conclusion and ended in a complete victory. I think I landed one bomb about on top of him and got some beauties into their trenches.

We were holding the trenches where the Prussian Guard attacked in November. The whole place is littered with their bodies which have been lying there ever since. There are numerous arms and legs protruding from the parapets too, which is rather unpleasant. Please thank Mother for her numerous parcels etc. which [I] found waiting here yesterday. I will write to her tomorrow. Best love.

Francis

15th–20th February   Usual work. Drill, orders, route marches, etc.
Sunday 21st February   Rode over with Johnstone to Neuve-Église to see the 120th Battery. Bulteel, Kaye, Nottidge, Congreve and Masters the only ones left of the brigade which left Newbridge in August.
22nd–28th February   Usual work. Drill, orders and training.

Victor Yeats-Brown was having a torrid time in the trenches with 3 KRRC. His last letter to Rachie had expressed how dreadful he found the whole experience and how ill he was becoming, unable to sleep and with stomach upsets. The trenches they were rotating through were not the deeply drained, duckboarded, heavily parapeted trenches, all joined in a continuous line; these belonged to the future. The line consisted of a series of detached trenches with intervals of around 30–80yd between them. There were either no communication trenches at all or, if there were, they were little more than waterlogged ditches, in which the water stood 2ft deep, and which consequently were completely unusable. All reliefs had to be carried out by night, and no one could approach or leave the trenches by daylight; even the wounded had to remain until it got dark. At night the reliefs or ration parties would flounder up through seas of mud, and would lose a good many casualties on the way. Individuals frequently got lost, and even drowned. Victor was a sensitive soul and the horror and the filth and the mud were all wearing him down.

Dora and George were so relieved to have got so much collateral information in January that Ted was alive and being cared for in hospital in Cambrai, but Dora still did not really know the full extent of either his injuries or recovery. She was determined to do all she could to track him down, through whatever channel she could find, and then to try and get him repatriated so she could look after him properly. She was in touch with relatives of other wounded and missing officers and more news was beginning to come through. Henry, her brother, had been officially posted to Camberley but was based at the War Office giving a series of lectures on 'trench warfare' around the country. He was also trying to help track down Ted:

5th February 1915
My dear Vorzes,

I returned this p.m. I made enquiries this morning. The last thing they had about Ted was dated 20th October last 'Going on well in hospital at Cambrai'.

Since then the WO has approached the American Ambassador, but they tell me

he has so much to do in this way that it is useless to bother him. He gets what news he can but it seems unlikely that he could get so far afield as Cambrai, which is comparatively near the front. They will let me know at once if any news comes along.

I am very sorry I shall miss you at Eton. I cannot get down till rather late on Saturday. I am going to Hindhead to lecture.

The War Office was also passing on any news it had and the following letter was sent to George only days later:

The Military Secretary presents his compliments to Colonel Foljambe and begs to inform him that Captain M. V. Hay now interned at Würzburg, Bavaria, in reply to enquiries concerning British officers wounded at Cambrai, has made the following statement regarding your son:

'Captain Foljambe, Rifle Brigade, convalescent.'

This information was received by the American Consul-General, London, from the American Consul-General, Berlin, under date 29th January. The latter states that he saw the letter which Captain Hay wrote and which contained the above information.

George now had two major concerns, the first was to try to influence whoever he could to get Ted repatriated at the earliest opportunity, and second, which reflected his long years of Territorial service, was to try and locate Ted's kit, or to get compensation. Francis had already claimed for his kit lost on the retreat from Mons and George wanted to achieve the same for Ted.

10th February 1915
The Military Secretary presents his compliments to Colonel Foljambe and, in reply to his letter, would suggest his writing to the Commandant of the Military Hospitals at Cambrai and Mainz to enquire about his son. In all probability Colonel Foljambe will receive news direct from his son before long.

With regard to the question of kit it would be well to put in a claim for the return of kit or compensation.

The proposal to exchange certain officers who are incapacitated for further service has apparently not yet been definitely settled.

For Dora, the women's information net was passing on any news any of them had, though it was very difficult to sort out who had said what and what was correct. Violet Warre, Dora's sister-in-law, sent the following on 11 February:

Mrs Kingsmill has just telephoned to me that 'Lieutenant Hay left Cambrai on 8th January and was moved to Würzburg in Bavaria. The American Consul in Berlin asked for particulars of prisoners – Foljambe convalescent – Major Johnson died of wounds – Captain Lloyd leg amputated – Chichester dead. The WO told Mrs Johnson they had checked the list and found it correct.' Mrs Kingsmill is a sister of Major Johnson's and she wondered if you had heard anything about her brother from Ted. I told her you had no letter from Ted since September. I have telephoned to Henry and he said he would make enquiries at the WO tomorrow. I am so very glad and hope you may soon get a letter.

I hope all are well at Osberton. Has the boy [Alan] cut a tooth?

Major Cecil Johnson, who was reported as died of wounds, was also in the King's Royal Rifle Corps and had served in South Africa where he had been awarded the DSO. He knew Henry Warre and Victor Yeats-Brown and had known Hubert Foljambe. He had gone to France and Belgium with the BEF in August 1914 and had been brigade major of 19th Brigade at Le Cateau where he had been wounded and taken prisoner. Phyllis, his wife, wrote to Dora:

I got your letter this morning here. Cecil has mentioned your son two or three times in his letters – at least I imagine it must be him though he has never said his Christian name. I haven't heard from Cecil now since December, written by him on the 28th, and he said, 'Foljambe is better, I am allowed to say.' In his recent letters he had said he was wounded in much the same way as he, Cecil, was and that he had suffered from sickness. I think the report about your son being wounded in the back is true, as it was Cecil who said he was wounded in the same way as himself. They were in the same room together – Cecil is paralysed in both legs. As far as I know none of my letters have got through, though of course Cecil may have got some since he last wrote and I have been trying new ways of writing one just lately.

The American Express Company – 84 Queen St, EC, who seem to be good and also Le Secretaire, Bureau de la Croix Rouge pour la Recherche des Prisonniers de Guerre, Geneva.

Both these have assured me they have got letters through but since I wrote that way I haven't heard from Cecil, so I don't really know. The American Express Co say they can forward parcels.

Could you tell me how the report about your son being wounded in the back came through? Was it through a man called Hay? I ask because as through this source there is a Major Johnston – died of wounds at Cambrai. But I am not putting an awful lot of faith in this – as I had a letter, just about the same time as this was written, from a German friend saying how much better he was, and I want to discover if I can if the reports about the other officers of this man Hay are true as it may be something to go by. I should be awfully grateful if you could tell me.

The address of the hospital is: Kriegs Lazarette, Institut Notre-Dame, Cambrai. Written in block letters I believe it ought to be.

Poor Phyllis had been married in April 1914 and had only had, at the most, four months with her husband. The report from Lieutenant Hay was true and Cecil had died from his wounds on 1 January in the hospital at Cambrai.

George had written to Ted's battalion to tell them what he had heard so far and to enquire about Ted's kit. Captain Liddell, the adjutant, replied:

10th February 1915
Dear Colonel Foljambe,

I am so glad you have some definite news, but I fear it is not very satisfactory. If only one could find out how seriously he was hit. Presumably, however, he is likely to be on the road to recovery now, and perhaps may be out of hospital. Let us hope so.

I am afraid his kit will have been destroyed and thrown away, like all our kit was during the retreat. We had orders to rid ourselves of everything except food and ammunition and we left it all burning on the ground. Of course he will be able to recover the price of what was destroyed, but I doubt whether they would pass a claim till he comes back and gives a list of what was there. It might be worth your while to try. Supposing you consult your paymaster at Newark on the subject? The original Army Routine Order on the subject was dated 27th December and was No. 487 and it was amended by Army Routine Order No. 563 dated 19th January 1915. Condensed it says that officers who have lost kits on active service or have abandoned them by order are to submit claims on AF 01784. If necessary I could get a certificate signed by the CO that your son's kit was so abandoned. Presumably it consisted of a valise, one or two blankets, a greatcoat, a change of boots, socks, shirt and underclothes, probably a suit of service dress and some sundries like an electric torch etc., in all about 35 lb weight. Most of us have claimed £25–£30.

If I can be of any further use in the matter please let me know, but I doubt the pay people doing much without your son's signature.

I trust when we do go forward we shall find him better than one dares at present to hope.

Dora's quest continued. Henry Warre had served with Lieutenant Prince Maurice of Battenberg, a brother officer in the King's Royal Rifle Corps, who had been killed with the 1st Battalion in October 1914. He went to visit Princess Helena, Prince Maurice's mother, to ask her to try and find out more about Ted through her royal connections. In addition, Victor Yeats-Brown was the godson of the Kaiser's mother but there is no record of how many royals were involved in helping Ted. Princess Helena, however, did write.

26th February 1915
Dear Mrs Foljambe,

So many thanks for your note. I was so glad we could send some good news of your son. As to exchanging him – that is a matter for the War Office and regret we cannot help in that.

It was such a pleasure to see your brother – my beloved son was so devoted to him and I have to see his dear friends and know that they never forget him.

Sincerely yours,
Helena

Just heard Major Morrison Bell lists Guards prisoners at Freidberg. Lieutenant Foljambe 1 Battalion Rifle Brigade severely wounded hospital Cambrai. Last news of him on 16th.

Crown Princess Helena

Dora received a letter from a Johnston Watson, father of another prisoner of war:

28th February 1915
Dear Mrs Foljambe,

I am sorry I am not in a position to give you much news of your son – Lieutenant Foljambe.

My son (a captain in the Gordons) who is a prisoner of war in Mainz, in his last letter dated 20th January, asked me to communicate with Cox and Co informing them that Lieutenant Foljambe of the Rifle Brigade was in hospital at Cambrai, wounded. He added (I do not know with what truth) that he was anxious Cox and Co should communicate with the parents of Lieutenant Foljambe as nothing had been heard of him in England.

I conclude that some fellow prisoner at Mainz who had been in hospital at Cambrai was carrying out some request of your son in getting the information forwarded. I am sorry to say that I get very few letters from my boy – on average about one a month. It appears that there is someone at Mainz who could give information about your son and I will write and ask for further particulars. In the meantime I hope you may have good news of him.

I do not quite know how my son manages about cashing cheques – but I understand from Holt and Co that they have an agent who periodically visits the places of detention and advances money to the officers who bank with them.

I need not say I shall be very glad to do anything I can to further your desires.

Finally, and to everyone's enormous relief, contact was made with Ted. Although the letters were posted in mid-February, they would not have arrived with the family before the end of February at the earliest.

No. 2

A short line to say that I am getting on splendidly and am much better already as regards the lungs as there is anyhow fresh air up here if nothing else. I have just been for a quick walk up and down the passage and I feel rather like an overgrown puppy about the knees. It has been very cold the last two days and I haven't been out at all. I wonder if you could get me some khaki trousers and another thin shirt, and a pair of brown shoes. I am not sure that it wouldn't be a good thing if you sent for my things from Colchester and have them out, as they were packed in a great hurry and will not be improving, especially the uniform. They could be done at Osberton by Cutler if you are too busy, which I expect you will be. I hope you are well and Mother and the rest of the family. It is ages since I last saw anyone – I don't think that I shall need an operation now, which is a marvel and a blessing. I will number my letters. Will you do the same in case any get lost? Best love to all.

No. 3

New regulations are coming into force here, namely that one is not allowed to write so often and also we are asked not to receive too many letters. Well as I haven't had a letter since I was wounded I can't say how many in the month one is allowed, but if you write fairly regularly it means a lot this end as a letter is a big thing nowadays. We have been fairly moved about and all the rooms changed to make room for some more arrivals. One of the five English was exchanged the other day and the remaining four of us are scattered one to each room for some reason or other. The room I am in now was fearfully damp and cold when we were moved but is better now. We have a collection of very childish games which are played with much feeling. There is also a kind of casino which is very amusing and you can generally pay for your butter from what you win with the bank. I have developed a very bad cold in the head but am otherwise as well as one could expect and can get about splendidly as long as there are no stairs or the path is not uphill when I am beaten at once. I do hope this stops this year as I am quite sick of hearing a foreign language talked and long to hear nothing but the proper tongue

ABOVE *Exhausted and injured British prisoners under guard by a solitary German soldier, rest themselves on the bank of a river.* Topham Picturepoint/ TopFoto UK

talked at meals. Best love to all. Anything of interest to put into a letter being nil this must be brought to a close.

No. 4

News as usual practically nil. Some more French have arrived here, and the rooms we inhabit are full now unless they put more beds in. We have some music at last in the shape of banjos and guitar and we sing or dance nearly every night. The Russians are very nice indeed but one of the rooms smells rather of bear occasionally. I am much stronger and my only difficulty is staircases and running, neither of which I can do at all. How are you? And all at home? There is a young Englishman here by name Miller, who knows Mother. Will you write to G. J. James, High St, Oxford, and ask him to send me out 100 cigarettes every fortnight. He had some for me. Starting at once. They are very good. Also some tobacco. I hope this doesn't go on very much longer. Books are difficult to get also; some would be very acceptable. The languages are rather confusing with French as the basis. Give my love to all at home. I hope all are well.

Please send out my black hat, my khaki one has gone.

George had been even busier at the beginning of February at Newark, despite being worried about Ted and finding time to support Dora. At the beginning of the month the 2nd/8th Sherwood Foresters had left the depot at Newark: 'The men were all present and sober, and the train moved out of Newark station whither a large crowd had collected to say goodbye.' The departure of the battalion to Essex left the Newark depot very quiet and George had a slightly easier month. He was still recruiting and ensuring that the new recruits were trained to the right standards to be able to be sent down to the 1st and 2nd Battalions in the south. The 1st/8th was almost fully trained and ready to go to France but the 2nd/8th still had a long way to go. They had gone to Luton where the biggest problem was the constant complaining about the shortness of rations.

The representatives of the battalion were expected to take their rations away, without seeing them weighed, and were forced to accept the weight on the tickets as correct. The CO soon intervened and the system was put right to the satisfaction of the soldiers.

A week later the battalion moved to Billericay to learn how to dig trenches. The weather was awful and there was a great deal of sickness amongst both officers and men, mainly influenza, which all officers suffered from at some time or other except the CO and the adjutant, who were billeted at Ramsden Hall in Billericay and 'lived in the lap of luxury'. The men were not so lucky and the billets in town were bad and the men scattered around. In the middle of the month they were further disrupted by having to send another reinforcement of 85 men to the 1st/8th and then they had an outbreak of German measles that swept through the battalion. In all, it was not a very happy period of training and they moved back to Luton and greater comfort with some relief at the end of the month.

George was still in touch with friends at the front and his old adjutant, Hugh Hole, wrote to him again on 5 February:

Dear George,

Thanks for your letter

Very sorry for your anxiety about your boy; what trouble, what hopeless waste it all is. However, while there's life, and please God you'll get him back one day. Notts has paid its toll this time alright. I expect my boy out directly, and went over yesterday to find my son-in law, but his ill-fated regiment, the Irish Guards, were still in the trenches, and I hadn't time to get down there.

I am in a billet of an ideal kind for a few days only. My host, a foreman at a great steel works, who has made a cottage spotlessly clean and a trim garden bordered by golden pheasant cages. His good wife teaches my Gunner to cook, and my horse and Indian also put [up] on the premises. I feel as if I were at a watering place, after a month in a miner's shack where everything one put on smelt of the house! They make out here a soup of pork and greens which gets into the walls and taints everything and everybody in the house. Spent some time with the 8th Gurkhas yesterday; one officer who landed still with them. My division had 38 out of every 100 who landed after Xmas week. Now we are made up again, and go up next week. But it's pretty thick to see all these fine fellows snuffed out like nightlights – I count myself lucky to be in it – few of my generation of OEs [Old Etonians] are here. I've shed 4½ in. round the waist, and put on 3 lb! Am riding any old thing that comes along, as I did thirty-five years ago, rather a long interval. Might even venture to back to the meet with the Rufford among all you bloods after this! Well, so long, I hope Huskinson's lot will do well. I wish I were with them, tho' I'm fond of these Gunners.

Notts men are top-hole when led. They grouse infernally, but fight very well indeed. They like their own people to lead them though.

The 1st/8th knew it was ready to deploy and the battalion was full of rumours about when the day would be. Confidential orders were received on 15 February but the following day the CO, Lieutenant-Colonel Huskinson, who had recruited, trained and been with the battalion for years before as George's second-in-command, was posted to France and a staff job at the base.

16th February 1915
My dear Foljambe,
    Just a line of news to you privately. We are off very soon now. Last night I received orders that I was to go to France, (with Captain Gerald Clarke as my adjutant) and take on [an] appointment [in charge of] base details. I am told it is an honour (which I never sought) but someone has to do it who is a colonel full blown, and the choice has fallen on me. Of course for the present, I shall be away from the regiment, and may rejoin after some months. At

BELOW *The 4th Notts & Derby in front of Neuve Eglise in 1915.*

present I do not quite understand what it is, except there are 1,500 men and two COs under me to look after. It's rather a pang to have to leave the old 8th, I can assure you, just at this time, but I can only obey orders, and do my best. I leave the regiment for the present in good heart, order and spirits. I thought I would let you know at once. We have been doing night work hard lately.

Major Fowler, the battalion second-in-command, was promoted and took over and finally on 25 February the battalion left Bocking with 31 officers and 996 other ranks and deployed to France. The men were in good spirits and raring to go, but the battalion journal gives an accurate description of how truly ready they were.

BELOW *Major Dawson at Kemmel.*

On the whole the battalion was well equipped, and physically everyone was fit. The chief drawback appeared to be that we had rather a large percentage of young and inexperienced officers and NCOs, but as all had much to learn of the kind of warfare actually going on, this was no great disadvantage. With so many late additions and the very recent reorganisation, few commanders had had the opportunity of getting to know their men. So far as training was concerned we had covered in a way the whole of what the books had to say, and were fairly well acquainted with ordinary methods of fighting. There was a tendency towards staleness at the moment, and it is doubtful whether prolongation of our training in England would have been beneficial. We felt somewhat ignorant of many practical points affecting trench warfare, into which most of the fighting on most of the Western Front had degenerated, and although we had received useful hints from Major Hume, who had been out, we had yet a great deal to learn; this we did in France, in the hard school of bitter experience. Whatever our shortcomings, we felt proud indeed to belong to the first complete Territorial Division to embark for France.

This Territorial Army that was being deployed to France was a very different beast to the BEF that had left only six months before.

March 1915

The beginning of March was very quiet for Francis and G Battery, but all was not well. Francis, who was now a very seasoned and experienced officer, did not take at all to his battery commander, Major Dawson. Dawson was a small, energetic 'old school' artillery officer, more interested in his comfort than the professional development of his battery. A fine horseman, he was much more interested in the polish at the wagon lines and ensuring the horses were looked after rather than the gun end of the battery or, even worse, than the goings-on of the observers at the front. Francis did not like his approach, had been free of him in February when he had volunteered to work with mortars in the trenches, but was now stuck with him again. Dawson was also a bit of a snob and, as an officer in the socially prestigious Royal Horse Artillery, tended to look down on Francis who had only been commissioned into the Field Artillery, which Dawson thought must be inherently inferior. Dawson did not seek to use Francis's experience so Francis just buckled down to work his section as best he could, and try to enjoy his stints at the front.

The Cavalry Corps was concentrated south of Hazebrouck in order to exploit a heavy infantry attack on Neuve-Chapelle that was supposed to break the German line.

Tuesday 9th March   *Orders in evening to be ready to move at 6 a.m. Heavy firing in direction of Messines.*
Wednesday 10th March   *No further orders. Stood ready to move all day.*
Thursday 11th March   *Marched as far as Bois de Nieppe and waited in a field all day harnessed up. Attack at Neuve-Chapelle. Watched wounded coming past all day. Bivouacked near Morbecque. For the attack there were 481 guns on a 2-mile front!*
Friday 12th March   *All ready to move. No orders.*
Saturday 13th March   *Ditto. Orders in evening to return to old billets.*

Later in the month, as Major Dawson recalled, the battery was deployed to Kemmel, a hill that was just down the line from the town of Ypres. They were to spend some time here, among a series of batteries in a line some way behind the infantry. Observers were either forward with the infantry in their trenches, or on the hill overlooking the trenches, with telephone line laid both back to the guns and forward to the infantry. The trouble was that the line was easy to break and was often cut by German artillery fire. The guns were arrayed in gun pits behind, with the gunners building shelters both for them to live in and to protect them from artillery fire. Further shelters were built for the ammunition,

which had to be in easy reach, and it all had to be concealed from the air. Further behind, maybe a mile or so, were the wagon lines with all the horses and where the administration of the battery was carried out. Francis takes up the tale:

Sunday 21st March   *Orders to join Second Army.*
Monday 22nd March   *Marched to St-Jans-Cappel. Dawson went on in a car to make arrangements. As usual he made a muddle of everything. Some vague orders about a digging party in evening. Result: Lutyens and I with the detachment are sent off ten miles in the rain and find nobody waiting the other end to show us the position. Return at 10 p.m. to find we were not*

BELOW *Renauld and Francis Foljambe.*

supposed to go at all. Furious with Dawson, who was thoroughly comfortable in his billet and had made no attempt to stop our unnecessary journey.

Major Dawson had found a position for the guns, but it was rather exposed and very little movement was allowed to and from the position by day, as the Germans might have been able to notice any movement. There were no distinctive features around, so nothing easily identifiable for the Germans to aim at and there was a deserted house close by which served as a billet for the guns. It had two stone-floored rooms on the ground floor which were occupied by the officers, signallers and cooks, and the men not on duty in the gun pits slept in a loft above. A nice farm was found for the horse lines to the rear. It was untouched and the inhabitants were still pursuing their daily occupations.

Tuesday 23rd March *Up early and proceeded with digging party to Barseye. Dug pits and got guns in in evening. No sign of Dawson all day.*

Wednesday 24th March *Quiet day. Registered zone.*

ABOVE *Lionel Lutyens (standing, killed 6 January 1918) and John Fitzwilliams MC (seated, killed 30 August 1918).*

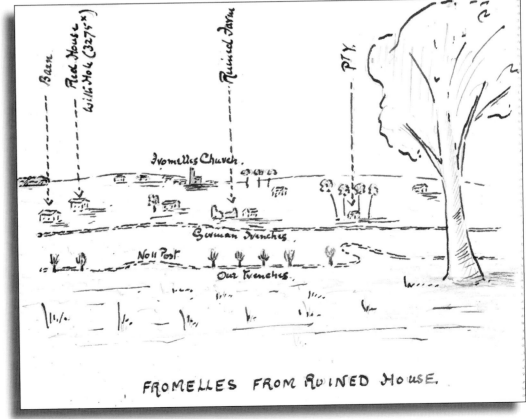

RIGHT *Fromelles from a ruined house, March 1915.*

FROMELLES FROM RUINED HOUSE.

Thursday 25th March   *Fired a few rounds.
Great trouble with Dawson about his
arrangements in the battery. Quite the
worst major in the Army!*
Friday 26th March   *Spent day at wagon
line. Very cold.*
Saturday 27th March   *Quiet day. Usual
routine.*
Sunday 28th March   *Eight big shrapnel
into battery. Our billet knocked in. Spent
very cold and nasty night.*
Monday 29th March   *Fired on register.
Moved our billet. Some shells close to
wagon line.*
Tuesday 30th March   *Wagon line shelled
again. Two wounded and two horses killed
and one wounded. Slept in infantry trench
H2 after most unpleasant walk down
Kemmel–Wytschaete road with plenty of
bullets flying about.*
Wednesday 31st March   *Rode down to new
wagon line in morning. Slept with guns.*

Neither Major Dawson nor Francis ever
worked out why the wagon line was shelled.
There were few aeroplanes around, and
there were more obvious and attractive
targets in the area. The horses and the men
were concealed from view and the NCOs
and men put it down to spies. There were
refugees camped in some of the outhouses
and no one seemed to know much about
them. Dawson was walking back towards
the lines when it happened and there was
mayhem in the horse lines. Two killed and
more wounded and the rest had broken loose
and took some time to round up. Dawson
gave the order for the more badly wounded
horses to be destroyed and to the sorrow of
the battery this included Bessie. Bessie was a
favourite of the men, a hunter that had come
to them on mobilisation in England, and the
story had gone round that on her departure
her family had gathered round her and wept
over her. She liked to be petted and the men
had spoilt her.

The poor farmer had also lost several
bullocks and pigs and his mother-in-law
was badly wounded in the leg. The soldiers
helped him to kill his wounded animals and
were invited to help eat some of them! The

last dead creature that Dawson saw as he
went to the guns was a cock chaffinch which
didn't have a mark on it – it was his first
experience of shellshock.

Victor Yeats-Brown had not been having
a happy time with 3 KRRC. His commanding
officer had sent him to the rear to rest at
the beginning of February and he had not
recovered enough to take back command
of his company. None of his letters survive
but the family were worried about him,
particularly Henry Warre in England who
was still very much in touch with the
KRRC battalions. Henry wrote to George on
10 March:

*I had a letter from the Rat [Henry's
nickname for Victor] yesterday and I think
it is only right you know about it as it
is somewhat disturbing. He has, as you
know, been seedy and was, as far as I can
hear, sent back for some time, which in a
way makes his statement more serious. He
writes:-*

*'My chill was a stupid affair. I can't sleep
and this makes one go rotten sooner than
anything somehow. The row of the shelling
seems to get on my nerves that when we
come out to rest I find it impossible to sleep
at nights. If I break down again I rather
think it will be a bigger job. The only thing
I can think of which would possibly enable
me to be of use would be as some very
junior instructor at Sandhurst . . .'*

*From the above I gather that he is losing
self-control. I never dreamed that he would
be like it, but it is on a par with his being
unable to contain his temper in his younger
days. He did not go through the attack
made by 3 KRRC and so did not have to
stand the racket of that, but I expect he has
been quite ill and you must be fit to stand
the strain.*

*I had to send Dolly Druisan home on
account of his nerves as he would in a
short time have become a danger and it is
not worth keeping a fellow in command of
men when he might crack just when cool
judgement and quiet decision might be the
absolute necessity for success or for saving
of life.*

I have written to Charlie Gosling [CO of 3 KRRC and a friend of Henry's], George, as I thought he ought to know. He is at present at home [Gosling had been wounded on 15 February] but will be with us again shortly. I am very sorry about it.

Victor's breakdown had been dealt with sympathetically by his battalion. It was understood that some people could not take the strain and many officers and soldiers from the battalion had either been sent behind the lines, or back to England with injuries or frostbite. Henry again wrote to George on the 12th:

I had a letter from Goose [Lieutenant Colonel Gosling] this morning. He said that the Rat had been away a fortnight when he was hit and that he had not seen him, but he thought old Linger [Major Ling who had taken over as CO whilst Gosling was recovering] would soon understand and he (Goose) said he would write to him sometime.

I daresay an adjutancy would suit the Rat well but it all depends on his state as to when he should take it up. He might, of course, recover quickly but he might require considerable time before he could do any work at all. One cannot tell. Some fellows crack under the strain, and others control themselves during the strain and crack on the reaction. I have seen it both ways, but in either I think a quiet time is necessary. We do not, of course, know how much Rachie knows but I wrote to her yesterday and put in a veiled way that I gathered Rat was not fit and that he had been probably worse than we expected, but I said not a word about a nervous breakdown.

I hope you will soon be all right again.

Lots of work here. Riding gives me rather gyp but, despite of it, it is nice to be on a horse again.

I am glad Ted has written.

Victor was sent back to England to recover and was then later posted back to France as a divisional signals officer. In this role he would be able to continue to serve but would be further behind the line than in the trenches and would not be exposed to the same noise, fear and degradation that had caused his breakdown.

March was a very good month for Dora. None of Ted's letters, written towards the end of February, had yet arrived, but she was shortly to hear from him. In the meantime, she was able to start sending him parcels of food and other necessities. Parcels could be sent either through the Red Cross or American Express and Dora chose the latter route, receiving the following acknowledgement on 1 March:

We would acknowledge receipt of letter and package for Lieutenant. E. W. S. Foljambe, who was recently at Cambrai. In a letter received from Berlin dated 17th February, they advise us that Lieutenant Foljambe had been transferred from the field hospital at Cambrai to some point in Germany. They were not quite certain where, but all enquiries have been made and they will notify us promptly. Immediately this information comes to hand we will advise you, and also send out the parcel you lodged with us.

The network of prisoners' relations was still working and Dora was thrilled to get another letter from Mr Irvine, her old correspondent in Ireland:

3rd March 1915
Dear Mrs Foljambe,
You may recall that you wrote to me on 29 November last asking about your son E. W. S. Foljambe of the Rifle Brigade. I have just had a card from my son, C. G. S. Irvine of the King's Own, who has been moved out of the hospital at Würzburg and is now in the Festung Marianberg, Würzburg, Bavaria in which he says 'We have been joined here by Foljambe of the Rifle Brigade – he has made a marvellous recovery – I knew him at Hythe.' As there appears to be only one of the name in the 1st Battalion, I believe it must be your son. Most likely you have heard from him but

it will be something to know what my son says of him. Letters come pretty regularly but it takes 20–30 days. The authorities in Würzburg do not post them until ten days after they are written and it is another ten more before they are delivered. On the whole the officers are fairly well treated but hitherto it has been hard to get parcels out. The delay has been mostly in our own post office in Mount Pleasant London, so far my son has only got four out of fifteen but we must hope the others will turn up.

I most heartily congratulate you and from experience I can fully sympathise with you in the anxiety you must have felt. It is well not to let the knowledge of his safety get into the papers. It did about my son and the German authorities promptly stopped Professor Mendelssohn-Bartholdy, who used to see him every day and bring him books and papers, going to see him altogether.

Now came a major breakthrough in a letter from the Red Cross from Paris:

4th March 1915
Dear Madam,

I thought it might interest you to know that yesterday a Polish lady, Mme de Rudincka, came in here with some news about some of our prisoners. She has been at Cambrai since August and nursed many of them there, including Lieutenant E. Foljambe. She reports to us that he was badly wounded, but had quite recovered and is now [a] prisoner in Germany.

Even better, there followed a letter from Madya de Rudincka with her first-hand news:

Madam,

I came back yesterday from Germany and I got the opportunity to cure your elder son, Edmond Foljambe, lieutenant in the 1st Battalion Rifle Brigade, until 1st February 1915, at the Hospital Nôtre Dame in Cambrai. As I don't know if you've got news from him, I'm very keen on giving some to you. Mr Foljambe is quite safe

ABOVE *Lt Boulez (left) and Hay at Notre Dame Military Hospital, Cambrai, in 1915. Ted was taken here after he was captured.*

and even if he is not dangerously ill he still needs some care. When I get his address I will give it to you because he is looking forward to receiving news from you and particularly to know where his brother [is], the Lieutenant Francis Foljambe whom he has not got news from since the beginning of the war.

I'm leaving to Serbia within a fortnight therefore I'd like you to answer me quickly in order to, if you wish, allow me to give some news to your son or a letter through some influential friends I have in Switzerland.

Would you please, Madam, believe in my best feelings.

M. de Rudincka

You can answer to me in English.

though his wound was very serious and he had been very ill for several months, keeping intact nevertheless his braveness and his good mood.

Since the 1st of February, Mr Foljambe has been carried out to Germany and I've not been able to know where but I'm trying hard to know in order to send him some supplies, because the lack of goods makes our dear prisoners suffer so much.

Through the same channel, I'm trying to get Lieutenant Foljambe [to] enter a sanatorium because his lungs are weak

This was the best letter Dora had had by far and you can imagine her excitement as she realised that Madya de Rudincka had not only nursed her beloved eldest son for nearly four months, but that she might have some influential friends who could help get Ted back to England. What she did not know and could not even suspect at this time, was that Madya and Ted had formed a very strong bond. Ted had been utterly convinced that Madya had saved his life. His wound when he had arrived in hospital had been severe and she had nursed him throughout, not only giving him the will and strength to get better, but also giving him hope for the future. She was a lively and attractive woman and for his part, Ted had told her about his life in England, his home at Osberton and the estates that would one day be his. Madya had set her cap at Ted and saw that he was a good prospect for the future, and Ted was so grateful to her, and had been so dependent on her, that they had an unspoken pact to marry at the end of the war. It was a relationship that was to develop and Madya was quite determined to do everything she could to get Ted out of the clutches of the Germans.

Dora knew that she must meet Madya to thank her for looking after Ted and to see what could be done for the future. She arranged to go to Paris.

Meanwhile, Dora was still getting advice from Ireland:

8th March 1915
Dear Mrs Foljambe,
I am glad I wrote. I thought you would have heard but trust [that] before this you have had a letter. Letters should take 3–5 days but they take 20–30 as the Germans do not post a letter till 10 days after its date and they keep it 10–15 or 20 days in our office, sometimes, before they send it, but save for that they go and come pretty regularly. The Post Office is always making new regulations, but get from the GPO the latest and follow the directions and now they go all right and so do parcels. Up to this parcels have been delayed in our post office (Mount Pleasant) but they told me they were short of hands and I found parcels had been there over six weeks unsent. If you send parcels fully addressed to the 'Comité International de la Croix-Rouge Agence des Prisonnieres de Guerre, Geneva' they will forward them on and if unable to deliver them will return them to you but they bill me now. All parcels addressed as directed by the regulations but marked 'Berne-transit' will be forwarded direct to prisoners by the Swiss Post Office, so now I am sending that way. If you get the Army and Navy February circular you will see the export prices and I get them to pack. The Medium Hibiscus are the best cigarettes to send as they are good. I send roast chicken and chicken breasts in glass, you see them in this lid and the poor boys' menu consists of 'pig' in every conceivable form but always pig, so chicken is a bit of a change. I send eating chocolate and chocolate food and Taureau or Beef in bottles 16 oz 5/- and good cups of leaf tea. Be sure to fill up the customs notes and dispatch notes you get in the post office accurately.
They get money all right by Post Office order, provided the address and note is accurate. Don't send more than £2 at a time or £5 in the month or they will not get it. I send £2, £1, and £2. Be sure to follow all the red tape in the forms. I suggest you print the envelopes, they go quicker if you do. I hope you will have good news.

More good news for Dora was that American Express was now starting to deliver her parcels.

12th March 1915
Dear Mrs Foljambe,
With reference to the package which you handed to us some time ago for Lieutenant Foljambe we would advise that same was duly sent forward to him at Festung Marianberg, Bavaria, along with the letter. We are also writing our Berlin House in this matter asking them to get in touch with Lieutenant Foljambe, and do everything necessary for his comfort and pay him any funds permitted under the regulations. We trust this will be quite agreeable and satisfactory to you. We will write to you immediately if any further news comes to hand.

Dora must have been concerned by this arrangement for the company wrote to her again on the 16th:

With reference to your favour of 13th inst., we would advise you that the camp of Festung Marianberg is very well known to us, and there is no doubt but what the package will be sent through to the right address. Due instructions have been given to our Berlin people as to the help etc. they should render Lieutenant Foljambe.

Dora and Madya met in Paris. At the outbreak of war Ted had been informally engaged to a girl called Celia Tollemarche, and the family's recollection is that he had hopes that Dora would not particularly take to Madya, which could give him an excuse not to marry her. But Dora and Madya got on. Dora for her part was so grateful for everything that Madya had done and saw also that she could be a help to try and get Ted repatriated early. Dora had not really taken to Celia Tollemarche and thought Madya would be a most suitable daughter-in-law. Madya saw that Dora could be a strong ally in her plans, and told her about the arrangement they had to marry and they started working out together how they could help each other and Ted. Dora agreed to try at the English end, and Madya would see what she could do with her contacts in the Red Cross and in Switzerland.

Dora did not get off to a good start. She asked Henry to write again to the War Office to try to get Ted swapped in the next exchange, but got a negative response:

War Office
18th March 1915
Dear Warre,
The question of making special application for the return to this country of a badly wounded officer is one that frequently comes before me. I only most sincerely wish that we could take any steps in the matter, but it is impossible. The bald, unsympathetic facts are as follows: the question of selection of those whom we are prepared to return to Germany, as being so seriously wounded as to be of no further service, rests with us. Equally, the selection of those who are in German hands rests with Germany. They have no say in the matter so far as those in our hands are concerned, and we have no say as regards those of ours whom they hold.
Many congratulations on your promotion. I wish I could do more to meet your wishes.
Yours sincerely,
H. Bulfield

My dear Dora,
Herewith Sir H. B.'s letter and I am afraid nothing can be done this side of the water. I only hope that the Polish nurse's efforts will be successful. Please thank George for his postcard. I cannot get up to him this week. Love to you all. Yr loving brother. H.W. 19.3.15

So Dora tried herself, writing to Princess Thurn und Taxis on 23 March:

My dear Princess,
I hear from my aunts at Genoa that you have most kindly made enquiries about
my son (Lieutenant E. W. S. Foljambe, Rifle Brigade) who has been wounded and missing since August. We have now heard that he has been moved from Cambrai to Würzburg and is a prisoner in the Festung Marianberg. I have heard from the Red Cross nurse, Madame de Rudincka, who looked after him for five months at Cambrai, that his state of health is so bad that he would be eligible for exchange – he was severely wounded through the lower part of the body. His lungs are also affected.
We should be most grateful to you if you could possibly mention his name to whoever manages the exchange of prisoners – so that he may be included in the next lot, either to return to England or to Switzerland. He has written three letters only and had not, up to 20th February received any letter or parcel from us.
Yours sincerely,
Dora Foljambe

Dora tried again, asking a friend in the War Office to approach the Foreign Office, with the following results:

Foreign Office
25th March 1915
Dear Colonel Bingham,
I am afraid it is impossible for any action to be taken here in regard to the inclusion of Lieutenant Foljambe among the incapacitated prisoners for exchange, as the selection of such prisoners must necessarily rest with the government which holds them.
I am sorry, therefore, that I cannot help in any way to bring about this officer's return.
Yours truly,
Horace Rumbold

War Office
26th March 1915
My dear Dora,
I am very sorry that the enclosed does not help. I only wish to goodness it could be done and that you will get your boy back safe. I am very sorry to have failed. It was so kind of you having us to dinner last night.
Frank Bingham

ABOVE *British prisoners of war on the Western Front, some of whom are wounded, are guarded by German troops.* Topham Picturepoint/ TopFoto UK

For Ted himself letters were just starting to arrive, and American Express managed to get some money through to him, as confirmed by a postcard he sent to the company on 21 March:

I am in receipt of your letter of the 18th inst but not yours of the 13th. I am taking the liberty to keep your cheque till the beginning of next month, when I expect to be in need of more money. Will you inform my Mother that my wound is now healed and that in time I may be perfectly alright. My lungs, however, are not in good working order and may need a rest in good air. Please also state that I have written frequently to my Father since I have been here. I am most anxious to hear any news of my brother 2nd Lieutenant R. E. T. Foljambe, Royal Field Artillery. If you should happen to have heard, I should be most grateful for any information.

Ted wrote to Dora:

Post Card No. 1
March 26th 1915
My dear Mother,
  I am so pleased to hear from you at last. I have your letters of 8.3.15 and 10.3.15, also one from Father. I am getting

on splendidly and am really quite strong again and there is hardly any visible change now since a year ago. Please suggest to any whom I might happen to know that letters are the only things that take one out of the ordinary routine, and though hard to answer are very acceptable. My best congratulations to Mary, and I hope all my new relations are well and some growing. You can't imagine what a relief it is to hear that Francis is well and safe. I have been horribly uneasy about him. By what I could write in a letter you could get very little idea what life is here – so I won't write anything. I hear that a packet is on its way from the American Express Company from a Mrs Falkner. Is it a misprint for you? I have been getting a few answers to letters written but it takes an indefinite time for any letter to reach England from here. They come much quicker. I am so glad you heard from my nurse. If it hadn't been for her I should not be writing to you now. I was given three days to live by one doctor, but she refused to believe it and pulled me out of the hole. It is very hard answering letters with four postcards and two letters only a month. Will you have my boxes opened keys or no and have my clothes out. The keys must have been lost in the post. So sorry to hear

that Father has been laid up. I hope he will
be all right by the time this letter arrives.
Give them all my love wherever they may
be. Smoke and food arrive out here and
very acceptable and I should be very glad if
they could be sent sometimes.

> *Best love to all.*
> *from E*

Finally, at the end of March Dora tried to
pull more strings to get Ted repatriated by
writing to Princess Margaret in Sweden.

Madam,
I venture to write on behalf of my son
(Lieutenant E. W. S Foljambe, 1st Battalion,
Rifle Brigade) who has been wounded and
a prisoner since 26th August. Your Royal
Highness mentioned him in a telegram
last month to Princess Christian as being
severely wounded and in hospital at
Cambrai.
We had never been able to communicate
with him as to where he was, and were
very grateful for this mention of him.
Since then we hear he has been moved
to the Festung Marianberg at Würzburg
and we also hear from the Red Cross
nurse Madame de Rudincka, who was
at Cambrai, that he has suffered much
from the effect of his wounds especially
in his lungs and he would be worthy
of consideration for exchange either to
Switzerland or to England. Would your
Royal Highness pardon me for troubling
you with this in the hope that should an
opportunity occur you would mention my
son as eligible for exchange.
I had the honour some years ago of
meeting your Royal Highness at Eton where
my father, Dr Warre, is provost.
I remain your humble servant,
Dora Foljambe

George was having a much quieter time
in Newark now that both battalions had
deployed, but was still very busy, particularly
with the paperwork generated by both
battalions being away. The 2nd/8th Battalion
was still near Luton and its training was
progressing, albeit with some problems. A

consignment of Japanese rifles had been
procured and these were dished out to the
men and they were ordered to go to the
ranges to try them out. Many of them had
had little training in musketry, and the course
was not only a waste of ammunition, but
may even have done permanent harm to the
men's shooting. The practice was carried out
in a snowstorm, and there was no shelter of
any kind for the men waiting to fire. It was
not a successful day.

The 1st/8th Battalion was in France as part
of the North Midland Division, commanded
by Major General Edward Stuart-Wortley, a
friend of George.

4th March 1915
My dear George,
Many thanks for your letter just received.
It was great luck getting the division out
as a complete formation. I am sure they
will do well. The Notts and Derby Brigade
go into the trenches tomorrow for short
periods, more for the sake of giving them
their baptism of fire, and for instruction.
The King sent us a charming telegram
yesterday wishing us God speed. This was
most kind of him – and very unusual. I
have to write to him once a week, which is
rather a trial!
I wish you were out here, but I'm sure
you are doing excellent work at home.
> *Yours ever,*
> *Edward Stuart-Wortley*
> *The men are all very fit.*

Lieutenant Colonel Huskinson, who had
handed over command just before the battalion
deployed to France, wrote again to George.

Commandant
Étaples
4th March 1915
My dear Foljambe,
So many thanks for your letter. I had
[command] of Rouen Reinforcements for
a month. I am now moved up nearer the
front to establish a large camp here (I
cannot give you the numbers) to be kept
permanently ready for the immediate move
for the front. You know what the work

means of fixing everything up, and also arranging with everyone, and along the lines of communication.

I expect the first regiment in at the end of the week, and there are already four hospitals here now. When the camp is full up, I expect they may push me further north again, as they will send a general here to command the unit, or they may keep me on.

It's a rum job to dodge me about like this, is it not, but so long as I am doing what they require, I must not grumble. I am under the General of Lines of Communication now, but I would rather be back with the old 8th in spite of it all. But I suppose they know best, and it would be rather hard luck on Fowler to apply to go back there don't you think?

I have been in my office now at 9.00 and I don't finish till about 6.00, and then sometimes at night, as the troops are going about all the time and the work will get larger.

I expect something is on the move, as 'The Boss from the WO' was through last week for three days.

I don't hear quite so much news as I heard at Rouen. The truth about La Chappell [Neuve-Chapelle] was the telephone broke down. The 7th Division did not push on but dug themselves in and waited which hung up the show; result [was] the cavalry were all held back, or else the Germans would have had a smashing defeat, and Ostend would now be in our hands, but it will come shortly. The general and staff, however, of the 7th Division have been sent home.

It is quite miserable to see the poor wives and fathers here to see their sons. One officer died last night and I did the best to cheer them up. I think a trip here would do you good if you could come and stay with me at my little hotel. The air and country are grand. You cross to Boulogne, and you will hear the guns occasionally, and an aeroplane is over sometimes. I have waited for a shot but have not got one yet. The French continually pot at our planes regardless of asking, and we are trying to stop it. A German submarine passed here the day before yesterday, but I think the French got it.

Patrick, my boy, will insist on going into the Army, so I want to get him into the Rifle Brigade or the 60th. Can you do anything for me? He goes to Sandhurst on the 14th I think. His name has to be put down in some list by the powers that be.

Sorry to hear you are so full of gout and pain: hope it will be better soon.

Yours very truly,

C. J. Huskinson

You would laugh seeing me interviewing the Mayor of Étaples through my interpreter, and my French dictionary; also a French count whose land we are on.

Lieutenant Colonel Herbert Fowler, now commanding the 1st/8th, was also writing letters home from France, including one to George at Newark on 5 March:

Many thanks for your letter. We have got over safely and are now somewhere in northern France. All the men very fit and anxious to get on at it. I wish you could see the battalion now – you wouldn't recognise them in their fur skins! It is quite mild now. I think they will hardly want them.

We are in good billets in barns and small houses in a tiny village.

You will be having a lot of our correspondence etc. to deal with now.

Yours ever,

G. H. Fowler

Fowler also wrote to Huskinson in Étaples on the 13th:

My dear Colonel,

We eventually got across all right, though the battalion got split up in going. We all went aboard on the Thursday, on a fine ship, but 780 were fetched off in the evening, so only 2½ Platoons of A Company and the transport went that night. They waited at Havre for us, except Ashwell and the two platoons who went up country to Oudezeele near Cassel. The rest of us spent two nights in the rest camp at Southampton. Then Becher and 100 men embarked on another ship with the divisional ammunition column, but were kept on board for three days. The 680 remaining stayed in a Clyde steamer one night but were fetched off again, and spent another night in billets, very comfortable.

The next day we really did get across – very smooth – spent a few hours in Havre, drawing fur skins, and came up nineteen hours in the train to Cassel, where we joined up with Ashwell's party at Oudezeele. Becher came in the day after, late on the night of the 5th. So we were at last complete. The result of all this is that we missed our five day's course in the trenches which the other battalions in the brigade have had.

They all seem to have enjoyed it very much, and each one has had a casualty. Still we had a very good time at Oudezeele, and saw a lot of the French troops.*

We left there Tuesday, and by the afternoon had joined up with the brigade at Merris. We were devoutly thankful of this. The Lincs and Leics to whom we had been attached were not quite the same.

We left Merris on the 11th, and are now quite close to the lines. There is a gun in action close by here as I write. We are lying near a lot of Canadians, who are very rough but quite good fellows.

I can't tell you but you may guess my meaning. 'What we have often wished for is going to happen, and we [are] expecting orders to move any time.'

I think the men are very happy. They hardly grouse at all in their letters, which they write in 1000's. Have you seen that Fosbury and Torrance have been in the Gazette. Officers are all messing by companies and headquarters now, using the dixies. This is working very well. In view of our probable marches, we have to reduce the men's packs, so are arranging to store the spare things in the pub here, for which I have agreed to pay 3 francs a week. I think this is fair for the battalion private funds, don't you? I have got an agreement made with the landlady on this.

I have heard from Mrs Huskinson, who is sending out things every fortnight. They

ABOVE *Dardi, the interpreter, who was attached to Francis' artillery battery.*

will be very useful as the men can't carry much. We miss you very much, and I hope you will be able to get up and see us soon. General Smith-Dorrien the other day saw us on the road. I think the men are looking forward to the idea of a scrap. I do hope we shall be able to ride in to N[ewark] together when this show is over.

So, at the end of the March, the 1st/8th was about to go into the trenches for the first time.

---

* On one of its route marches from Oudezeele, the battalion marched through the little village of Wormhout which had a battalion of *poilus* resting in it. All the French soldiers gave the Notts men a warm welcome as they marched through the streets and the entire 1st/8th whistled the *Marseillaise*, which went down particularly well with the French.

CHAPTER 7

Ypres, Mount Kemmel and Loos

By early April Francis was now firmly entrenched on Kemmel Hill which overlooked Ypres from the south. The infantry trenches snaked in a long line to the north and south with the fire trenches within 100–200yd of the German front line. Between the front lines were shell holes, rusting wire and decomposing bodies, and a pervading stench of death. Behind the fire trenches were the second line and communication trenches crossing the landscape and further back the battalion headquarters' dug-outs. Everything was covered in mud, knee-deep in many places. On Kemmel Hill the guns were

placed in pits, with dug-outs for the men when not firing and the horse lines some distance behind.

Francis spent some of his time with the infantry in the forward trenches as a liaison officer. There was no direct method of communication between Francis and his guns, and ammunition was in very short supply as the allowance for a battery of six guns at this stage of the war was only three shells a day. The idea of sending an officer to sleep in the trenches was to equalise discomfort with the infantry and he was known as a 'hostage'.

Most days in April were quiet with

OPPOSITE Ypres: the Cloth Hall after the first enemy bombardment, November 1914.

BELOW The communication trench between front line and support line, Neuve Eglise Sector, 1915.

BELOW *Sector G,
facing east from No
4 Bloke Row, Kemmel
Hill. Position of
Wytschaete–Messines
Ridge, April 1915.*

the main work of the day to improve the
positions, adding depth and additional
protection. The battery's new position had
in fact been well prepared and a farm about
a hundred yards away was available for the
horse lines and the officers and men when

not required at the guns. The place was very
dirty but they succeeded in making it very
comfortable, particularly as their last billet had
been hit by a shell and had become cold and
draughty. Francis's diary resumes:

Monday 5th April   *Moved my section into*

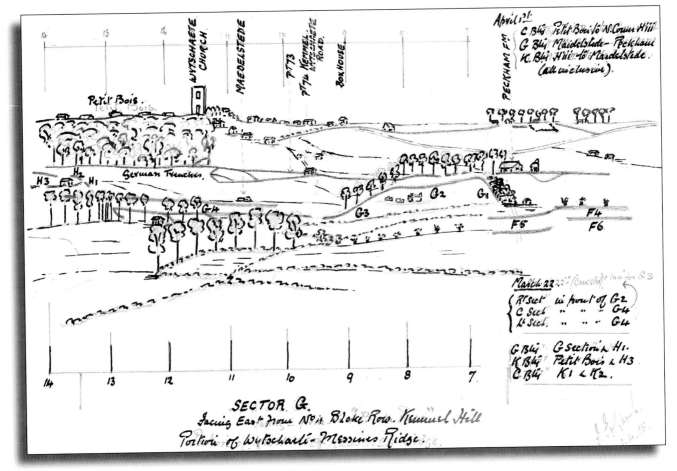

LEFT *Patrick and G.H. Johnstone in their dug-out on the Kemmel–Neuve Eglise Road.*

new position behind Kemmel. Dawson has worked an exchange with a Terrier [Territorial] battery simply so as to get the horses and guns together. Great amusement with Terriers moving out.

Tuesday 6th April   *Rest of battery move in. Furious with FitzWilliam in evening for muddling up my arrangements. Slept with guns. Pouring rain and icy cold.*

Wednesday 7th–Thursday 8th April   *Made dug-out. Very pleased with it. Got corrugated iron from the RE for roofs.*

BELOW *The guns at Kemmel.*

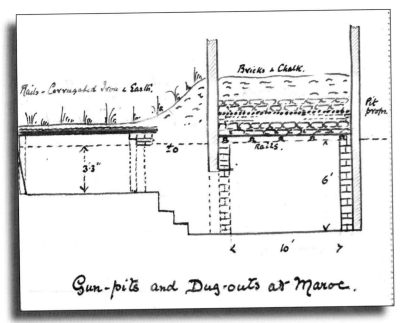

ABOVE *Gun pits and dug-outs at Maroc.*

Friday 9th April   *Rode over to Westhoff to act as instructor to infantry in trench mortars. Usual staff work, no mortars, so found Masters and had tea. General Sir Horace Smith-Dorrien round on tour of inspection.*

Monday 12th April   *The major calculated a short range for night firing. Result, some shell into our own trenches and one killed and three wounded. He was sent for by the general to explain and we became quite hopeful. However, he was let off with a warning.*

Major Dawson takes up the tale:

That night at about 1 a.m. the infantry in front called for fire. I was asleep in the farmhouse but was wakened by the signallers who told me of the call. I rang up the officer at the guns who told me he had been asked to fire a salvo but as far as he could make out all was quiet. After waiting at the telephone for some time, I gave orders that I was to be called if anything else happened and I lay down again. At 4 a.m. I was informed that two more salvos had been called for and fired and all was quiet again. This was corroborated from the guns and once more I lay down, and at 6 a.m. went up to my observation station at Little Kemmel. At 10 a.m. I received a message from the colonel to say that one of the

second series of shells had fallen short and killed a man in our front trenches. I went to the colonel and explained that I could not believe this as all the guns had been properly laid and that the other shell had been all right. We both went to the colonel of the battalion to express our regret and asked for a search to be made for any piece of shell which might determine whether it was ours or not. He said that this would be done but that there was no certainty that it was one of my shells that did the damage and, in any case, he was sure I had taken all reasonable precautions, and that the matter must be regarded as a regrettable accident. I expected to hear no more of the matter, but the next day General Byng arrived on a visit and the affair was reported to him. He came to see me and I explained to him exactly what ranges were on the guns and also that, although the battery had fired twice during the night, nothing was said to me until 10 a.m. He then went away.

Shortly afterwards I got a copy of a note from the colonel to the general saying that, under the circumstances, he thought it better that I should give up my command. On reading this I telephoned to the colonel demanding an interview, and then and there strongly protested against such treatment. I showed him the calculations which had just come from home as regards corrections for atmosphere, temperature and wind, and insisted that these had all been complied with at dusk. I had a pocket aneroid and thermometer but the wind I had to judge. He agreed that I had done all I could and said he would withdraw the letter. I considered the matter urgent and asked leave to go to Hazebrouck with it myself. It was a long ride, but, after much difficulty, I succeeded in finding a car belonging to a French interpreter, who was going that way, and I started off.

I reached Hazebrouck in the afternoon and saw the general who told me that Colonel Rotton's letter had already gone on (I must say that I thought unseemly haste had been displayed) but that if the colonel wrote another letter he would get it withdrawn. I returned to Kemmel, saw the colonel and the letter was written and dispatched that night.

Next day General Byng appeared again. He had apparently forgotten his promise to withdraw the letter and produced several reasons for my not remaining in command of G Battery. These reasons were easily demolished but even then he would not give way entirely and left me saying 'he would see what could be done'. As he appeared to have taken a personal dislike to me I had not much hope of his doing anything, but I determined to have the matter fought out, although I thought I would probably come off second best in the contest. The injustice of it all hit me very hard, especially as I knew, and had told the general, that a similar, though more serious incident had happened some miles further up the line and the battery commander had been held to be blameless.

Three days later, Brigadier General White-Thomson, who was then CRA [Commander Royal Artillery] of the Cavalry Corps, came up to make an official report. He did it very carefully and at some length, and, at the end, told me unofficially that he personally was quite satisfied, and he thought I might assume the matter had ended.

Major Dawson had certainly had a rough ride, but he did not have the confidence of his officers, as Francis went on to note:

As a result of the accident General Byng inspected the battery. Dawson withdrew all except spare men from the guns and turned all his attention to smartening up the wagon line.

I believe the harness was excellent and the battery was praised for the smart turn-out. The gun line was never visited! Dawson is typical of a class of RHA officer which takes no interest in anything behind the wheel horses.

BELOW *Lutyens' horse.*

RIGHT *The 7th Notts & Derby in the trenches on the Kemmel Sector.*

BELOW *Corporal Johnson and Sergeant Mappledoran.*

Friday 16th April   *Spent a quiet night in F6. Raining hard. Slept in Mellor's dug-out. 7th Battalion Notts and Derby.*

Saturday 17th April   *A peaceful day. Left at 7 p.m. A demonstration in evening to try and prevent Germans sending troops north where a heavy attack on Hill 60 was being launched. A fine sight from Mount Kemmel.*

Thursday 22nd April   *The major came to inspect the guns for the first time at 3.15 and at 3.30 the Germans started shelling us with 5.9-inch continuing till 5.00 and sending over some thirty shells, three of which landed within fifteen paces of our shelter where major, Lutyens and self were sheltering. Some chips off the guns but no casualties to personnel. Sergeant Graydon stopped a runaway horse in a very plucky way.*

Major Dawson also records this day:

I had just arrived at the battery when the Germans started firing and took refuge in the officers' dug-out which was cut out of the road embankment and covered over with corrugated iron and turves – a most inadequate protection but we knew no

better. The guns were across the road and the protection for the detachments was of a similar kind. The bombardment stopped and started again and in one break I ordered the detachments from their guns. All got away but two before the next shell landed and for the next forty minutes we stood on the road and looked on and prayed for the best. After it was over we went round and made an examination. The road was cut to pieces and deep holes surrounded the gun positions. The telephone wires were blown into fragments and one or two of the carriages had received slight damage. Not a single man received any hurt worth mentioning, and this was all the result achieved by over a hundred shells.

When we looked at the farm behind, however, the results were more apparent. The buildings had been badly knocked about; about a dozen pigs were dead or dying, and cattle and poultry had also suffered. There was no sign of the inmates, but the family dog, a species of mastiff, appeared from somewhere and seemed glad to see us.

Friday 23rd April   *Quiet day. Dawson didn't come again!*
Saturday 24th–Monday 26th April
Watched Ypres battle going on.
Friday 30th April   *Dug alternative position on Dranouter–Neuve-Église Rd. Some big shells behind guns in the morning.*
Saturday 1st May   *At 6.30 p.m. the*

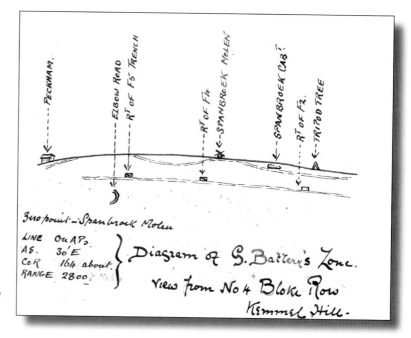

RIGHT *The view from the observing house, April 1915.*

Labels on drawing: *Wytschaete Tower.* *Bos House.* *Spanbroek Molen.* *Spanbroek Cabaret.*

VIEW FROM OBSERVING HOUSE

Germans started on F2 and F3, 4, 5, 6 with big shells. A very rapid fire for ½ hour. All the local batteries turned on to their trenches in reply. Went up to observing house to look on. I think this was a reprisal for some bombs which we fired the night before. Most of the shells fell over and no one was injured.

Sunday 2nd May   Lutyens in trenches. A gas attack at Ypres. Strong smell of chlorine!

Monday 3rd May   A few rounds. Dawson sends down the usual Extraordinary string of orders. This time he altered the original range seven times before deciding what to select to start with.

Wednesday 5th May   A peaceful day with 7th Notts and Derby. Watched the 8th Notts and Derby getting bombed and shelled in the H trenches.

The gas on 2 May did not affect anyone at the battery badly but many did not understand the funny coloured cloud rolling up the valley of the Bollartbeke. A few people tasted it, but not many, but the old woman in Major Dawson's cottage was violently sick and collapsed from an attack of nerves. The 8th Notts and Derby was another name for George's 1st/8th Sherwood Foresters, which was next door in the trenches, so Francis was supporting a brigade from his part of the country.

Saturday 8th May   Trouble with horrible Sapper officer who wants to dig trenches on crest line in front of the guns.

Monday 10th May   An attack on E1 at midnight by bombers. Great excitement among the Leicesters who evacuated the trench. The Sappers returned to the trench and found it empty except for one dead German. We fired a few rounds while the Terriers shot like mad for about two hours. The Germans were much amused at all the excitement caused by about four men and chaffed the infantry about it all day.

Wednesday 12th May   A few crumps over in evening. The whole female population came and sheltered in our dug-out.

Thursday 13th May   Rain and cold wind. Walked up to OS and wagon line in

morning. *Walked up to F6 via Regent St and Pall Mall. The Germans bombed down most of the parapet of G2 and a few rushed the trench. Fearful excitement again. All the reserves marched up from Locre. Laid a line to F6, tapping into old line. Slept in F6.*
Friday 14th May *Relieved by Hewson. Walked back by road before daylight.*
Saturday 15th May *3rd Cavalry Division lost heavily at Ypres.*
Sunday 16th May *Dawson's brother reported killed. Bombing again in G2.*

Poor Major Dawson already knew that his brother, Gordon Dawson, who was in the Blues, was wounded and missing. Major Dawson takes up the tale:

The battle in the direction of Ypres now increased in fury and we received a message that the Blues had been badly cut up, which made me exceedingly anxious. I tried to find something out over the telephone and was told that Gordon was missing. I sent my orderly over to Bailleul to see if Bill Campbell would lend me his car to go up and obtain details. I eventually arrived at Vlamertinghe where the Blues were quartered in some huts, or, should I say, the remainder of them. I saw Tweedmouth, who was commanding, and he took me to the corporal of Gordon's troop.

He said that the troop was charging across the open to recover a lost trench. Gordon and one of his privates ran faster than the rest and were out in the front alone. He saw Gordon hit. He fell and began to crawl to a shell hole and his corporal ran past and saw no more, but a man behind him told him that Gordon was hit again as he got to the shell hole.

His body had not then been recovered and, as the place was practically in German hands, I found nothing else could be done. The officers promised that they would let me know as soon as they found anything out. It was possible he had been captured or picked up wounded and evacuated through some other unit.

A day or two later I was telephoned to say that he was reported wounded and missing, which gave me some comfort as

it was evident that his body had not been found. However, a few hours later, Boyd, the chaplain of the 3rd Cavalry Division, arrived and gave me the things which had been found on his body. Only a pigskin cigarette case and some letters. Watch, money, compass and all else had disappeared.

On the 20th I went back to the front with Boyd and found the corporal who had discovered Gordon's body. He undertook to lead us to the place where he was buried and started off across the open behind the trench line. All went well for a short time and then apparently we became visible for rifle bullets began to whistle round us. Both Boyd and I protested against this procedure so we took to the trenches where the corporal immediately lost his bearings.

Fortunately we soon found our way and we arrived at the temporary grave. Poor Gordon was buried behind the parados of the front trench – such as it was – and we crawled over to it and lay there whilst Boyd read a short funeral service. The enemy snipers were very active and the parados was an inadequate protection. It was now almost dark. The trenches were very shallow and muddy and all the way up we had been compelled to advance on our hands and knees; the return journey was worse. It was an exhausting day and by the time I reached my billet on Kemmel I was done up.

Such was the end of the dear 'Infant', a most lovable character, and, after he developed, a most accomplished man. One wishes he had been spared for a few years longer, but he died as I am sure he would have wished to die, at the head of his men in a charge across the open in the greatest war in history.

Thursday 20th May *Germans blew up mine under E2 right. Fifteen men killed and wounded. We replied with bombs in evening.*
Friday 21st May *The general announced his intention of visiting the battery but as usual did not turn up. Pay up at wagon line.*
Saturday 22nd May *With the Lincs and Leicesters in F4. Found our dug-out had just been wrecked by a bomb.*

Sunday 23rd May *A few whizz-bangs over in morning. Replied with some rounds on their trench. Relieved at 9.00 by Hewson. Went to be shown some second-line trenches which the artillery have to dig. Archdale to dinner. Bridge till midnight. Won five games.*

Monday 24th May *A beautiful day. Got up early and rode back to show ammunition column position of second-line trenches. Thence to Kemmel. Italy declares war. Cavalry driven back near Hooge. Walked round deserted farms behind trenches in evening to look for linseed cake for the horses. Unsuccessful.*

Tuesday 25th May *Johnstone in trenches. Germans firing incendiary shells and three* farms alight, including our old billet in N16A. 85th Brigade lose heavily in counter-attack at Hooge. Very hot day. Sat in dug-out and read all day.

On the 25th, then, Francis was up with the guns but Major Dawson was back near the wagon line and reported on the fire:

The only excitement was that the farm next to our wagon line went on fire. The picket sentries noticed it and turned the men out who streamed over to render assistance. The outbuildings were full of Belgian refugees, to whom no doubt the fire was due. But on the first alarm they fled from the place, and then collected at a safe distance where they made a bloody row and never did a hand's turn to help anyone. Duff, my groom, saved all the pigs except those which insisted on running back into the burning styes. One man carried out the farmer's wife, another saved a child whose clothing was on fire, and dipped him in the moat. Others devoted themselves to cattle. The farm was burnt out, but all the humans and most of the livestock were saved.

Thursday 27th May *Dug up larches on Kemmel and planted them for concealment. A shell nearby in evening.*

Friday 28th May *Lutyens in trenches. Cold windy day. Two big HE shells burst in air with a terrific row just outside the billet window whilst I was shaving! Walked back to GHQ line and met Parker, Budge and Gregory. News that Dawson is going to command a 6th Division brigade!*

Saturday 29th May *Up at 6.30 at Kemmel. A beautiful day. Watched heavies shooting. Germans crumping usual places. One shell into Kemmel village killing three children.*

Major Dawson left the battery. He had no regrets at leaving Kemmel: 'It was a place associated with unpleasant memories and, although one pursued an existence free from any great danger, the life was monotonous and dull. I left Kemmel and rode off to the south with Duff and the two mares. The

BELOW *The personnel establishment of E and F Subsections of 'G' Battery, RHA, at Kemmel in May 1915.*

faithful Browning followed in a cart with my kit.' He did, however, regret leaving the battery he had commanded for five years and had taken from India, to England and then out to war. Francis, however, was glad to see him go.

Tuesday 1st June   *Did some jumping with battery horses.*
Wednesday 2nd June   *In trenches. Returned in evening. Ran guns out onto road. Moved back to wagon lines at 8.30. Slept at billet in Kemmel.*

The rest of June was a quiet month for Francis. The battery moved back to billets near Blaringhem, out of the line, and Francis once again became an instructor on trench mortars. He selected a field for trench mortar practice, built earthworks and started training the cavalry. He also received his first letter from Ted from his prisoner of war camp in Bavaria.

Tuesday 15th June   *More trench mortar practice. I had built up an earthworks resembling a grouse butt for the mortar and made everyone get under cover in case of a premature burst. One bomb, however, burst just as it cleared the butt and it is difficult to see why it did not account for everyone standing behind. It took all the buttons off my coat and made a bit of a bruise on my chest, that was all! Another dangerous situation was frequently occurring when the gun missed fire, usually owing to the novice instinctively drawing out the fuse as he lit it. After unloading about ½ dozen I made it a rule that people had to unload their own misfires. At one particular misfire Bombardier Singleton looked over the top of the butt just as the bomb prematured and all he got was a black eye though the report was deafening and there was nothing left of the gun. Personally I think these home-made mortars are far more dangerous to the users than to the enemy. Harrison of the Blues who was sitting thirty feet away got a splinter in his foot right through his boot.*
19th–29th June   *On leave, but found England very dull so returned four days*
early much to the RTO's [Railway Transport Officer's] surprise. I don't suppose anyone had done such a thing before.
29th June   *Left Victoria 2 p.m. Rough crossing. Fortunately got a lift in a car back to Blaringhem.*

Francis was not telling the full story of his leave, though he told a fuller version to his son Michael. Francis was having dinner in the Army and Navy Club, wearing his uniform, and smartly turned out, but wearing non-regulation boots. His feet were in quite bad shape – he had had trench foot during the winter and they were still rather tender – and his regulation boots did not fit comfortably. A general at a nearby table summoned him

BELOW *Francis at Kemmel*

over and ordered him to report to him at the War Office the following morning. Francis did so and was given a lecture by the general (who had not even been to the front) about standards and the necessity of being correctly dressed at all times. This so incensed Francis that he cut short his leave and returned to his unit in Belgium.

Dora now knew Ted was alive and fairly well as a prisoner of war in Bavaria, but was determined to try to pull every string she could to get him repatriated to England. She had high hopes that Ted's wounds would be grave enough to allow him to come home. She wrote to Crown Princess Margaret of Sweden, who replied on 6 April:

Dear Mrs Foljambe,
Having received your letter today I wrote at once to send an answer and say I will do what I can to get someone, either from the Swedish or American Embassies in Germany, to go and see your son and let us know how he is.
I feel the question of exchange is beyond my powers, to mix in that is I regret to say impossible!
Rest assured that I will do all that is possible.

But a week later Dora had some bad news from the Red Cross in Geneva:

Dear Mrs Foljambe,
We are informed by the officer commanding the Gefangenlager of Würzburg, that Lieutenant Foljambe, who has been lightly *wounded, cannot be sent home as unfit for further military duty. It would be useless to make any demand with this object.*

Crown Princess Margaret of Sweden had indeed asked the American Ambassador to enquire for her, and Ted was allowed to reply to him on the 21st:

Your Excellency,
I have the honour to acknowledge the receipt of your letter of April 10th and ask you to convey to Her Royal Highness the Crown Princess of Sweden my sincere thanks for her kind inquiries. I am very much stronger now and as well as can be expected. Thanking you for your very kind letter.

The Red Cross was still trying to get Ted out, but to little avail, as Dora was told on the 24th:

Madam,
We beg to inform you that we made the request that Lieutenant Foljambe might be amongst the prisoners to be exchanged. But to our great regret, this demand has been refused by Germany. We are very sorry about it, and express all our sympathy.

Meanwhile, Dora was still trying to ensure that Ted had enough money and that his food parcels were getting through. American Express told her:

We would like to tell you that our Berlin Office wrote to Lieutenant Foljambe, Festung Marianberg, Würzburg, on the 21st inst, conveying the information you gave in your last letter to us, and we have no doubt that he has received it by now. When they were writing to him they were acknowledging a letter of his that came to hand the same day enclosing a cheque for £5, the equivalent of which was forwarded in exchange. Apparently he had not then received the parcels and comforts that had been sent him. This latter feature, however, is made the subject of special investigation and we trust that your son has got the packages meanwhile. The cheque we cashed for him is dated 7th April Würzburg.

Dora was also still in contact with the families of other prisoners, as shown in a letter of 12 May:

Dear Mrs Foljambe,
Mrs Hay Newton has sent me your letter asking for information about Würzburg. I assume it is Lieutenant Irvine about whom you wish to know. Officers are treated well or perhaps it would be more exact to say they are not ill treated. Parcels and letters

ABOVE Prisoners of War at Mulheim in 1916. Ted is seated third from the left in the middle row.

are very welcome and almost always get through. Cigarettes, biscuits, Huntley and Palmers, cakes, shortbread, chocolate in fact provisions of almost any kind should be sent. The food provided in the camp is well cooked but hardly sufficient in quantity and not the sort that one usually gets at home. Books are also a good thing to send, puzzles, jig-saws, etc., etc.

Yours very truly,
V Stacy
Mr Irvine is very fit and cheerful.

Henry Warre was still helping as much as he could:

31st May 1915
My dear Vorzes,
I went to St George's Windsor last evening and found myself sitting next to Princess Victoria. She told me she had had a letter from the Crown Princess of Sweden dated three weeks ago. In it she stated that Ted was quite recovered and well. I thought you would like to know.
Hope you are getting well.
Just off to London. Best love.
Your brother, HW

Finally, more of Ted's letters home were getting through:

Festung Marianberg
8th April 1915
As usual no news. I am fairly well, but this kind of life tells on one's inside and mine is fairly well out of order now. We have had no English letters now for some time, so I suppose they are holding them up somewhere. Easter as you can imagine was really exciting. Parcels arrived just before and most people grossly overfed, none too easy to do here. They keep all letters here apparently about ten days before sending them which accounts for the length of time they take in coming. I got a packet the other day from someone, biscuits and a cap, etc. which were very acceptable. Biscuits are very useful and better than this bread. Books are necessary and very scarce. All these Frenchmen talk at the top of their voices and it might well become a madhouse. The way we are treated would surprise you, but I suppose it is all one can expect. If you get any news of my regiment please send it. Hope the gout is better. Best love to all the family.
E

10th May 1915

No news and I'm much better, in fact to all appearances as well as ever. Lovely weather but we aren't allowed to pause during our walk up and down the b'way, so it is rather trying. Thank you and all for your letters and please tell Mary that she is allowed to write more than once a month! Piles of letters have to go unanswered, I'm afraid. I have had two letters from Francis now and will write when I can. Please thank Aunt J. for her book and the cigarettes and also that some more of them will be always acceptable. I heard from my nurse the other day; she can't stick that photograph, and I thoroughly sympathise. I had one taken when I left Oxford at Gillman & Co, St Aldates, Oxon. Will you tell them to send her one. It's slightly less human so she may recognise it more easily. An escaped parrot relieved pressure the other day and sat on the trees for some time. So far six of your letters since 8th March and four from G. and F. Five parcels: one Mary, two G & F. They open and turn out every tin so don't send anything perishable. I shall be glad when this nightmare is over. I wish treatment was the same for all prisoners of war!

Best love to all,

E

26th June 1915

Dear Mother,

I am so sorry to hear that you have been laid up and I do hope you are better now and about again.

Will you tell Daniels, Bury St, my tailor to send me some black stars for a coat I am having made here, and also a complete set of black buttons for my service coat and greatcoat. The parcels have been arriving for which very many thanks. All the Frenchmen are having their heads shaved this morning and one of them looks just like a dormouse and the rest like clowns. I am very well and burnt black. It's been very hot and I suppose will be hotter before long. I have at last gone to a dentist and came away minus most of my jaw and the prospect of having the other side out in a week, but I think I will try what persuasion and a crown will do.

At least we can keep more or less clean with a shower bath, cold, every day. It feels quite funny not being continually dirty. Please give my love to the bits of family that are around and make my excuse for not being able to write to all.

Yours,

E

George was still at Newark, struggling now to find the men to send to both the 2nd/8th Battalion, still training near Luton, and also the 1st/8th, now about to enter the trenches in earnest for the first time.

As was noted earlier, the battalion marched

BELOW *Map of the Kemmel Sector, spring 1915.*

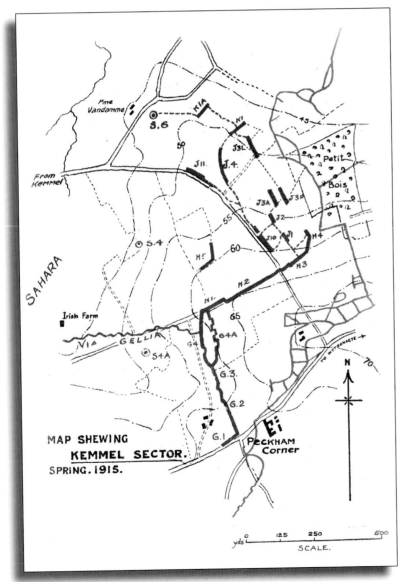

to Locre in Belgium at the beginning of April in preparation of taking over a section of the line at Kemmel and was part of the brigade that Francis Foljambe was supporting with the artillery. The first trench relief was not pleasant. It was a wet night; the men were all loaded with packs and greatcoats and had to carry sandbags full of rations and petrol tins of water. There were of course no lights when they were led away in their platoons, finally being settled in by about 11.00 p.m. Their first day holding trenches on their own was Easter and was fairly quiet. Some men of C Company sang hymns and the Germans made overtures for peace by showing a white flag. About forty of them appeared on the parapet and a brisk conversation ensued for several minutes across no-man's-land. A very unflattering remark from one of the Germans who had a knowledge of coarse English ended the armistice rather hurriedly.

The men of the battalion found themselves totally outclassed in equipment by the Germans. They lacked trench periscopes, telescopic sights and well-constructed loophole plates, all things the Germans seemed to have in abundance. The German snipers operated with some impunity and the first fatal casualty they inflicted was Private Hyde, who was shot in the head on 6 April. The battalion was to lose a steady trickle of men during the next weeks, many of them to sniper fire.

Lieutenant Colonel Huskinson managed to visit the front and then wrote back to George Foljambe:

6th April 1915

I got a friend to drive me up to the front and found the 8th who had just gone to the trenches for four days. I thought it wiser not to visit them in the trenches in day time but saw Hales who is fit and well, and also my old hunter who knew me again. It was Easter Sunday and not a shot was fired all day. I saw our new 15-inch gun hidden in a novel erection, at the back of the 8th's position. They are in comfortable billets and those that have not billets, have what I describe as hen coops in wood which they sleep in.

At 4.30 every day the Germans open fire on a certain hill as regular as clockwork,

and then Mother, that is the 15-inch gun, replies with four shots, cost £200 a shot I am told. The German trenches I could see little of through my glasses, except the line and a few [bits of] earth turned up. The Germans have made iron balls with spikes which they sprinkle on the roads to lame the horses with, and the Scots Greys had a very narrow escape of being blown up the other day on a road which was mined. Anyway, at the front there is nothing doing, and whichever side attacks first must lose heavily.

I expect you have been to Le Touquet. I am here, and if you can come over, I would try and arrange a trip up to the front like I did – the most interesting trip I have ever taken.

George was in close touch with Huskinson and wrote to try and arrange a visit so he could finally see exactly what was going on in France, both to his battalion, and possibly to see Francis at the same time. Huskinson replied:

My dear Foljambe,

Your letter, so many thanks.

I see your point about age and agree. I shall stick to my job here as I think it best for the regiment, but it's rather hard.

About crossing over: I think it will do you good and an ordinary bag will do. I am staying at a most comfortable hotel at Le Touquet. The air will do you good; there is nothing for you to do but look round here, and if I can manage it a trip up to the front on a Sunday: spare change of clothes and boots advisable: ordinary boots and leggings: soap: Get to Boulogne then by train to Étaples, twenty miles off.

I think if you saw your friend at the War Office for a pass; you will have to get one to get over – they are most particular with all passes.

We shall have to have a motor, as the front is now fifty miles off.

Don't come next Sunday.

At the same time George was trying to fix up his trip he also wrote to Lieutenant Colonel

Fowler commanding 1st/8th Sherwood Foresters, who replied on 13 August:

Dear Colonel Foljambe,

Many thanks for your letter. I do indeed wish that you could come out and see us; it would be a pleasure.

We are doing our turn in and out (four days each) of the trenches, and having some very good experiences. Some of our trenches are only thirty yards away from the German ones, and bomb throwing is a constant amusement of Martyn's men. The only thing to do if they throw is to send double the number back, and the Sutton men are rather expert at this.

Our headquarters billet is nearly a mile from the trenches – a deserted doctor's house – and we are making it quite comfortable, although courting destruction by doing so – it has been gutted by shells once.

Do try and come and see us, we could really look after you quite well.

And Fowler wrote again on the 18th:

Dear Colonel Foljambe,

I do think the men have done splendidly. We have had to take over a beastly line of trenches, some within thirty yards of the German lines, and the men have tumbled to it in a wonderful way. There have been just a few cases of what we would rather not have during the first four days, but by dealing with these severely I hope and think they have stopped. There was only one case (smoking on sentry) during the last four days in. Their coolness is wonderful, and I have several cases to recommend to the general for notice. You will have seen our officer casualty (Gray) a very slight clip in the head. We only put it in to get him a DSO in the future. He is a son of the Master of Jesus, Cambridge, and is a masterpiece of cool deliberation in any possible situation, and a very plucky fellow indeed. I do hope you will be able to get leave to come and see us. I don't see in the least why you shouldn't. While we are 'out' for the four days, we have quite good quarters, and when we are 'in', though you would not go

in the trenches, you would be able to get a good general idea of how the land lies from a mile behind. We are in rolling open country, with one or two big hills, which makes it more interesting.

We have just had a splendid present from Miss Gilstrap of Winthorpe: five galvanised baths and a boiler, a perfect benefaction they are – the men can't keep clean in the trenches. They are with the cookers [which] makes us a very well-equipped battalion. Our chief wants now are periscopes and telescopic sight rifles. The former are an issue, but we get a fearful lot shot away.

George wrote again to Huskinson at Étaples. His reply was written on the original and sent back as Huskinson was rather overwhelmed with work. Both are shown below:

Newark
16th April 1915
Dear Huskinson,

I was rejoiced to hear that you had received such an excellent report of the old regiment on its introduction to the trenches. Thanks for your letter of the 12th.

I shall try to work it to cross on Thursday or Friday night in next week, so as to return say Tuesday night in the week after. If it is put off any later, I doubt my getting across just yet, as I can hardly be away when we start the 3rd Line depot, as they now call the new units. I have now got about the required 100 to be attached to the 2nd/8th for drafts, so expect to start work here any time now.

Orders as usual are so conflicting that no one can understand what the intention really is. If my trip comes off, I should like to see the regiment (1) [figure added by Huskinson] if possible. I heard from my son, now in G Battery RHA, 3rd Cavalry Division, that he is close to them, wherever that may be. If this trip comes off please let me know when it is convenient to you, whether my suggested dates suit. Is a Kodak (2) allowed?

Yours,

G. S. Foljambe

Commandant
Étaples 19th April 1915
Excuse this answer, no room for letters.
You must get a passport.

(1) I cannot promise this, but I would
try. I hope to get up Thursday – it all
depends if a car runs or not. They are
getting very particular now. They are at
Locre near Ypres.

Yes, but I know you don't mind taking
the risk. The trip will do you good, but
you may see nothing. If you could get
Wednesday night I might manage it
Thursday. I cannot after.

(2) No.

C. J. H.

George Foljambe got out to Étaples and
was able to see Charles Huskinson, but he did
not manage to get up to the trenches, either
to see the Sherwood Foresters, or to find
Francis on Kemmel Hill. The Ypres Salient
was particularly busy and from the 1st/8th's
trenches they could plainly see the shelling
and burning of Ypres. On 21 April they lost
2nd Lieutenant Eddison, their first officer
killed, whilst he was with a wiring party,
and on 22 April the Germans made their first
gas attack on the French and Canadians at
Ypres. Although it was a few miles to the
north of them, several men had smarting eyes
and others were sick. The gas attack caused
commotion on all sides and before too long
the first consignment of respirators reached
the battalion – pieces of gauze that had to be
filled with tea leaves, damped, and fastened
round the mouth in the event of an attack.
Bells and gongs made from shell cases were
hung in the trenches to be sounded by any
sentry who saw a cloud of gas.

On 24 April the battalion suffered a heavy
bombardment causing severe damage to at
least three of its trenches. In B Company
Lieutenant Vann and his platoon had a
particularly difficult time. Vann was digging
out wounded from his trench and another
bomb landed close by, killing four and
wounding three others, and blowing Vann
himself several yards across the open at the
back of the trench, and practically wiping out
the garrison. All in all, an hour's bombardment

killed fourteen men and wounded two officers
and a further fourteen men.

George Foljambe, meanwhile, had been
told that he was in the running to command
the new Notts and Derby Brigade that was
being formed in England and he wrote to
tell the CO of 1st/8th Sherwood Foresters. In
addition, he was continuing to recruit and train
reinforcements. Men had been recruited into
the 2nd/8th, trained, and then drafted out to
the 1st/8th when reinforcements were needed.
Now the Army planned to use 2nd/8th as a
combat battalion and a '3rd Line' was set up
to recruit, train and then send drafts to both
battalions. Herbert Fowler replied:

1st May 1915
Dear Colonel Foljambe,
Many thanks for yours of the 17th. We
were very glad to hear that you would be
appointed the brigadier of the new Notts
and Derby Brigade. I only hope it will soon
be a going concern. There is going to be
tremendous demand for men. As you know
we want a draft of at least 100 to fill up.

We are about eight miles south of
the heavy fighting of the last few days –
holding on to our line of trenches. We
had an experience a week ago, when
they bombarded us with trench mortars –
enormous great shells, with a high explosive
charge in them. They wrecked the parapets
of two trenches, and we thought they were
going to attack, but they didn't. We got our
reserves up and help from the 7th Battalion
and things quietened down, but it was
quite exciting whilst it lasted.

You will have seen what our losses are.
Everyone says that our men are marvellous
for their discipline, and for the work
they do. I only hope they will keep up the
reputation they have won – I think they will.
I will look out for your son – we are covered
by C and K Batteries, a pity it isn't G.

Not all was going on as well as hoped
in England. The demand for men was
outstripping supply. Not only was the
1st/8th taking casualties near Ypres but the
2nd/8th was still recruiting to try to come
up to strength. The pool of manpower was

shrinking as the war had now been going on for almost a year and the first huge flush of volunteers were now either in France or still training to deploy. Colonel Fowler was getting concerned about reinforcements and wrote to George Foljambe on 19 May:

> *I am very sorry you are having so much trouble about the formation of the 3rd Line troops. We can't imagine here how we are going to get recruits if the 2nd/8th are to go somewhere [i.e. to a combat zone]. Reading all the accounts of their recruiting march through the county makes us think that we have been absolutely forgotten. I suppose it is a compliment really, but the question of a draft is a very serious one for us now. We have lost more than any other battalion in the division, and the line we hold is thinner than I like. We have had a fairly quiet time lately, but of course casualties are always mounting up.*
>
> *I haven't found your son yet, but mean to have another try, when we come out of the trenches next time.*

George Foljambe was also writing to other officers in the regiment, some of whom he had known for years and others whom he had got to know whilst training them at Newark, and then dispatching them out to the battalion. Lieutenant C. L. Hill wrote back in early June:

> *My dear Colonel Foljambe,*
>
> *Thank you very much for having sent me that letter.*
>
> *I am glad that the recruiting for the 3rd/8th is progressing – I hope we shall see the result out here. We have had very bad luck as regards our casualties. Up to our coming out of the trenches last night we have had about 18 officer casualties, some of course quite slight, and 181 men.*
>
> *You will already have heard of [Captain H. G.] Wright's death. We had just finished sniping from a loophole and a shot came through both holes of the double loophole and shattered his whole head. The trench was only thirty yards away. The weather here is very hot, but that is better than when we came out first.*

> *Hoping you are very well, or as the men say in their letters 'hoping this letter finds you well as it leaves me, A1 in the pink at present'.*

Both sides were trying all through this period to mine under each other's position in order to blow trenches up from underneath. For 1st/8th Sherwood Foresters C Company was the mining company, filled with miners from the pits of Nottinghamshire and Derbyshire, but the trenches were mostly built on waterlogged ground and it was not easy to sink shafts and drive galleries. The Germans succeeded where they had failed and on 15 June they exploded three mines which blew up part of a trench. At the same time there was a storm of artillery and trench-mortar fire and a hail of machine-gun bullets, followed by a raid by German infantry. It was fought off, but the battalion lost another 2 officers and 9 men killed and 29 wounded. By the end of their stint at Kemmel they had lost 49 killed or died of wounds and 120 wounded. They had only received 20 reinforcements.

July–December 1915

Francis had left Kemmel behind at the beginning of June, and then had a quiet month in which he did some more trench mortar training well behind the lines and had some leave. He arrived back early at the very end of June and rejoined the battery near Blaringhem. July was a quiet month – normal training and looking for ways to keep the men interested. Towards the end of July he ran an exercise and over a period of days practised moving the guns forward in support of an advance. The 3rd Cavalry Division was being kept in reserve ready to exploit any success that an attack might bring.

In mid-August the battery moved up with the brigade to Armentières to deploy and for the next six weeks Francis prepared for and took part in the Battle of Loos.

> 13th August   *Left Reclinghem by bus at 8.45 and travelled to Armentières – billet at 45 Rue de Lille. Walked round 4th line*

trenches with Major Stanley. Next day – Started work at 6 a.m. Knocked off at 3.30 p.m. from digging trenches.

15th August   *More digging – heavy thunderstorms. Went down to look at McIlwain's trench mortars. He keeps some in action and some mobile – the latter dash down the trench whenever the Germans do anything and come into action like an RHA Battery. We fired a few bombs and listened to the Germans whistling. Then brought McIlwain back to dinner – a lot of shells fell in the town causing several casualties.*

16th August   *Thunder again but finished off trench in spite of the rain. Tea in the town. Sampled the contents of Monsieur Decasse's cellar. The latter had shifted off owing to the shelling.*

24th August   *Ordered to bus back to Reclinghem. Started at 5 p.m. and arrived at midnight. The ASC [Army Service Corps] guide who comes along the road several times each week lost his way three times. A chilly wind combined with clouds of dust contributed towards a beastly cold. When I arrived back I found that the order was a mistake and that I ought to have stayed at Armentières.*

3rd September   *Marched up from Lapugnoy with other four guns at 5 p.m. in pouring rain. Met a guide at Noeux-les-mines. After losing his way once and nearly taking us up to the front line, we got in at 9 p.m. Spent most of the night unloading ammunition and getting settled into action.*

4th September   *Up at 5 a.m. and started improving the position, making roofs for the guns and sandbagging the rooms of the houses – Went up in the evening with a party to strengthen the OP.*

15th September   *Spent in working on our position and OP and in preparing a forward position and OP at Maroc (by night). The latter became extremely strong with good overhead protection for the guns and bomb-proof shelters and ammunition stores adjoining. Each gun pit was connected up with the control station by a speaking tube made of drain piping which proved a most efficient way of passing orders. The signallers were also accommodated in a bomb-proof dug-out. The position was overlooked by the pylons at Loos. Batteries were continually arriving and coming into position. We registered many points all along and behind the front we were covering. The Huns shelled us very little whereas we used to keep a battery or two shelling transport every night. The French batteries were very active. The Frenchman in silk slippers who observed from next door to us would, I suppose, feel bored and would suddenly order about 200 rounds to be fired at some target or other, usually the village opposite or some houses, which would disappear completely in a cloud of dust and smoke. One evening they set fire to 11A which burned for several days. We certainly could not complain about lack of information. Reams of paper and aeroplane photos etc. came in every day. Altogether a very interesting time.*

16th September   *Orders came in unexpectedly to move and rejoin the cavalry. Moved out at dusk and bivouacked at the wagon line.*

17th–21st September   *Marched to billets at Bourecq and then to Reclinghem. Spent the 19th and 20th packing up all but the bare necessities of life and sent them to store at Fruges. Finally on 21st marched via Pernes to Bois des Dames, arrived at*

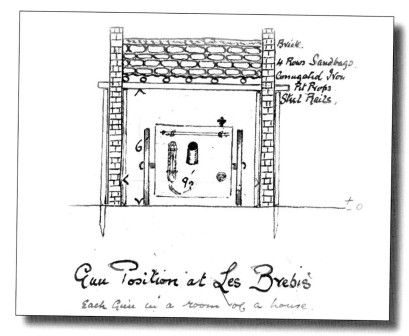

BELOW *Gun position at Les Brebis. Each gun is in a room of a house.*

midnight and bivouacked in the wood. Whatever the object of those four day's marching was I do not know but we had apparently marched some seventy-five miles for nothing.

22nd–23rd September   Spent these days hiding in the wood. Strict orders to keep under cover of the trees.

24th September   Rode up with Johnstone to reconnoitre cavalry routes. These consist of tracks with bridges across the trenches to enable the cavalry to pass through the gap which it is hoped that the coming attack will make.

Attack at Loos

25th September   Rode up again before daybreak with men to picquet one of the routes. Arrived beyond Noeux-les-Mines, just in time to see the gas cloud. A little rifle fire from the direction of Loos, otherwise quiet. Posted sentries right down to Grenay and nearly got picked off by a crump as we were walking down the road past Grenay. Met Jackson at Brebis who said that we had taken the first line of trenches and were approaching Loos. At 12 noon was ordered

to rejoin battery, which I found with some difficulty near Vermelles. An extraordinary sight altogether, all the roads blocked with (a) infantry going up (b) wounded coming back in hundreds (c) German prisoners coming back in hundreds too. Spent a most uncomfortable night where we were in the rain. Nothing to eat except a sandwich and no blankets. Got into a small dirty house but finally decided to sleep with the horses as the 60-pounders were firing straight over our heads from close behind and we were afraid of a stampede. Slept in a huddled heap with Johnstone with our waterproof sheets round us both and got a fairly good night's rest in spite of the cold and a German field battery which sent whizz-bangs into Vermelles all night – only two shells arrived where we were, one of which blew two horses and a man to bits in the transport just behind us. No orders. We heard afterwards that we had twice been ordered to move forward to the Carvin Canal by Haig, but Briggs, who was the only man who kept at all in touch with the progress of the infantry, refused and

BELOW British troops advance to the attack through a cloud of poison gas, as seen from the trench which they have just left. This remarkable snapshot was taken by a soldier of the London Rifle Brigade on the opening day of the Battle of Loos, 25 September 1915. IWM HU63277B

explained to Haig that the Germans were still at Hulluch and Hill 70.

This was fortunate for us as there was otherwise every likelihood of being wiped out. Several batteries were pushed onto Hill 70 and had to be abandoned, though the following day they were recovered without much loss.

26th September   No orders so walked with Allardyce to see Capper and Rotton, neither of whom knew much (Capper was shortly afterwards killed). We got permission to move back a little to Noyelles. The rest of the cavalry stayed where it was and no one of the staff seemed to see anything funny in keeping two complete cavalry brigades standing in mass in front of the gun positions and in a place which was frequently shelled. Streams of wounded coming back all the time. At about midday we were ordered into action behind the railway near the Halte and learnt that the Germans had counter-attacked and retaken Loos. We fired a barrage east of Loos. As a matter of fact the Germans never retook Loos as the Blues (who had been sent up dismounted) stood firm and were not affected by the disorderly flight of the 21st and 15th Divisions. At 3 p.m. the shelling quieted down. Slept with the guns.

27th September   Went up Fosse 3 in the morning. The whole plain in front dotted with batteries and wagon lines, all in full view of Hulluch and Hill 70. Several batteries getting shelled vigorously. Two crumps came close to us and killed a horse. At 1 p.m. we were ordered forward and came into action a gun at a time in the original German front line, without incident. Spent the rest of the day registering and digging. At about 4 p.m. the Guards Division with all its first-line transport marched solemnly up the Loos road and then attacked Hill 70. They were supposed to have been supported by their own artillery which, however, had not come up in time. All other batteries including us were positively forbidden to shoot, although we repeatedly asked permission to engage a redoubt which we could see on the Lens–Hulluch road and which was firing

hard. The Guards attacked without artillery support and lost heavily and gained nothing. Streams of wounded coming back whom we directed to the dressing station.

The chief features of the German trenches were the dug-outs which extended nearly the whole length at a depth of thirty feet under the parapet. Frequent shafts led up into the trench. Otherwise the trench was much the same design as ours, except not so tidy, having all sorts of homemade sandbags. Our wonderful bombardment had not been very successful and the success of our attack was entirely due to the gas surprise. The trenches were comparatively little damaged; many machine-gun posts were untouched and of course the dug-outs were absolutely intact. The only damage one can do to these is to blow in the entrance and prevent the Huns getting out in time to repel the attack. The wire was only indifferently cut and in front of each bad place was a whole heap of our men. There were a few Germans in front of these trenches, where they had run out to meet our infantry and there was

BELOW *Sketch map of the area around Vermelles, Loos and Hulluch, September 1915.*

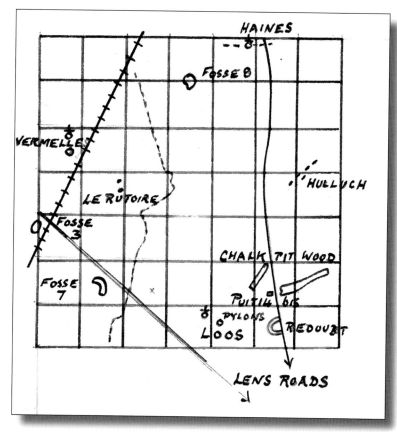

ABOVE *Battery Sergeant Major Macartney.*

Pit Wood supported by a hail of shrapnel, a good proportion of which appeared to fall short among our infantry. The attack never looked like succeeding, and only very few got near the Puits. The wretched men were being swept by rifle fire and shrapnel and must have lost heavily. The ground at any rate was pretty thickly covered with khaki dots. It was a most interesting spectacle and it is not often that one gets such a view of the actual assault. Returned to battery in evening – pouring rain. Fired on a barrage all night from 7 p.m. to 5 a.m. Took it in turns to control. A most uncomfortable night as each time the guns fired, bits of the dug-out roof would fall in. Fired all HE.

29th September   *Orders in the morning to move back to Labuissière at 5 a.m. The usual muddle with the cavalry staff. Waited two hours in the rain in Bois des Dames, and finally marched to Hesdigneul. Very sleepy. These were wrong billets but rumour had it that the staff had misread the orders to make use of a certain comfortable château.*

30th September   *The 47th Division march in late and find our brigade in their billets so they have to sleep out in the rain. French infantry passing all morning wearing their new steel helmets. They are taking over the line south of Loos inclusive.*

besides a good sprinkling of dead Germans in the trench itself. Most of these had a handkerchief tied round their mouth as a respirator. The communications trenches behind, over the brow of the hill, were completely untouched.

28th September   *Spent the day in the old German trenches from where one gets an excellent view of Hill 70 and round to the left of Fosse 8. Hear that most of the batteries that had moved forward are still observing from their old places some two miles back, so no wonder the fire was so bad. Registered onto the Lens–Hulluch road but were immediately forbidden to shoot, because we had not officially been allotted to that particular portion of the front. Had therefore a most interesting day looking about in the German trenches and watching the bombardment of Puits 14 by two batteries of 8-inch howitzers. Mann went into Loos to keep in touch with the situation and caught a prisoner and then let him go which was weak. At 5 p.m. the Guards attacked Puits 14 from the Chalk*

It had been a frustrating time for Francis. The infantry had not managed to break through and so the cavalry had not been deployed. He had watched the battle unfold and had seen the heavy casualties the infantry had received and the prisoners of war trickling back, heard the noise of the battle and again there was the smell of mud and death. That was all the fighting Francis would see in 1915 and the remainder of the year would be spent in winter quarters. On 1st October the battery marched to a new billeting area at Labuissière and Francis spent the next two nights sleeping in a monastery.

3rd October   *Moved to Burbure, a perfectly filthy mining village with hundreds of dirty children running about.*

9th–18th October   *Usual training. Bought a football and got some exercise kicking about.*

19th–28th October   *Left Burbure and then back to winter billets in Laires.*

2nd November   *Johnstone and McIlwain leave for Meerut Division which is shortly leaving for Mesopotamia. Bracecamp, a second lieutenant who has twice failed to come out with the division on account of sickness, arrived. The most appalling person one ever met. The men now consist of the major, a businessman from Peru, a cattle-lifter from Terra del Fuego, Bracecamp and myself. What I shall do when Allardyce goes on leave I don't know. An amusing letter from FitzWilliam which shows how difficult things are in the new batteries. Here are some extracts:*

'This battery A.71 is curiously enough the battery which was in action next to G close to Fosse 7. The day after G left, the battery was shelled out, losing two guns by direct hit and thirty men; it is at present very rattled and Major Cook has returned to England with shattered nerves. I have two subalterns, all from the staff, who know absolutely nil but who are excellent fellows

and anxious to learn. The NCOs are simply awful – the QMS [Quartermaster Sergeant] is an old veteran, and the BSM [Battery Sergeant-Major] was once an officer's groom many years ago. Not one but is far worse than the worst acting bombardier in G Battery. There are seven telephones in the battery; two are working badly, the rest are out of order. The signallers are hopelessly ignorant. We are firing a great lot now, last night I fired 200 rounds and would have fired more but the guns jammed. There is no fitter and the artificer was killed, so I had to take one of the guns to pieces myself. What do you think I found? Somebody's penknife in the spring case! By the way I can give you an excellent tip to stop horses kicking. Never feed them and give the hay to the drivers to sleep on! We have no kickers in A71.'

8th–9th November   *Nothing in particular. Continually getting messages asking for NCOs for various odd jobs in other divisions. Finally we get a message that we are to become a sort of training brigade for*

ABOVE *Major John Fitzwilliams MC (right) was killed on 30 August 1918.*

the winter. After giving us thoroughly to understand that we are to be a fixture here for some time, and after we had accordingly done some ten days' solid work improving stables, cleaning farms, building roads, etc., we suddenly receive a telephone message that we are likely to move in a few days' time.

14th–16th November   Rode over to the HQ at Fruges and then proceeded with the colonel to look at the new billeting area. Then the 15th – a white world and very cold. Slid over with Sergeant Parker and five men per subsection to prepare new billets. A long day interviewing farmers etc. And finally the 16th. Battery arrived at 11.30 a.m. and fitted in very comfortably in the farms allotted. No trouble.

31st December   Received orders to move into action as a brigade with the dismounted cavalry division. The divisional

artillery is to be composed of the Cavalry Corps RHA: i.e. D, E, J, H, I, and Warwick, RHA G, C, and K Batteries.

Francis also included some details on how supplies came to his battery:

Imprest Account
The following are allowed:
   ½ lb Veg per day per man
   (price lists are sent round)
   2½ wood
   1½ coal per man per day
   4 lb oats per day per horse
   ½ lb beetroot per day per horse
   6 lb straw per week per man

Each Sunday morning, i.e. from Saturday midnight to Saturday midnight, a return of supplies in duplicate is sent in together with

ABOVE *The funeral of a prisoner of war in Switzerland.*

one copy of receipts to the supply officer. He checks amounts and if correct he signs and returns one copy. At the end of the month the 4 returns and the original receipts are forwarded with the rest of the Imprest Account to the Paymaster Base.

Dora Foljambe now at least knew that Ted was safe in a prisoner of war camp in Germany and that letters were getting through to him. Dora had met Madya in Paris but nothing of their correspondence over the next few months survives. Madya had said in March that she would be going to Serbia for a while and it is possible that she went. She was still very interested in helping Dora and Ted and was trying to pull her own strings, and the news she heard was passed back to Dora in England. Her first contact was a Roman Catholic charity, who wrote to her on 7 July:

Madam,

I'm very pleased to let you know that Mr Priest Dèvand, when visiting Würzburg camp got the opportunity to take care, in particular, of Lieutenant Foljambe whom I had recommended to him. Here is what he told me about him. 'Lieutenant Foljambe is in good health and feels very well. He thanks you very much.' He has got some comfort to see a person interested in him and talking to him kindly.

This was a very quiet period for Dora. She had at the moment come to the end of the road of writing to princesses or ambassadors or the War Office so she concentrated on getting letters to Ted and making sure he was sent parcels with all the things he could want. Ted's letters continued to arrive and were a bit more positive.

Kronach
26th July 1915
Dear Father,

As you may see from this we have moved to another camp, which is much better in every way. There is a tennis court and much more means for exercise. The rooms hold about four each and are very comfortable. Please let as many people know as you can of the change or I shall be without news for some time, including my nurse at Cambrai. Food would be very useful, biscuits, jams, cakes and anything like that, cocoa and cigarettes as they are not to be got here. I am very well and feel a new man for the change. Much love to all.
E. W. F.

In early August Dora got a letter from Sophie, Countess zur Lippe, telling her that Ted had been moved on 25 July to the POW camp at Rosenburg bei Kronach in Bavaria. She reported that his state of health was good, and that his wounds had healed normally. Dora visited France at the beginning of the month, possibly to call upon the Red Cross to see whatever else she could do to try and get Ted repatriated and possibly to meet Madya. She called on Lieutenant-Colonel Huskinson at his camp in Étaples, but he was not there to see her, so the details of Dora's visit remain a bit of a mystery.

On her return Dora wrote to Herbert Bury, the Church of England Bishop for Northern and Central Europe, who was then in London, to try and see if she could get any news from the church about Ted. He replied:

17th August 1915
My dear Mrs Foljambe,

Thank you for your note of the 14th. I will do my best on behalf of your son, but at present I fear it can be but little. We cannot get any answer from the German Foreign Office about the admission of clergy, even as prisoners of war, into the camps in Germany, and it is hopeless to expect poor Williams, of Berlin, to be able to do more than he is managing at present. I am convinced that we cannot get at the prisoners in any satisfactory way until we have one of our clergy in every camp. We are willing to do it here and it seems so strange that that they won't meet us in the same spirit.

I will keep your letter and let you know if the situation should alter. It was a great pleasure to me also to meet you for I remembered afterwards that I had known of your son when he was at Oxford.

Believe me to be, sincerely yours,
Herbert Bury

P.S. I was talking with the Duchess of Bedford yesterday about the prisoners' question and she seemed to think that we should do better if we made an application through the Red Cross, and perhaps I may try that approach next. She thinks that we ought to co-ordinate all the branches, including the German, and then from time to time take action as one great organisation.

Ted, writing again from Germany:

25th August 1915
Dear Mother,

Thank you so much for three parcels received this morning. Please [can] you stop them sending any more bread as it never is edible; cakes arrive alright. Tinned vegetables and things to heat up are most useful, as cooking is also a source of amusement. Better weather here now and more tennis. I am very well tho' things seem about the same. Hope all are well in England and elsewhere, and I imagine we all are heartily sick of it. The Bishop of Central Europe certainly had never met the set of beauties we have among us here, or, he has very peculiar tastes. A lot of paper-covered books arrived some time ago which I suppose must have come from Father. What about sending some ping pong materials out? They would be a very good thing when the days get shorter or it rains. My very best love to all the different families and to you and to G. and F.

Dear Mother,

Very many thanks for your letter and parcels of which I have had twenty-four altogether, the last one sent 17th August. The breeches arrived today but are too thin and not ones I wanted. Pair very light coloured riding breeches around somewhere, please have sought and sent. For heaven's sake stop all bread sent out, the freshest arrives green and some even brown; cakes seem to come safely and are very good. Will you also keep sending me relays of tinned stuffs again as we cook them up or heat them in our spare moments and being besides good also waste time. We make all kinds of materials on spirit stoves – smells mostly. The golden pudding was simply excellent and went down fine. The first of that breed of food for a year. Chocolate running short. We drink gallons of it. What a foody letter. Please thank G. E. F. for her letter and some books that she has sent from the Religious Tract Society (the second consignment). You needn't tell her, however, that I sold the first lot to the French for 3 marks 50! I am feeling very fit though my lungs are just the same as ever and don't seem to improve. They can't find anything wrong exactly with them and the last explanation was 'recovering from pleurisy'. I was badly cut about with scissors last birthday – I hope this one won't be so painful. My very best love to Father, Mary and all the rest. £3 per month badly wanted.

28th October 1915
Dear Father,

Your letter of 10th October arrived. Of course I will do anything that can be of any help. Your plan is good if it can be sanctioned. Any papers that would have to be signed in such an event are best sent via the American Embassy and ought in that case to arrive safely. I do not know if you are still paying in my allowance; please don't hesitate to stop it, if it is of any help. I know every little must count now. As far as 'good considerations' are concerned, marriage is difficult from here, but I am ready to do my very best when all this is over. As letters take time and as this scheme if possible ought to be done quickly, I will put myself entirely in your hands to make any arrangements you like. Mother's letters [of the] 6th, 11th, both arrived also G. E. F. 9th October. Hope you and all are well. A little snow last night and very cold now. Lungs much as usual but it's difficult to get enough air in the rooms, as our companions love a closed window. Mother's parcels 24th, 29th September have come, very many thanks. The puddings are excellent. Can they be sent regularly, also tinned meat, vegetables etc. and butter? Also will you number letters carefully, from July if you have no record before, and please tell everyone else to do the same? Have you any more news of my regiment? Whereabouts am I on the list? The breeches I want were left behind in my base kit so ought to be somewhere about with coloured khaki riding ones. I heard from Francis the other day. He seemed well. How is Mary? Mother said something about sending a warm Shetland waistcoat. It would be very acceptable as I lost mine last year and shoes are wanted badly. Very best love to all. Please thank Rosamond for a letter.

10th November 1915

Got your two last letters, 11th and 23rd October, also M.'s of 25th. Please tell her I would love to officiate in any capacity whatever. Please have all letters numbered beginning from July. Breeches arrived safely. Father's leg must have been a good deal smaller than mine. I must have a pair, so will you order one to be made and sent out as soon as possible. Sandon in Savile Row will be as good as any. Light coloured cord riding breeches, so I could use them hunting afterwards as well as uniform. These are roughly the measurements: waist 30 inches, seat 39, length, waist to centre of knee, 24, inside leg to knee 15, above knee 14¼, knee 14¼, below knee 12½, calf 14. Leaving some room for alteration afterwards, if wanted. Fairly wide and side straps. I expect he will know the kind of colour I want. Brown will, I'm sure, be glad of a waistcoat, though he rather sniffed at the thought it was a discard of mine. What had happened to Father, I never heard? And how is Francis? Have had no news of him now for ages. We have three more officers here now which makes it more interesting. Please don't talk of language; I want to talk nothing but my mother-tongue for the rest of my life. Please continue the puddings, etc. They are excellent. Please thank Mildred Malet for her letter and please don't forget about the numbers. You might ask Cox again about my base kit which was left behind at C. when we left there and ought not to be lost. Perhaps it is left lying in one of the lost places. Did you ever hear about footballs? If not please send me one. I hope M. is all right. Please give her my love, also to everyone. Also Osberton. I have G. E. F's letter of 9th October. Any news of friends or regiment?

29th November 1915
My dear Father,

I have just got your letter No. 13. I'm afraid that things are not going very smoothly with you. The brutes, they will never let well alone. Thanks or any form of recognition one can never expect. I am so sorry to hear about your leg. I hope there is nothing serious the matter – it's probably the cold weather got to it. We have suddenly plunged into about 30 degrees of frost, a bit cold but very fine and dry so far. Rowley is here now, he was a 'mud' at Clumber for some time, but I don't know if you ever met him. There is, as usual, *absolutely no news and nothing to say in a letter. I am fairly well and just getting over water on the knee from playing football in the moat. Now as usual a word about food. Will you ask Mother to have some condensed milk and some butter, as little salted as possible, every week sent to me. Also a tin of the Ideal Milk, which can be drunk as the real thing or with porridge, would be very useful every week as well. I believe the best way to send money out here is by post by the Post Office; it saves time and bother. After four lots will you stop it being sent out as I will have enough for the time being. Also every spare penny I may possess I should like invested. What about promotions in my regiment? Has it come anywhere near me yet? Will you please send these other two sheets on to the Grandmother at O. and the detached one to Doris at Maes. I have had four parcels from Mother since I last wrote 11th November and two letters Nos. 38 and 39. Very best love to all the family and I hope you will be soon alright again. Many apologies for an uninteresting scrawl.*

5th December 1915
I expect by the time this reaches you, you will have finished the Christmas meal, so I will wish you no returns of that, but all good wishes for the New Year. Hoping you are all well. And with much love to all in their different homes, and a hearty handshake for the Godson!

George was still soldiering on at Newark, trying to recruit men for two battalions and sending out, whenever possible, another lot of recruits to the 1st/8th in France. The battalion had moved from Kemmel and been deployed into the Ypres Salient towards the end of June. It occupied Trenches 7–12 at Sanctuary Wood and the trenches were narrow and deep. It was a very dangerous place. It was a heavily shelled position and there was hardly any water fit for drinking in the front area so water carts had to brought up every night (a round trip of 7 hours) and left in the rear of the position in the shelter of whatever trees remained.

Rain made the trenches very uncomfortable and they had to build shelters which were little more than two or more waterproof sheets laced together and held in position across the trench by stones placed on the parapet and parados. Only 4 soldiers were killed in the first week at the end of June, although 20 more were wounded. They then had a marvellous 2 weeks out of the line in superb sunshine and received a much-needed draft of 69 men from England and a further 11 rejoined from wounded, which boosted the numbers.

In mid-July they moved to the Hooge sector and occupied trenches B2, 3, 4, 7 and 8. Some of these were only 25yd from the Germans and they had to erect wire meshing to stop them throwing hand grenades directly into the trenches. There was now a brigade sniper section under Sergeant-Drummer Clewes which 'worried the Huns on every occasion and made some splendid bags'.

They were in the trenches on 30 July when the Germans attacked under cover of a heavy bombardment and advanced behind flame throwers (*Flammenwerfer*). The trenches to the left of the 1st/8th were taken and their position threatened from the side and rear. They were fought off over the next 2 days (Private Tyne behaved particularly well, throwing back unexploded grenades), but losses were heavy with 21 killed and 40 wounded and over the next 2 weeks the numbers increased by another 15 killed and 50 wounded. Lieutenant Colonel Huskinson at Étaples wrote to George:

6th August 1915
I have nearly 30 of the 1st/8th here in hospital, and am looking after them all. It appears we lost 18 killed and 70 wounded at Hooge. We did not let the Germans through the lines. After the fire attack a wounded officer of the KOSB now here tells me what a splendid lot of chaps they were. The 1st/8th machine guns mowed the Germans down. Sorry our casualties are now 400 from the old battalion, but it is not for publication.

I was sorry not to see Mrs Foljambe when she called last week.

LEFT *Map to illustrate the Sherwood Foresters' fighting at Sanctuary Wood, July–August 1915.*

The rest of the month and September were much quieter, though with some spells in the line, but manpower was an ever-present concern. In August 41 NCOs and men left the battalion. Many of the Territorial Army had only signed up for one year's war service and this was now completed. Many amongst them were old hands who were very difficult to replace. The battalion did get a reinforcement of 2 officers and 107 other ranks, but numbers were still lower than they would have liked. George received a letter from Lieutenant Colonel Fowler, the CO, in September:

All the recruit officers have now joined up. I am particularly pleased with Skinner. He looks just the right stamp, and the others will do well too, I think, if they stand the conditions. We lost two, Date and Moore from the 2nd/8th, very soon. Weetman has

come too, and of course we are delighted to get him; he will be a most excellent adjutant I am sure. We are now practically full up, and I hope we shall get some time to let them shake down before serious work occurs, though I'm afraid this is doubtful.

We had a quiet time in the trenches last time, except that our headquarters were crumped the first few days in and we had to flit, to a place which hadn't been marked down yet.

We returned last week the two travelling kitchens, which were given to us before the battalion came abroad by the kindness of our friends and relations in Nottinghamshire. For over six months they have been in continual use, and have proved of the greatest help to the battalion. The authorities decided that they were rather too heavy for very active work, and have issued us with four of the FS [Field

Service] type, which are considerably more mobile, and rather more convenient, as each company can have one for its own use in billets or near the trenches.

I hope that the 3rd/8th will find the ones that we are sending back useful and that you will understand that they have only been sent back because we have been compelled to do so.

I hope that you are well, and that the 3rd/8th progresses. We are all very fit and very busy in the neighbourhood.

Payling has unfortunately shot his own finger off with his revolver.

George wrote to 2nd Lieutenant Payling to commiserate with him after this accident and got a reply at the end of the month:

I shall not attempt to apologise for not writing before, as you will understand, we have not much time in the trenches to cultivate this accomplishment. I have now been in the trenches twenty-four days, with an interval of six days in rest billets, eighteen days being spent in the fire trenches. You will probably wonder what my impressions of trench warfare are. Well, I should say the principal qualification is an abnormal capacity for doing without sleep. Night before last we were ordered to 'stand to' three times – as we thought the Bosche were coming over – during my short period allotted for rest.

As you are probably aware there was a tremendous bombardment all along the line with our people attacking at certain points. I am, of course, not in a position to say much, but I believe these attacks exceeded expectations (especially the French).

We came in for our share of it and the din was terrific.

The things which create the most noise are the trench mortars, 'small' souvenirs of about 260 lb. They come hurtling through the air for all the world like huge sausages, and burst with a tremendous explosion – fortunately you can see them coming. The men call them sausages.

The German trenches are only about thirty yards away, and the other day we gave them the surprise of their lives. Their

snipers had been busy, and our fellows had peppered their loopholes without effect, as they were protected by iron plates. An elephant gun was brought up which went through the plates like butter, much no doubt to the surprise and discomfort of Fritz. If there is anything you would like to know in connection with the conditions out here, I shall be pleased to tell you if possible. I trust the battalion by now is rapidly approaching full strength.

October was to be a traumatic month for the 1st/8th Battalion. It was to take part in a divisional attack on the Hohenzollern Redoubt. Losses were heavy and letters to George from Lieutenant Weetman, the adjutant, take up the tale:

25th October 1915
Dear Colonel Foljambe,

Thank you so much for your kind letter. Truly we have been tried during the last fortnight and I fear you would hardly recognise the fragment of your old battalion. Our losses in officers – especially seniors – was appalling; they fell fast but all nobly leading their men in the attack. We got across the open to attack a portion of a well known spot, which you probably know of now, though I think I had better leave it nameless. It was just before dawn on the 14th. Bullets were flying everywhere and we were at very close range from 200 up to a finishing point of 70 or 80 yards from the cross trench running at right angles to the one we were attacking, in which we got close enough to bomb along. Of course they heard us coming and we soon knew it.

Young Goze was the first down, a nasty one I'm afraid. Then Strachan disappeared along the trench and I fear was killed. Young Hanford fell, I don't know when, but was killed at once and I saw his body later on after it was light. We moved the bombers out of a bit of their trench and consolidated the position and I think I may say by our action saved this particular part, as they couldn't have held on much longer. Becher was outside before the attack directing us with a flashlight and got a bullet in the thigh – explosive – and lay out for nearly two days. He is very bad I believe. Before we had finished Ashwell and Vann both got very nasty ones through the shoulder, and that left only the CO and myself, of those officers who originally started, in the attack. Basil Handford was bringing a party across in the morning with rations etc. when he got killed – they came under very heavy rifle fire and MG at close range. Skinner got a twisted ankle in getting over the parapet. We re-organised our trench and put it in some sort of order, but were very tired as you may imagine and knew little of sleep. We got up one or two other officers during the day and kept on going. The promised relief at night never came and we had to carry on through another whole night.

The CO looked absolutely haggard and told me that night had added ten years to his life. At last at 5 a.m. next day parts of the 5th and 6th came to our relief. About half an hour before the relief was finished our dear colonel was killed instantly by a sniper, whilst trying to locate Becher's body, as we then thought he had been killed. It was the last straw and I took on the remnants to reserve trenches and then broke down. I thank God I was spared, but it is awful to think of all those brave fellows who have gone. It has been hard work since trying to re-organise, but we are straightening up now. Blackwell of the 6th is in temporary command. We are at present in rest billets. I think your letter to Colonel Fowler was sent on with his other papers. Three other officers have arrived today – Kebblethwaite, Peerless and Andrews.

Goodbye and many thanks for your letter. I hope you are all well.

General Stuart-Wortley also kept up his correspondence with George, writing again on 27 October:

My dear George,
Many thanks for your letter.
The division behaved in the most gallant manner on 13th and 14th October. We were given a very big job to do. The result of the artillery bombardment was disappointing;

the enemy's trenches, which it was hoped would have been knocked flat, were not much affected; consequently when the infantry attack took place, they were mown down with machine-gun fire. They advanced in successive lines in the most gallant manner and got on a considerable way, but as all their officers had fallen, they could not reach their objective. But they retired in very good order and held the Hohenzollern Redoubt against several counter-attacks. Fowler is an irreparable loss: he was a most gallant officer, and a splendid example to everyone. He lost his life looking for Becher, who was badly wounded. He

BELOW *Lt-Col G.H. Fowler, commanding 1st/8th Battalion the Sherwood Foresters, who was killed in action at Hohenzollern Redoubt, 15 October 1915.*

stood up looking over the parapet, and was shot through the head. I have recommended Vickers for the Victoria Cross.

Yes, we want drafts very badly, and many officers. It is a great pity that the training in England is not of a more practical nature. Bombing and bayonet fighting are of the first importance, and all trench digging and trench work. I should not worry about coming out: you are doing excellent work at home. You may tell everyone that they have reason to be proud of the Sherwood Foresters.

Lieutenant Weetman was again writing on 30 October:

Dear Colonel Foljambe,

Many thanks for your last letter about the draft of forty-five. I daresay they will get more practice at the base before coming up here. We have lately had reinforcements of nearly 200 from entrenching battalions, which has put us up to strength again. The sick are rather on the increase, and I'm afraid we can't hope for much improvement, as the weather is beastly just now. The battalion is vastly altered and it makes one grieve to see the change especially in officers. They may be useful, but it is not what it was. All the same the

men came out well for the review by the King yesterday. It was a fine sight, though a miserable day, and the brigade presented arms on a filthy ploughed field as if on the best barrack square in England under ideal conditions. They certainly pleased us immensely, and I hope they will do equally well when they get up to the trenches again. Blackwell is acting CO and we are beginning to get to know him better. He is all right but doesn't quite 'lay hold' of the battalion as I would wish. We have not promoted any others at present. At present we have neither second-in-command nor junior major – only two captains, Davenport and Turner.

It would be nice to be at Newark for the memorial service, but of course quite impossible. Padre is going on leave on Sunday, and may be there for it.

George naturally was also writing regularly to his family, including this letter to Rachie, his daughter:

31st October 1915
Dearest Rachie,

So many thanks to you and your good man for your kind thought of the old man's approaching sixty [and going] into another decade. It is unfortunate having to

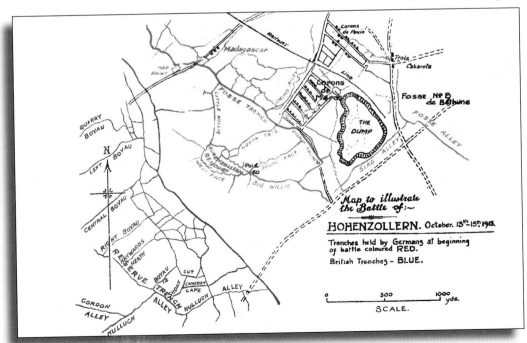

flit. In these days one has to sit very loose in respect of house and home as absolute mobility is of paramount importance, as every specialist says about his own particular crack.

It has been a horrible day, cold and east wind, meaning rain which has been coming down in increasing volumes since church this morning. I had intended riding over to luncheon with the Grenalls and getting a little fresh air and exercise, but luckily refrained from starting. I sent a draft away last week and the conducting officer has just returned very happy, as his was the only party that had all their papers and equipment complete, besides being the best drilled and disciplined. I only wish I could get recruits more freely. The neglect of this battalion on the part of the county is getting scandalous.

The 8th Battalion one way or another has been about wiped out as far as regards the original lot that went out. They were in reserve the other day so did not lose so heavily in men as some others did.

One battalion lost 19 officers and 480 men. I had a letter from Eddy Wortley saying how gallantly the division had behaved; apparently the artillery work had been ineffective.

The losses are heavy, but I think that there is no call for despondency. I feel sure that Germany is being bled to death at an ever increasing rate and this new Balkans venture of theirs will fail and open a new line of attack to us and our allies.

The end is not yet, but we have to remember we must stick it out for one day longer than Kaiser Bill and his Huns. Goodbye dear, with love to Victor and your young man, from your loving Father.

Lieutenant Weetman was again in touch on 10 November:

Dear Colonel Foljambe,

Thank you for your letter. I am not at all keen on having more junior officers at present. We have I think thirteen or fourteen 2nd lieutenants at present, and it takes a good deal of time and trouble getting them used to trench work, and I have had a fearfully busy time lately.

Cox is signalling officer and quite keen. We thought it would be a fairly quiet job for him. Peerless is grenadier officer and apparently keen. Something of him I don't quite like but I dare say he will do well. We are, as I say, fearfully short of any to instruct. Company officers are about a minus quantity! Kebblethwaite and Hammond are, I'm afraid, washouts. We have had three others from the 2nd/8th, Simonet, Michie and Rawlings, willing I think but ignorant.

We are at present about 800 yards back, which might easily be a very hot corner, but so far I am thankful to say they have left us fairly quiet. The trenches are awful and look like disappearing in parts with all this wet, and entail a tremendous lot of work. Still the men are wonderfully well – only three excused duty or sent to hospital today, which says something for them. I am glad the memorial service went well.

Our new CO, I'm afraid, I don't love exactly – it's such a change from my last dear colonel. He is not the worker that I'm used to so it makes rather a difference. Still it is good for me to be busy, and I think we are getting on well. I am more than pleased to hear of your new grandson, and hope they are both doing well.

Weetman wrote again the next day:

I remember making rather a bold sort of statement in my last night's letter as to the new officers being ignorant. *It struck me since that it wasn't quite what I ought to have said, but I wrote in such a hurry that I hadn't time to think what I was putting. What I meant was that they don't seem to have much idea of their duties from the point of view of platoon commanders: that is that they bear the entire responsibility of looking after every detail connected with not only the training and keeping efficient of their men, but also of looking after their general well-being. In several cases lately I have found that they quite ignore this point: on moving for instance to fresh* billets there is a great tendency for them to be enquiring at once 'Where is the HQ?' 'Where do we mess', etc., etc. – in a few cases before even seeing their men off the road into a billet. It is the realising of their responsibilities that requires impressing on them and I think if you could [at] some time get your old hands to give them some talks on this matter it would not be a bad thing.

Miserable weather now: I hope you are keeping well.

And there was a further letter from Weetman on 27 November:

Dear Colonel Foljambe,

Many thanks for your two letters.

What we want now is men of experience and used to handling men, which I am afraid is not knocked into the young officers who are sent out after a short course, and just with the general knowledge of things. There is hardly one of the new men who realises at all how much he is responsible for his men, and their well-being, and in fact everything connected with them, and the men cannot in such cases, look up to such men to lead them. The stamp is so different from our old lot, but we must keep hammering at them, as indeed we are. If you could arrange for your young officers to have entire control of a few men for a time, it would I am sure be a great help – so they might know before coming out here what sort of things they have to do as well as know. They are also, I'm afraid, apt at times to go their own way, and not carry out orders: the other night Powell took up a working party to carry out a four hours' relief with the RE but seemed to have had enough at the end of three hours, and so brought his men home! Needless to say it went as far as the general.

Cox will be good but at present knows rather too much! It has been unfortunate putting him as signals officer so soon, as he is at HQ all the time, and you can imagine what happens there, but we are putting him with a platoon for a bit now to work some of his knowledge off.

Nothing further to add about the others.

At one moment we had seventeen 2nd lieutenants only about ten days ago; so you can imagine what it is like carrying on the work of the battalion, and regular trench work as well. I shall be very sorry indeed if you leave the old 8th before the war is over – it will be a most horrible shame after all your efforts, though I'm sure you would be much happier without all the worry they give you all of the time. But I sincerely hope, for the battalion's sake, that they won't take you away at this hour of the day.

The changes at Osberton must be making the old place seem very strange. They tell me everyone has gone off almost now. What a war! And when will it be over? It seems to get more complicated every day, and yet they are, we all think, beaten any time, but I fear it will drag on yet for some time.

It is awful wet in the trenches – the ground is so very flat that drainage is practically impossible, and we are having to build up breastworks everywhere. Needless [to say] we don't do long tours in the trenches, and relieve as often as possible.

I hope you are all keeping well.

My kind regards.

But for George Foljambe his time in the Army was coming to a close. He was now 60 years old and not in good health – he had had problems with his leg for a while – and the Army had decided that he should retire and hand over the 3rd Line of the 8th Sherwood Foresters. He was not happy with this development. He had been involved with the regiment for over 30 years, had sent the 1st/8th off to war, had raised the 2nd/8th and had spent 18 months scouring the county for recruits and ensuring that officers and soldiers were trained and sent to reinforce the front. His total focus had been on the war effort. His brother (Hubert) had been killed; his brother-in-law (Henry Warre) had been through the worst of the battles in 1914; his eldest son Ted was a prisoner of war in Germany; his other son Francis was still with the artillery in France; and his son-in-law Victor Yeats-Brown had had a breakdown but was now working again in a headquarters in France. George did not want to sit on the sidelines and do nothing; he wanted to continue to serve his country any way he could. But the Army was adamant, and he had to retire.

Lieutenant-Colonel Coape Oates, commanding the 2nd/8th Sherwood Foresters, still training at Watford, was sad to see George go and wrote on 6 December:

I was very sorry to hear your health had broken down, and that you were giving up command of the 3rd/8th. I think everyone in the battalion feels as I do that nobody did harder or more useful work than you did, and the 1st/8th in particular must realise what a lot they owed to you just after the war broke out.

It will be awful hard work for you looking on, and I hope there will be some work offered to you which will suit you.

We are hard at work here doing company training, two companies at a time, struck off duty for three weeks. It's the only real sound bit of training we've had since we left Newark.

The adjutant of the 2nd/8th had been selected by George and also wrote from Watford a week later:

I must apologise for not having answered your kind letter before. I am indeed sorry to hear you are about to retire and if I may say so I am sure yours will be a very difficult place to fill. May I thank you for very many kindnesses both in the old and happier days and since the beginning of the war. Someone said to me that no one will ever know what the country owes to the 2nd and 3rd Territorial Lines. Do you know that since 1st November 1914 and including officers attached we have had no less than 63 officers in this battalion? A grave responsibility for an amateur adjutant and out of the 980 men sent from this brigade 441 have gone from us! So I think the 8th has kept its end up and I know what a lot of officers you have sent, and men too.

They have now reduced us to 23 officers and talk of our going out in February but I hardly think we should get more officers and men before then. I shall never forget the day you suggested my being adjutant as I was filled with alarm, but I have loved the work and in spite of many grievous mistakes have done my best so am glad I followed your advice.

With all good wishes.
A. D. Leslie Melville

LEFT *During the First World War, the Post Office was responsible for censoring post from the troops. Censorship took place at Base Post Offices and at Le Havre and later Boulogne.*

CHAPTER 8

At the Front and Prisoner-of-War

The new year saw Francis return to action with the dismounted 3rd Cavalry Division. Winter had been cold and pretty boring, trying to keep the men busy and the horses occupied in billets which they had lived in for the last six weeks of the old year. The next weeks were busy on the front line before Francis and the battery were again drawn back and spent the rest of spring preparing for the great offensive that was due to take place in July on the Somme.

1st January   *Rode on with advanced party to Estreé-Blanche and arranged billets for the battery in the large disused factory there. Two sections complete under cover. Mess in the post-office. Crease found a brand new saddle in a stable so exchanged it for my old one. Chalmers and Ironside returned to the ammunition column, thank goodness. Elliot arrived to replace them. C Battery with us. K at Fléchin. The usual trouble with supplies and staff. A move of*

OPPOSITE *George visiting Ted and Madya in Switzerland.*

BELOW *Ironside, Rivers, Burchell, Board, Beshaw and Godwin.*

a few miles seems to upset all our supply arrangements. More staff work in evening when a battalion of tired infantry with their transport arrived, having been told that the village was empty. A great squash!

7th January   Marched the remainder of the battery up via Lillers, Béthune, Sailly Labourse to Vermelles. Watered and fed at Pont de Reveillon. Rain and wind. Some trouble on account of roads being blocked by infantry on a route march. Arrived wagon line 3 p.m. Corporal Searles who had been left by the BSM to give all local information pretended to know nothing. Later he was removed from the battery. Took the guns up to the position and brought the teams back. Settled down by about midnight. An uncomfortable wagon line and billet, dirty and insanitary. The horses have to stand on the pavement at the side of the road and only a few yards of tarpaulin up in the way of overhead shelter. Two men wounded by playing about with a bomb.

8th January   Mapped out a scheme for the gradual improvement of the wagon line. Then up early at the guns for breakfast. Decided on position for new gun pits (the battery we relieved was a Kitchener one with only four guns) and spent the remainder of the day constructing them. Started work also on a new and better placed signallers' dug-out.

9th January   Continued work on position. Germans shelled the water tower area with 4.2-inch howitzers. General Birch and Gillson round in afternoon to inspect.

10th January   Continued work. Completed signallers' dug-out. Drew up large quantities of material from the RE store. Colonel came to tea. Elliot liaison officer with infantry. Fired about sixty shells on various targets.

11th January   At OP. Fired about forty rounds at various points in our zone.

12th January   A beautiful frosty, clear day. Hun aeroplane very active ranging a 5.9-inch battery onto Chapman's single gun near Le Rutoire. Our anti-aircraft efforts quite unavailing. Fired 100 shells into Quarries in evening. Chapman's gun

seems to annoy the Huns very much. He is admirably placed for shooting at movement behind Fosse B and gets all sorts of quaint targets.

13th January   A cold stormy day; took a wire into the water tower and observed Allardyce's shoot onto the Dump etc. Corrected the lines which were by no means parallel.

16th January   At wagon lines all day. Things much improved but the billets for the men are still disgusting so started a new plan of sandbag huts and tarpaulin roofs with wood floors. About half the horses are now under cover.

17th January   Observing again from the water tower. Rather unpleasant as the Huns started trying to hit it with a 4.2-inch howitzer battery and some shells passed very close. A field gun battery also firing at the railway crossing just in front.

19th January   Vermelles shelled by 5.9-inch, and the cavalry had a good many casualties. The Germans fired a mine at Hog's Back but no activity resulted.

20th January   Drew more stores from RE making a good total including 12 tarpaulins and 2,000 timbers besides stove, sandbags, etc.

21st January   A long court martial at 7th Brigade HQ on a drunk WO [warrant officer]. Walked to OP afterwards with Ironside and fired some rounds on new trench. More tarpaulins put up at wagon lines and stables are now nearly complete. I stupidly forgot to order them to be muddied over at once and a Hun aeroplane flew over, which may have accounted for:-

22nd January   Three HE shells burst in air very close to the horses just as I was going in to breakfast. No damage, however, and no more shells came. Saw Wells-Cole in evening.

25th January   Started work on a new men's dug-out.

26th January   Up early at OP and registered Haisers and other points. Rode back with Allardyce to the wagon line. A very heavy German bombardment started as we were returning to the battery at about 5 p.m. On arrival at OP we found that a portion of our front system, some 400 yards in length and 300 yards in depth, was being plastered with 5.9-inch and 4.2-inch HE. The bombardment lasted two hours and some 10,000 shells must have been fired. The trenches were much knocked about, but no infantry attack took place. Everything quiet again by 10 p.m. Several concentrations were fired by us on various possible assembly points in the German line. Milne at the OP all night.

27th January   Another Hun bombardment on same lines as on previous day, this time on Chapel Alley. Fired in reply as before.

5th February   Took over command of the battery from Allardyce who becomes acting colonel during Kay's absence.

6th February   Walked all round front-line trenches and inspected our zone from various points of view.

7th February   Went up to water tower in morning and corrected the lines of fire. Then took a wire down from battery HQ to Alexander Trench. Registered Parsifal, Stag Alley and Zeppelin Trenches. Saw a lot of Huns walking about behind the dump, but they are most difficult to hit as one is so much to a flank of the line of fire.

8th February   Walked up Bart's Alley to look for possible new OPs. Fired a barrage round a mini [Minenwerfer] from 10.00–12.00 midnight, near Bill's Bluff. Our infantry occupied the crater.

9th–10th February   Usual routine, fired about sixty shells a day on various German communication trenches.

11th February   Laid a new line via Rifleman's Alley to Alexandra Trench and registered again on Zeppelin Trench, Slag Alley and the junction of Zeppelin and Parsifal Trenches. Pouring rain and trenches in extra bad state of filth. Covered with mud. Fired a barrage at night round a mini at the Kink. Walked round the Kink and out along Sap 3. A nasty dangerous spot.

12th February   Allardyce back again. Walked round to see FitzWilliam's battery near Fosse 7. The batteries here are short of cover and their flashes are visible from many points in the German lines. The result is that the area gets shelled regularly

day and night with every known sort of gun and howitzer and shell. FitzWilliam has given up any idea of concealment and has gone in for brute strength with dug-outs ten feet deep with rails and cement roofs. These work well and up to date he has had few casualties in spite of many direct hits. A most unpleasant home, nevertheless, as it is always dangerous to wander about in the open. One battery close by had just been shelled out; the ground pitted with large shell holes nearly touching everywhere.

13th February   At OP with Fletcher. Huns shelling our front line all day with big howitzer. By way of minor retaliation we

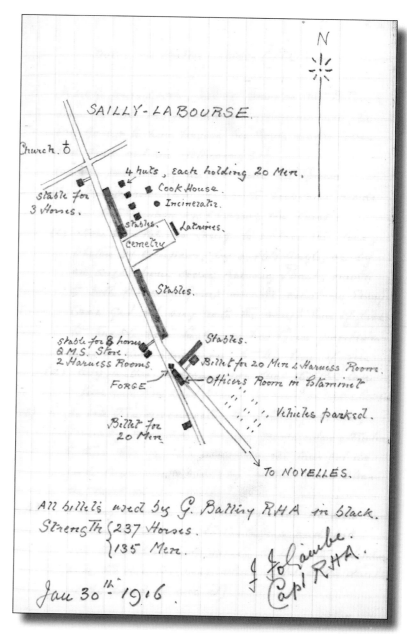

ABOVE *Sketch map of 'G' Battery at Sailly-la-Bourse, 30 January 1916.*

knocked some holes in the German front line parapet with HE. We were just thinking of returning to the battery at about 5.30 p.m. when the Huns sent up two flares from behind the line. This was evidently a signal to start a bombardment which came down at once. From 5.30–9.00 p.m. they deluged the front line and back to a depth of about 1,000 yards with HE. At 8.30 they fired a mine near the Kink, a very fine sight in the dark. A raiding party of Huns came over into the Kink but was driven out again during the night. All quiet again by 10 p.m.
14/15th February   High wind, range shortened by 150 yards.
16th February   The battery took part in a retaliation bombardment, in reply to the Hun strafe. At 1 p.m. a concentration was fired at a selected area of the German front-line system and a certain amount of damage appeared to be done but on the whole, compared with the Hun bombardment, it was a poor show. The 15-inch howitzer then did a shoot behind the Dump, which was quite worth watching. The shell makes a splendid splash. Several duds.
21st February   Our section withdrawn to wagon line.
22nd February   Withdrew remainder of battery and made a long night march to Wailly (35 miles). The roads were covered with ice and we had great difficulty with the GS Wagon which did not reach Wailly till late the following day.

Francis by this stage had spent nearly 18 months in France with only 2 short spells of leave. He had been through the mill at the beginning of the war and had seen action since, particularly at Kemmel in 1915. George was concerned that Francis had not got recognition for his actions and tracked down his original brigade commander from Ireland before the war and through the Battle of Mons, the retreat and then the fight on the Aisne. This officer had since been promoted and was a brigadier in Salonika; he wrote to George as follows:

10th March 1916
My dear Foljambe.
    Your letter of 18th February (posted on the 19th) reached me today.
    The post in this place is very slow. I certainly sent on the name of your son Francis for mention in despatches, as he had done such good work in the 27th Brigade RFA. As I dare say you know the names are cut down at every stage, and it is most probable that his name was omitted as there were too many to forward. I never cancelled my recommendation. He left the brigade and then I left it, so it

RIGHT A 15-inch Howitzer and crew preparing for action.
IWM Q1990

was impossible for me to do any more for him. I am very sorry indeed that his name has not been mentioned. To the best of my belief nothing took place in Ireland on or during mobilisation that was in any way against your son. If there had been I must have heard of it. Your son's name should have appeared in the Gazette in February of 1915, or June 1915. I do not see how anything can be done about it. The real truth is that the officers who went to the Horse Artillery at the end of 1914, or at the beginning of 1915, have never had a chance of doing anything. The RHA have practically had no chance of fighting since the Aisne in September 1914, except a few fortunate batteries that have been turned into divisional artillery. All the work has been done by the Field and Mountain Artillery, and of course the Garrison with the heavy guns and howitzers.

I do not suppose your son's battery has been in action, except perhaps three or four days, since he joined it. It is very unfortunate, as if he had been in the Field Artillery, he would probably have got a mention in one or other of the last Gazettes.

I do not think you need anticipate any prejudice to your son's future career. Although the mentions are very numerous, it is impossible for everyone to appear in the Gazette, especially the captains and subalterns. All the Horse Artillery have suffered in the same way, as they have had no opportunity of distinguishing themselves.

I wish I could do something for you, but I'm afraid I cannot.

I came out here on 12th November 1915 – a poor change from France. Nothing doing here.

Yours sincerely,
N. H. Onslow, Brigadier General

But George cannot have been satisfied with that letter because Onslow wrote again on 15 April:

I hope you did not think I wrote an unsympathetic letter about your son Francis. I do not see how anything can be done now. The unfortunate thing is his having gone to the Horse Artillery. I expect by now he is a temporary captain, and commanding a battery. I can assure you there has never been anything against him, and I am sure he will do well.

I cannot tell you what we think, and the French think, about the nonsense of conscientious objectors etc. Why cannot we have compulsory service at once; it will have to come.

In France if a man refuses to fight, he forfeits his property and all his civil rights.

Francis was blissfully unaware that all this was going on and finished his spell at the front towards the end of February. The next few months were very boring. He was not impressed with the new officers and remained in command of the battery until Major Joyce arrived in mid-February. He takes up the story:

23rd February–24th June *Allardyce and Kay both left on promotion being replaced by Joyce and Wheatly. A dull depressing and uninteresting period spent in endless schemes, tactical exercises and other training for open warfare which is expected to develop as a result of the grand attacks to be staged in the late summer. Joyce, though a charming man, is unfortunately quite hopeless at all military subjects, and map reading presents to him a puzzle which he cannot and never will solve. After his two glasses of port he retires for the afternoon every day to sleep and write letters and all military worries are over, for him, till 10 a.m. the following morning when he looks on for a short while at whatever training may be going on. Early in June he went on leave and became ill and failed to return. Though his name remained on the battery books for a long time we never saw him again and I remained in command of the battery till Fleming arrived in the middle of July.*

The great plan for 1916 was the Battle of the Somme. It was intended to be a decisive blow, massing troops preceded by a huge artillery bombardment to smash through the German lines. Once a gap had been made the cavalry divisions in reserve would pour through, with Francis and his guns in support. That was the plan. The reality was very different. Attack after attack ended in failure, or at best made only very limited gains. Francis was a mere spectator. As the next diary entry shows (dated 24 June but containing information relating to August) in this period he must have been writing up his journal some time later:

24th June   Started off at dusk for the Somme. First march to Vironchaux, thence to St Ouen thence to Bonnay. Here we remained for the first five days of the attack ready to move at ½ hour's notice. The situation being still unsuitable for the employment of cavalry we then returned to Pont-Remy for three days when we once more moved up to Bonnay for the attack on the second line.

No opportunity for the cavalry having developed we finally came back on 3rd August to St-Pierre-à-Gouy then to Drucat and so to Hesdin. A most unsatisfactory period, always waiting to move forward, and gradually realising that the hope of breaking through was becoming very remote. We went several times to look on at the battle – twice to Shamrock Tree where we saw the assault on La Boisselle and once to Fricourt and to near Contalmaison.

From Hesdin we made one more preparation for a 'gap', marching in one step to a bivouac near Corbie. No result, as before, so returned to Vecquemont and then to Lespinoy. Saw Congreve, Lutyens and Gilman, all in field batteries taking part in the attack.

So yet again Francis had missed the battle and withdrew back out of action.

For Ted, after Christmas 1915, and its rush of parcels, was over, the new year looked like settling back down into the same boring routine.

28th January 1916
My dear Mother
Thank you for letters up to [No.] 48 received, and numerous packets. As for food, I am not eating very much these days, but as long as it arrives regularly is all that matters. I can get vegetables and bread here, but I shall be always glad to get the former in parcels. Will you please thank Rachel for a parcel and Mr Mallet as well for some jam and a letter. Father and G. E. F. also. How is everyone? I hope Father is better and will be put right again, but I expect it will take time. It goes so slowly now, one loses count entirely. I am keeping fairly well and more or less sound, though my watered knee gives a good deal of trouble. After one cold spell it is warm again, but I suppose we shall get some more. I am having another go at the dentist now more to fill up the day than my mouth. I don't know what he was up to last time but he filled the latter with acid and I cursed him for hours afterwards. Everything tasting as if it had been wiped with a dirty rag. I am starting on the Spanish language. If my greatcoat can't be found don't send one out, but I should like a few more black stars sent out to put on my coat. Very best love to all and I hope for all your sakes life is more interesting than it is here.

4th February 1916
My dear Father,
Thank you for No. 17, just received. In these times of stress, twenty shillings a week for such a useless thing as my stomach, so we will cut that list down as follows, omit entirely: cheese, marmalade, soups, meat, and puddings; and following alterations: Ideal Milk one tin per week not two; biscuits one tin fortnightly not weekly; jam or golden syrup, one pot fortnightly not weekly; in addition one tin margarine fortnightly. Add macaroni also to the list of needs, and half a pound each of two different items on the list, fortnightly – not weekly – and Quaker Oats occasionally. That ought to cut it down by half I should think, and will make the study of economics more interesting this end.

I am very fit and keeping my figure well but my knee is giving me a lot of trouble. I hope it won't get permanently stiff. If this arrives in time for the Grandparents'

*diamond wedding, send them my love and
congratulations. I am afraid that it will be
a longer job than anyone imagines, but if
he pulls through, it's the main thing. We
have a piano installed here now, and you
can imagine what the noise must be like
when I tell you that yours affect. is the only
performer on it.*

*We have a book of songs and ease our
nerves a bit that way. Football still goes on
and I limp about in the middle somewhere
and curse. I have quite got my nerve back
which is a blessing as I thought at one
time it had gone for good. I wrote to Cox
the other day and told him to use his own
discretion about investing any money I
may have, which seems the best thing to
do under the circumstances. I do hope
your leg is really better – I hope it isn't
legs – one is always bad enough. Will you
please send on these sheets the other side
of this to Captain G. W. Liddell DSO, Rifle
Brigade, The Grange, Camberley, and the
other to Mrs Heap, Dorrington, Shrewsbury.
How are all the family? I hope well and
flourishing in their different abodes. I hear
from Francis occasionally. He seems well
and still complains of the danger! Well, I
must to bed now, so goodbye with very best
love to all.*

16th February 1916.
My dear Father

*The parcels continue to arrive all right,
and I hope you got my letter cutting down
the list somewhat. I have just had three
bills sent out here to me. Will you please
deal with them for me – (No. 1) R. A.
Cooper, 84 Jermyn Street, London, 19/- July
1914; (No. 2) H. L. Griffin, Head Station,
Colchester, £5 7s 10d storage of my kit
etc.; (No. 3) H. W. Salmon & Son, 77 High
Street, Winchester 3s 2d for photograph.
Would you see if the Colchester one is all
right? You may possibly have receipts for
the other two among those bills I sent before
I left. Will you ask Mother not to send any
more Buzzard cakes [sic] as they are too
powerful in captivity, but that the light
cakes, sultana, etc. are excellent. How is
everyone? Very pleasant dirty weather here*

*– rain and snow alternate days and a spot
of mud about! I'm pretty fit but want some
strenuous exercise badly. I'd give a lot to
go and dig in a garden, and would spend
a week in bed afterwards, I expect. It's
too bad to play football now so our livers
stagnate. Will you please send on these
other sheets to the names on them. Best of
love to all.*

28th March 1916
My dear Father,

*Thank you very much for your letter,
just received. I am having this forwarded to
Thorny Court and I hope you will get it in
time, though I suspect you will have left [to
visit France] long before this even starts. We
are allowed out for walks now on parole,
but I'm not sure it doesn't make the life
inside here worse. Playing a semi-liberty is
a very poor game and I never could take
much pleasure in a crocodile. The woods,
however, are perfectly wonderful and the
way they are kept is marvellous. They have
the thinning to a fine art.*

*Lyle is not up to much I don't think. He
can't pack his parcels so they have any
hope of arriving all together but the stuff is
not bad. A couple of pots of fruit per week
would be a good thing during the summer,
and I would be very glad if you would
get them to add that to their list. I am
sending a photograph of myself and some
companions. Don't let it get about that I
look too well as it would spoil my chances
of blood money afterwards. It's taken in the
courtyard below the windows of this room.
Not an over-cheerful spot.*

*I heard from Francis who seems in
usual health and not very pleased with
life. I should imagine they are only one
better off than us. If this lasts much longer
I really think some of us will go mad and
I'm afraid it will be years before we are any
good again mentally for work. We have
even to hunt about for words in English
sometimes, or at least I have to very often.
I hope you are quite alright again by now
and have got the complaint out of your
system. How are all the rest of the family?
Quite well I hope.*

Irise Foljambe Park Royal 1916

15th May 1916
My dear Mother,

There [are] a good many things I have to thank you for: shoes, two capes from Barker and boots, also for the butter from Switzerland which is excellent but whether it will arrive good in hot weather I don't know, as it's not hermetically sealed up. Lyle is a bad number. None of the parcels are packed properly and they generally arrive like scrambled eggs. Anyway please stop the Golden Syrup as it always leaks, and jam or marmalade are better. Please thank M. Malet, I always forget whether she's an aunt or cousin, for a letter. She said she was sending two parcels, I believe, but unfortunately neither have arrived. If you happen to be in the way of it, Rosamond and Albuda both have to be thanked for letters. Notwithstanding the family complaint I seem to peg along alright. The doctor says my lungs are too large and for some reason won't contract and that's what is causing the trouble – owing to too much exercise and too many games! Yes, I don't think! As for the rest I am sound again. By the way, after some wandering I got some cigarettes from Violet B. for which the need was great and a due proportion of thanks owing. Nothing seems to have happened as regards bread from Winter in Birmingham and the Bern bread still arrives. If Grandmother doesn't want to send it, will you order it to come every week. I do wish they would come to some conclusion soon, we are all getting horribly aged here and quite unfit to talk to. I hope everyone is well, with best love to all.

Dora meanwhile had again been working behind the scenes to try and get Ted either exchanged or taken to Switzerland for health reasons. Dora and Madya must have been in touch during this period, although no letters survive. Madya had also been trying to pull strings with people she knew both in France and Switzerland. She had written to the Baronne de Montenoels, who was going to try and influence the Swiss Medical Commission in order to get Ted repatriated, as she told Madya in reply:

24th May 1916
Madam,

Immediately, we are making requests to the appropriate authorities and the Swiss Commission for the prisoners, to try and get the transfer, in Switzerland, of the English prisoner you speak me about and whom we took care about before.

It will take several weeks if we achieve the happy end I wish and hope. Yet the first transfer of prisoners is over tomorrow but the doctors will begin their control soon in view of the exchange of Germans and Englishmen and we will recommend particularly your protégé.

I am pleased to have got news from you and assure you of my affectionate and best feelings.

At the beginning of June Madya was back in Paris (there is no clear record of where she had been during the preceding few months) and in contact with Dora, who still thoroughly approved of her. Dora had sent Madya a photograph of Ted in Rifle Brigade uniform, taken before the war, and Madya was very happy with it and wrote to thank Dora:

3rd June 1916
Dear Mrs Foljambe,

Thank you ever so much for the photograph you sent me. I loved to compare it to the last one. May I keep it or shall I send it back to you?

I am very sorry I left England without seeing you and I shall look forward very much for meeting you again.

I don't know yet when I start for Salonika and I don't suppose the present state of affairs down there will make it any easier. I don't lose hope anyhow and meanwhile am very busy here; you can do some good work everywhere if you really want to.

I hope you got the letter Baronne de Montenoels sent me. I applied here too, both to the American and Swedish Embassy, so let us trust Captain Foljambe will be sent to Switzerland in the next exchange. It can't be very soon, though what is really to avoid is another winter spent in Germany. Dear

madam, I do hope he'll keep his nerve all right up to that time.

Let me thank you again for the kindness and sympathy you showed, I appreciated it so much as I do sometimes feel so awfully lonely since this horrible war broke out and brought such terrible perturbation in my life.

And so, to get busy and help others is a kind of selfishness as it takes your own worries out of your mind and the sight of other people's suffering makes your own so much very easier to bear.

But finally things were at last moving for Ted and either through pressure applied by all sorts of aristocracy and contacts through Europe, or quite simply because he had been badly wounded in 1914 and was not back to full health, Ted was finally examined by the Swiss Medical Commission to see if he was suitable to be moved to Switzerland. Ted wrote about it to his mother:

Mainz
20 June 1916
My dear Mother,

Just a line to tell you that I have been sent here to look at the Swiss Commission. As a matter of fact they looked at me yesterday and the result is as yet unknown by ordinary people. You can't think how I long to pass and get away. But even if we do have a bit of luck here, they may do the dirty on us at Constance where they hold another inquisition. There were a lot of English officers here when we came but they have now gone en masse to another camp. So only forty commissionaires and some French, Belgians and Russians are left to squabble and grouse at everything and one. So sorry to hear the Grandparent has been unwell but I suppose it's inevitable now; give them my love if you write and please tell GEF I will write to her at the first opportunity. Tell Mary she is a perfect dear for her letter; I thought it was never coming. It has been raining a lot and is filthy cold and we all feel like worms. Well, very best of love to all the family and if I get through I hope I shall see some of it.
Your loving son,
Edmond

OPPOSITE For a while in 1916 Avice worked in a munitions factory at Park Royal in North London.

ABOVE *Women drivers and their ambulances lined up for inspection at the Joint War Committee's ambulance station, Boulogne, France.*

George had now been retired from the Army and had handed over his responsibilities at the depot. The 1st/8th Battalion was still in France and Lieutenant Weetman, the adjutant, wrote again to George:

29th January 1916

I have been wanting to write you a line to tell you how sorry I was to hear that you have really left the 3rd Line, and am afraid I have rather let it slip. It was a sad blow to those of us who know something of the battalion, when we heard you were really going, as we had all hoped in the end that it would not come to that, but that you would be allowed to continue at the helm for some time longer at any rate. We all feel very doubtful as to how things will go now, but of course must hope for the best. They have not sent us out any reinforcements for some time, so we haven't got much practical information as to how they are going on, but we hear they have a good many of the 'old hands' there again, and several to come out. We have picked up well after our holiday, and are now in pretty

good form, though rather under-strength. It is pretty wet and dreary here – but not really cold for the time of year. At present we are well behind in rest billets.

I hope you and your family are well and that the Squire and Lady Gertrude keep up. The war must be trying for them I fear.

George did not hear much more from the battalion. The occasional letter came through but he was no longer at the hub of the England link. However, he was not prepared to be idle and if the Army no longer wanted him, he would find some other way of keeping involved with the war effort. In early 1916 he volunteered to join the Red Cross and went to France to join the missing persons bureau. He understood how parents felt when their sons went missing, and he felt he could help those who were prisoners of war. In addition he would be nearer to both Francis and Ted and might even be able to help Ted in Germany. So he left England and headed for Paris. He also regained contact with the 1st/8th Sherwood Foresters who were not far away at Vimy Ridge. George got a letter on 5 June from Lieutenant Wright, whom George had recruited and sent out to the battalion in 1915.

Whitten let me read your letter to him the other day and I was greatly interested to hear you were in France, also to hear that your son had got to a decent place after all his troubles.

I am getting on alright and have not missed a day when the battalion has been in the trenches. In fact I have not had a day's sickness since I came out, so it is not so bad for one no longer quite young, although I have been somewhat weary on various occasions when I have to do with very little rest.

This part of France is very fertile and the crops are very good. It is a rolling country and quite well wooded, though some of the woods are in a very sorry plight, owing to artillery actions. We had a little partridge shooting in 'no-man's-land', and the bag brought in at night was two brace, these we had for luncheon the next day, and found them quite good – they were not red legs, but English birds. There are also a few hares, but as they are often a long way outside our wire it is not worth shooting them as one could hardly find them at night. The battalion is still the 8th in spite of many drafts, and is by no means the least smart and efficient in the brigade. I hope you are fit and keep free from rheumatism, and hope to have a yarn with you again some day not too far distant.

July–December 1916

The summer was very quiet for Francis. Much of the British Army was involved in the continuing difficult fighting on the Somme. Other units were licking their wounds after their efforts there; G Battery was in reserve. Francis spent his time continuing to train the battery. Much time was spent riding, practising the advance, looking after horses, practising signals and all manner of other things now so necessary at the front. Some battery documents from the period have been kept with Francis's diary:

G Battery Instructions for On the March

1. -Towards the end of a march when the battery is approaching the field where it is to bivouac, the Section Commanders with their No. 1 should ride forward to the head of the battery and find out where to put up their horse lines.
2. -Keep the horses tied up in the same order always, so that they will get accustomed to one another and not kick.
3. -Never tie a horse up to a gun.
4. -Cooks will report at once to the QMS who will show them where to light the fires, etc.
5. -The chief delay in settling down in bivouac is watering the horses, so section commanders must find out at once where the water is and the first section to enter the field will at once file off to water before the harness is taken off.
6. -Harness will be wrapped in the saddle-blanket and placed in rear of the horse.
7. -Peg down the poles of the wagons which hold up the lines.
8. -Drivers nearly always tie up horses too long.
9. -Don't allow any horse to be tied up within reach of a packed wagon.
10. -See that the position of the latrines is known to all before the men are dismissed,
11. -Cooks will save time if they collect bits of dry wood on the march.

Towards the end of October, the battery geared up again for war.

21st October   *We finally received orders unexpectedly during the night to march next day. Started off as an RHA brigade via Vitzvilleroy, St Ouen to wagon lines near Englebelmer; pouring rain made the field into a sea of mud. Went up with Fleming to look at positions and marched up early on following day to the edge of Avelmy Wood when we came into action between the railway and the River Quare. This corner of Avelmy Wood lies opposite a sharp salient in the German line and thus one might expect a certain degree of immunity from disturbance, but this, however, was far from the case and every night the battery area was shelled which interfered with the pleasure of shooting duck on the Anse marshes and indeed resulted in several casualties to the sentries. One sentry received a direct hit from a 5.9-inch as he was attending to the siege lamp of one of the guns. Our OP was situated in a trench in front of Mesnil and observation was peculiar in that one was often looking back towards the gun for the shell burst. During the first week in November we registered many points on our front and prepared for the attack on Beaumont Hamel and Beaucourt which was rumoured to take place shortly.*

13th November *Attack astride the Ancre. Our battery was due to limber up at zero plus 2 hours in readiness to advance to a forward position in front of Hamel. All appeared to proceed normally and in due course I led the battery down the river road. As we approached Hamel a regular stream of bullets started crashing through the tree tops along the roadside from the direction of the German lines in front of Schwaben and Stuff Redoubts and it soon became evident that the information as to our progress to the east and south of the Ancre was not accurate. We reached our position, however, without mishap and were about to come into action when a heated orderly arrived with orders to return to our old position and prepare to take part in a renewed bombardment for a further attack on certain portions of the German line which were still holding out.*

It seemed to me far more dangerous to return than to stay where we were, as the only gateway into the field was being shelled by a field gun and the portion of the field near the gate was being ploughed up by bullets. We passed out the guns one by one and an hour later were shooting again from the position we had left in the morning.

No further orders to advance were received that day and we settled down to a disturbed night. We were just having our meat course at dinner when a shell fell close, followed by another just outside

our shelter, which put all the lights out. Someone was just relighting a candle when a third shell could be heard coming very close. It fell, unfortunately, in the cooks' partition of our shelter, just the other side of a sandbag wall from us and killed the cook and two servants.

Thinking it was time to get out of the place, we were just emerging from the doorway when a fourth shell landed close outside, wounding Fleming in the foot and wounding Woods, my servant, in the head. We carried them to the local dressing station and got things put straight but had a restless night as shells continued to drop close to the battery all night.

What Francis does not report is that on 13 November he was mentioned in despatches. The full citation no longer exists but the certificate (which was signed by Winston Churchill, Secretary of State for War in March 1919) states that the award was for gallant and distinguished services in the field.

16th November *Reconnoitred new forward position in Sausage Valley beyond Hamel and took Baker's section in by night.*
17th November *Took remainder of battery up together with 600 rounds per gun. Worked all night and by daylight had the guns concealed and ammunition more or less protected and some shelter trenches dug. Sent Baker and Fletcher out on a reconnaissance but they never came back and enquiries traced them back through the advanced dressing station. They were both wounded by a single shell shortly after they started on their reconnaissance.*

We stayed in this position for four days firing on barrages and engaging various targets with success. We had to spend a considerable time collecting corpses which were strewn round the guns, the position being situated in the original front line. Our casualties (Royal Naval Division) must have been regrettably heavy at this portion of the attack.
21st November *Received orders to move out that night so ordered up the teams (for after dark) and took the opportunity of an*

hour's more daylight to expend some more ammunition on the Germans and save labour in carting it back. Fired some 500 rounds into the Miraumont area and then loaded up ready to move. In spite of all the precautions I had taken to post men along the road to mark the crossings at trenches and other difficult points, it was 5 a.m. before the last vehicle reached Hamel. It was creditable not to lose anything as the night was pitch dark and the mud half-way to the axles. The last wooden bridge across the last trench broke as the last vehicle was crossing but with great exertions the wagon was manhandled out. In Hamel the trumpeter was waiting with Sunny Jim and I rode back to the rendezvous where I found the battery forming up and finally reached the brigade starting point at 06.30 a.m. in time to march at 7.00 as ordered.

Thence we marched back to Lespinoy and Rousseaux where Major Young joined. I never liked the latter much. He started off the first day to retrain the horses and rearrange the drivers, who in several cases were separated from the horses which they had had throughout the war and of which they were naturally fond. There was much dissatisfaction and I applied to return to the Field Artillery.

Francis had spent two years with G Battery. He had been unlucky with some of his battery commanders. He had not liked Dawson at all and had ended up commanding the battery himself during the absence of Major Joyce. He was an experienced soldier, had been involved in some pretty traumatic battles, but had come through as a respected and reliable man. The posting in of Major Young was the last straw. Francis wanted his own command and knew it would come sooner if he transferred back to the Field Artillery, which had a heavier gun and supported the infantry. He knew he would be posted back to the trenches (or just behind them) and would be in the thick of the future battles.

Ted now just had to wait and hope against hope that he would be moved to Switzerland. Dora told Madya that Ted had been moved to Heidelberg and was now in the hands of

the commission. Dora's hopes were so high that she immediately started planning to go to Switzerland to see Ted, if he was sent there, and asked Madya if she would be prepared to accompany her. Madya was thrilled with the offer, not only to see Ted but also because Dora was including her in her plans.

Madya had written to Ted to tell him not to look too well when he went in front of the Commission and to give him hints on what he should say to try and influence them to be

ABOVE AND BELOW
Francis' mention in despatch on 13 November 1916.

sent to Switzerland. Madya was still in very close touch with Dora:

18th July 1916
Dear Mrs Foljambe,
   It was kind of you to send me the magazine and I was so very interested.
   I have had a letter from Captain Foljambe dated 24th June, place Mainz. I believe he followed my instructions as he says: 'I am not quite up to the usual form as I have crows' feet round the eyes.' You see lumps are funny things and appearance doesn't mean anything very often and I think it is just a matter of luck for him.
   I hope to get a letter from my father in a fortnight or so – it will be the first one for over two years so I am awaiting every post anxiously already.
   Dear Madam, I do hope and trust both your sons will be given back to you soon and that all this terrible war is at an end before long, but how glorious are all soldiers and how comforting it is to see that all of them are heroes.
   Thank you once more for sending me the magazines and please believe me.
      Your most devoted,
      Madya de Rudincka

But it was not all proving to be simple. All parties to the process were being difficult and the following note appeared in *Le Matin* on 29 July: 'In retaliation, German authorities have turned back to prison 500 Englishmen chosen by a Swiss medical commission to follow a course of treatment in Switzerland. The convoy had already reached Constanz when it was given the order to turn back.'
   Madya and Dora were on tenterhooks until finally they got a postcard from Ted:

10th August 1916
Start for Switzerland tomorrow morning – new address MÜRREN. Please acquaint all shops of change of address and stop bread.
      Love to all
      E

Dora got a postcard from Maud Wyndham in the British Legation in Berne:

12th August 1916
Dear Mrs Foljambe,
   Your son arrived last night and I gave him your letter. He seemed well and was most cheerful and pleased to hear news of you all, and all about his sisters, etc. He has gone to Mürren; there are 35 officers and 400 men and we expect more tonight. Your son wanted clothes but he will doubtless write to you. All the officers had been for the last six months at Heidelberg where my brother is imprisoned, so I heard all about him. Let me know if you come to Switzerland.

Now Ted was able to write his first letter from Switzerland:

Palace Hôtel & Grand Hôtel des Alpes
Mürren
13th August 1916
My dear Mother,
   At last I can write in ink again. We arrived yesterday morning and are very comfortable indeed. I am most awfully badly off for clothes so if you are thinking of coming out for a bit will you please bring some – dinner jacket and white shirts, black waistcoat and trousers and evening shoes, white ties, studs, black silk evening socks, 2 pairs white flannel trousers, 2 flannel shirts, 2 sweaters (1 Oxford and the other with buttons down it), safety razor, 2 dozen blades, 1 pair black boots, black serge. This must be made at Daniel who has my measure. I'm not so large as I was so he mustn't make it too big. Impress on him black and not green. Well I think that's about all in the way of clothes. I forget a tennis racquet in case of accident. They had better be packed in my uniform case, I should think, which will hold them and would be most useful for my materials here, which lie about in wooden boxes.
   By the way I have forgotten something, another khaki coat, trousers and a black officer's greatcoat, some stars and cord to put on this coat for badges of rank.
   We hardly realise yet that it's a hotel but will I suppose in time. We took the boards last night for a few minutes. There is absolutely nothing to do here which is a

ABOVE *Prisoners of war arrive at Berne Station, Switzerland, in September 1916.*

nuisance. I must stop as I have some more letters to write before the post goes.

Best love to all.

Yr affectionate son,

Edmond

All parcels sent to me here must have two covers. Inside addressed as usual to me here, the other one addressed to His Excellency His Majesty's Minister – Berne. He undoes it and sends it on.

Madya immediately planned to go and see him. Dora was unable to go straight away as Rachael was about to have another baby in England.

Paris

18 August 1916

Dear Mrs Foljambe,

I am leaving tomorrow night for Mürren where Captain Foljambe has been transferred – will you be able to come and see him too?

I am so happy to hear of those good news, and Mürren is such a lovely place. I am quite sure he will soon be quite himself again. It was so kind of you to tell me every little bit of news you happened to hear, and I am really thankful to you for it.

I do hope to see you soon and I am sure Captain Foljambe will be really happy to see you.

Ted wrote again to his mother:

27th August 1916

My dear Mother,

I expect you will have got my letter by this time asking for clothes. They are urgently needed, all of what I mentioned in that letter, except the dress clothes for which there is no particular hurry as we have to be always in uniform. So will you substitute for the white shirt some soft white silk ones which I used to wear occasionally in the evenings, and some had a white double collar. A dressing gown is a necessity and a small and cheap wrist watch is also really a want. As soon as the uniform and things can be got made I should like them sent out to me as when it rains I can't go out as I have only the coat I was wounded in two years ago and it's inclined to be untidy for dinner and dances? Any other niches of ordinary comfort which I did not mention but which make life worth living, please include as well. As for a box, I think that if father comes out, if he could bring

ABOVE *Ted Foljambe,*
Riddie, Irvine and
Parke arrive at Festung
Rosenberg prisoner of
war camp in Bavaria.
The fortress of
Rosenberg is situated
on a hill above the
town of Kronach.
Officer prisoners were
concentrated in two
wings of this high
citadel. Among the
allied prisoners was
a young Charles de
Gaulle.

my uniform case, so that I can make away
with some of the dirty old boxes I have toiled
round Germany with. I do not think you had
better think of coming out here at present.
The journey is fearful with only the back
of beyond and a few dilapidated officers at
the finish of it. You see there is absolutely
nothing to do here and we can't get away to
any place without great difficulty.

Please make them hurry with my black
serge – this coat does stink.

Best love to all.

E

George was based in Paris, still working
with the Red Cross, and also planned to visit
Ted in Switzerland:

29th August 1916
My dear Father,

Just a hurried line in answer to yours
of the 18th. As far as staying here there is
no difficulty as the place is nearly empty. If
even one had fifty people to stay they would
be something like pleased. So if you come,
which I hope you will soon, you can have

a room here for the asking at any moment.
There are clothes which I want and must
have in fact, as I have nothing left not
really in rags, as is likely to happen after
two year's hard wear. I sent a list to Mother
of articles necessary, but of course there
must be some other things forgotten.

As far as my clothes go, I don't want
any new-fangled ideas as worn by the 33rd
Battalion in London and Southsea but the
patterns worn before the war. I want a
new black serge made in place of my old
green one.

Well, I must stop and tempt the weather,
so goodbye and I hope to see you soon.

Finally Madya managed to get out and
reported back to Dora:

Paris
27 August 1916
Dear Mrs Foljambe,

I have spent a week at Mürren and have
been very happy to see Captain Foljambe out
of the Hun's clutches at last. As regarding his
health it is far from being so good as before

and the doctors want him to go to Leysin to a sanatorium for tuberculosis. He does not want to go but I hope by and by he will be more obedient as I think six months of strict and looked after life will cure him forever.

Of course I quite understand that for one who has been imprisoned for two years, this perspective is far from appealing but if he goes on as in Mürren, smoking, dancing and drinking, I am afraid he would ruin his life for ever and why so if a few months can put him straight again.

I hope dear Madam that the baby came alright and that you soon will be able to go to Switzerland. I believe that you are rather wanted there too and a little rest would do you some good too.

The journey is awful, you are stopped and searched and must have letters from the people you are going to see. I had none but luckily was passed all the same as my passport was issued by the Prefect of Paris himself, but many are stopped.

Dear Mrs Foljambe, I am so glad for you that your son has crossed the frontier and I hope soon that, health coming fully back to him, he will recover all his lightness and lose that slight sense of bitterness which I never noticed before.

Let me know if you intend to go and see him and when and would you like to stop at the Grande Bretagne [Madya's Paris hotel] on your way? I think you are obliged to stop one day to have your papers and visa [checked] once more. I am not quite sure though. If I can do anything for you please remember I would be but too glad.

So Ted was transferred to Leysin to follow a cure to recover his health:

Hotel Sanatorium du Mont Blanc
Leysin
6th September 1916
My dear Mother,

I am here answering the prayers of some of my relations and I don't think there can be a worse place in this country. I am perhaps a bit iller than what was thought and they say I must be here at least six months doing a strict cure. You,

of course, must not come out here on any consideration whatsoever. Father, I must see if he can manage to come out but otherwise I would much sooner be alone and get done with it.

I'm afraid I can't describe the place as my language would not be suitable. There are nearly 200 English soldiers here whom another officer and myself are now helping to look after, so there is not too much time for a cure. But there won't be too much to do soon I hope. Before anything else I have to make up two stone in weight which will be well nigh impossible with the present meals, food and drink, the idea that you always rise from your meals hungry. I was awfully sorry to leave Mürren as it was beginning to become quite amusing and we were getting to know the people quite well.

Please congratulate my niece on her arrival and Rachel and everyone else concerned. Though you mustn't come out, don't forget to send my clothes which are of secondary importance to nothing.

Madya had now returned from her first trip to see Ted. This was first time she had seen him since he had left hospital in Cambrai in early 1915 to go to Germany and she noticed the change that two years in captivity had had on him. George Foljambe, meanwhile, had set out to visit Ted in Switzerland, no doubt aware of Madya's concerns:

14th September 1916
Dear Mrs Foljambe,
Captain Foljambe made up his mind so quickly.

I had a letter from him yesterday and he does not seem to like the place very much. I own I found his character very much changed and a touch of bitterness which he had not in Cambrai. After all it is not very surprising and we have to thank God that nothing worse happened after all the terrible trials he had to undergo.

Do you intend to go to Leysin soon? I would be so glad to see you again and do believe that he needs somebody with him and little by little his bitterness will melt

– there's no better sunshine than family affection, I think.

I am so pleased to hear about the baby and hope they are going on well; I did hope to see Mrs Jelf again, she is so frightfully sweet and I know a great friendship ties her to her brother – and is Captain Francis going to see him too?

If you don't [think] it very rude of me I would like to hear Colonel Foljambe's opinion when he comes back – to see the change that occurred since the war as well physically as mentally – you excuse me I hope – but I am very interested.

What a pity the colonel started for Mürren – it is such an awfully trying journey nowadays and then he probably has very short leave – it is so wonderful of him to do such work in France!

If you go to Switzerland this month I will be very pleased to join you for a fortnight or so – my trip to Salonika is quite over, so except home work and my few families and soldiers I am looking after I am quite free – but, considering what Captain Foljambe says, Leysin is the dullest place on earth so perhaps you could remain for instance at Monthey which is not very far from him and go and see him twice a week – and Monthey is a lovely place.

Finally George had been to Switzerland and had visited Ted. Ted then wrote again to his mother from his sanatorium at Leysin:

6th October 1916
My dear Mother,

You must excuse my not writing to thank you before for all the things you sent and especially the ones for my birthday which are perfectly delightful but, with father here and my cure, there has not been much time for writing. The doctor will give you an account from here as to how I am.

I have contracted the tuberculosis bug alright without any mistake, but the affair has not gone very far and from what I gather I can be quite cured in time.

This is no place for any human being and that is why I suggested you should not come out. It is also hard to keep to the hours of the cure when alone but when there is anybody out here it's much harder.

Switzerland may be the most delightful place in the world and it's certainly a million times better than Germany, but give me London smoke any day and I'd exchange gladly. These mountains are so fearfully cold and stagnant and life ceases to be.

Well Father was in very good form and was, I think, looking well, though of course many years older than when I last saw him. He felt better for the high air and I hope he enjoyed his visit. There is another large meal in progress so I must needs attire myself and descend.

Thank you again very much indeed for the gifts. With love to all.

Ted wrote again to his father after his visit to Switzerland:

28th October 1916
My dear Father,

Please excuse pencil but the ink has become more like glue than anything else and is quite impossible. Thank you very much for having that money put into Cox's for me. I shall be able to carry on alright now.

Talking of the waterproof and B[ritish] Warm, I understood you were going to do that so as to be able to choose colours and what make. It would be better if you could because it's hard to trust the tailors these days. Also I should like the waterproof lined with detached inside.

If the cap has not been sent off yet could you have a patent leather black strap instead of the crown put on it. Greatcoat and boots are in the building but have not yet been sent I don't think. Good account from the doctors here of me and I put on a kilo by mistake the other day. Wrong place I'm afraid as I developed a pain shortly afterwards.

I hope you found everyone well at home and all goes satisfactorily at Osberton.

The weather is too awful for words here now and has begun to snow these last few days.

I have started golf as the only means of exercise, down at Aigle and have had two lessons so far. I do nothing but cricket shots and the ball goes past extra cover like anything. The pro gets furious. Anyway it's just amusing and passes a moment or two.

If this is going to catch the post it must go now, so goodbye and love to all.

The year ended with Madya and George having both visited Ted in Switzerland and Ted finally starting to get better. George was working with the Red Cross in France and Francis was still at the front.

A couple of George's letters of the period to Rachie survive:

2nd August 1916
Dearest Rachie,

So glad to hear you and Nino are thriving. At last we have some summer weather and it must be pleasant under the pine trees. I see the promised visit of the Zeppelins has come off. There is not much of an account but they seem to have been pretty promiscuous along the east coast. It is strange what poor judges of human nature they are. Every bit of frightfulness will be brought up against them one of these days and maybe some of them will be sorry for themselves.

Is old Grey coming to you temporarily? I think he will be a comfort to you. We have a Mrs Widdington here – her husband was in the 4th/60th at Pindi and now commands a brigade somewhere. She has come over to see her brother. There is also a Mrs Sims whose husband was a Rifleman of many years ago. She lives at Fleet not far from Aldershot. Altogether we are a very big party just now and the poor parlour maids have a bit of a rush but they are quite first rate.

Today has been the easiest day we have had for long. A very small convoy in and no letters from Carlton Terrace! It has been a hideous drive the whole of last month.

Has any more been heard of Ted? I do trust he won't be disappointed. This is a mangy sort of letter, but there is so little that one can say. Goodbye dear and may all go well with you.

Your ever loving father,
GSF

ABOVE *A nursing contingent from the Red Cross.*

Saturday [undated]
Dearest Rachie,

Many thanks for yours and mother's of the 27th which arrived last night and very glad to hear you are on your legs again, and well enough to think of going to the sea. If you go I should say the sooner you can manage it the better, before the weather gets cold and breaks up. I am afraid you won't find a horse to ride, but maybe there will be a jackass to be discovered. I don't know if there is anything with four legs I can commandeer at Osberton unless it be the shorthorn bull!

Rain has fallen here again heavily and I fear will impede operations as it must be very difficult to get the guns into fresh positions in the wet soil. However, it will make it difficult for the Huns to get theirs away and things seem to be going grandly. Just been reading Lloyd George's speech, I wish he had spoken like this some time back. It will be pleasant reading for Fritz! Paper arrived all right thanks. Well I must get on. Best love to all in the flat, you are indeed a party there and so glad to hear the smalls are flourishing.

Your very affectionate father,
GSF

CHAPTER 9

Last Battles and Homecomings

January–July 1917

Francis started 1917 waiting for orders to move to a new battery. He had decided to transfer again, both to get away from Major Young, whom he did not like, and also because he wanted to get back into the war and command his own troops. He knew that his experience would make him a strong runner to command his own battery. In the event this was to be his most satisfactory period as a soldier and he had much less time to devote to his diary:

14th January   *I received orders to join the 4th Division artillery and on the following day left by car to take over command of the 135th Battery RFA at Longpré. Went into Amiens to have dinner with Dennis.*

17th January   *Marched to Camp 14. The battery is a very slovenly concern after G Battery and the guns appear to be much the worse for wear. Very cold, and snow fell all day.*

18th January   *Got a lift in a car driven by a Frenchman and after skidding about the roads arrived at a point about a mile from our position, whence I walked to the French battery which we are to relieve. The French have eight batteries in one long line with excellent deep dug-outs and guns lightly screened. It was difficult to find the place in the snow, although I went to the exact map reference, as there were no tracks or any sign of life. I found the required*

battery at length and, penetrating a deep dug-out, found the commandant and the lieutenant of the battery; the former had a long beard and was in bed, the latter was listening to someone who was singing down the telephone for the amusement of the brigade. The working of a French battery was curious. The gun lines appear to rather disperse the échelon and treat it merely as an arrangement to supply the needs of the battery. Much attention was paid to the mathematical side of gunnery and great reliance was placed on the results calculated. For example, neither of these two officers has visited any OP. When they had first come into this position an NCO from the group had gone to an OP and tested each gun onto a point de reglement. Subsequently an NCO manned an OP to keep a look-out for the group; the remaining personnel seemed scarcely ever to move from their dug-outs, which were incidentally very lousy.

19th January   *Moved four guns into action as soon as the French 75s were clear.*

20th January   *Remaining two guns into action. There followed a remarkably cold spell, our thermometer registered over 30 degrees of frost. The extreme cold may have accounted for some very short rounds which fell about half way to the target. We established an OP near Marrières Wood some 1,000 yards in advance of the French look-out post, and carried out the usual routine of shooting and liaison. No work*

OPPOSITE *Ted, Madya and 'Flick'.*

possible on account of the extreme hardness of the ground.

6th February   A bombardment was carried out to liven things up. We fired about 1,000 rounds.

11th February   I cut the German wire in front of Sap 16, observing from the latter place and having two guns in the Marrières Wood area. The Germans did not interfere.

Not all was well back at Osberton. The Squire finally died at the age of 82. Francis was not able to get back to the funeral but wrote to his father on 20 February:

Thanks for the letter. I saw in the papers on the same evening that I got your previous letter that the Squire had died. I hadn't seen him for more than two years and am glad I did not go there last time I was on leave. I prefer to remember him as he was, the kindest and best grandfather anybody has ever had. Osberton will indeed seem strange now.

Rain has come again and with it the mud. This place is really the scene of utter desolation. Dead horses and broken carts and guns everywhere and shell hole touches shell hole as far as the eye can reach in every direction. Every other one is the grave of some unfortunate and marked with an old helmet or a shell stood up on end. I think, however, that we have about done our tour of duty here.

I acquired an MC some time ago, as a matter of fact towards the end of last year. They are slow in publishing anything. As a battery commander of six guns I get the temporary rank of major, but only while this war lasts.

Francis was very matter of fact about the award of his MC. The citation has not survived but it was a very satisfactory award for Francis. He was a most effective artillery officer and very professional in his understanding of his business, but did not get on well with his superiors. He must have been a difficult man to command but he was respected and liked by his soldiers.

23rd February   Moved up to Marrières Wood and carried out the usual routine of constructing cover, registering our zone and reconnaissance. There was a marked decrease in German shelling about this time and it is likely that they were starting to withdraw guns in accordance with their plan to evacuate the whole Somme salient, which was shortly afterwards put into execution.

Still very cold and I think I caught a chill; at any rate I woke up one morning and couldn't move at all without great pain. I sent for a doctor and took some medicine to try and get a sweat up, which I managed to achieve after six hours or so when I felt better. He said keep dry and warm which was not very sensible or constructive in view of the fact that the dug-out was dank, always full of smoke, the roof dripping water continuously and several inches of liquid mud on the floor.

Either something in Francis's letters had concerned George or he was not hearing from him as often as usual, so he wrote to Francis's CO, Colonel N. C. Tilney, commander of the 4th Division artillery, who replied on 1 March:

In reply to your letter of 23rd, I am glad to say that your son is alright, and I fancy it must be on account of the badness of the post that you have not heard from him. Letters often take ten days to reach us here and I believe that they take nearly as long to get home. He was bothered a day or two ago by his neck, and had to stay in bed for a day, but he is better now, although still a little stiff.

Since he joined this brigade, he has been working very hard with his battery, and is an excellent battery commander.

Please excuse my writing paper, but I have run out of the proper article.

1st March   Orders with regard to a minor attack on Fritz Trench were issued and I was well enough to stagger to the OP and test our barrage. There was an official test barrage late and ours was passed as very good.

3rd March   *Spent the day cutting wire at Fulda Point from an OP called Rachel North.*

4th March   *Attack on Fritz Trench by 8th Division. Zero hour at 5.15 a.m. A complete success and all objectives gained but rather heavy casualties were sustained later during consolidation, by shell fire. All quiet at 6.30 a.m. except German shelling on the lost trenches.*

6th March   *Orders to withdraw ½ battery to the wagon line.*

7th March   *I took remainder of battery out and bivouacked in wagon line. Bitterly cold and snowing hard.*

8th March   *Marched via Sailly-le-Sec, St Gratien, Talmas, Outrebois to Couchy-sur-Canche. A very different show to marching G Battery. These poor old horses can hardly struggle along after a winter in the Somme mud. Ended up the march some thirty horses short. The roads, after the break up of the frost, were almost unpassable. We got bogged twice in the main street of villages! We went into billets at Couchy and rested, cleaned up generally and did some training.*

22nd March   *Battery moved up into action near St Nicolas. 10.C.2.2. There are about three brigades in line here; in fact the whole area is stiff with guns of all sizes. OP is in a large building off the square in Arras. About twenty other artillery officers observe from the same place.*

22nd March–2nd April   *Usual routine of registration, look-out, liaison and preparation of barrage tables. German air supremacy very marked. Their red squadron is on this front and every day several of our planes were shot down. The Germans here seem to be superior in every way to our airmen. There is a rumour that we have got some better machines ready but are waiting for the offensive to start before letting them loose. On the 24th a shell landed on the trail of No. 6 gun and killed Bombardier Webb and three of the detachment. The No. 1 was unhurt, though the shell must have nearly hit him. The gun was knocked out.*

On the 31st our wagon line was shelled by a gun called Percy by the drivers. The brigade HQ lost some men and a good many horses, so the wagon line was moved to Lazerette. On the 25th I went to reconnoitre OPs down a trench which led forwards from the crest of the hill in front. I turned down a cul-de-sac trench and looked for some time with my glasses at the German lines when a 5.9-inch battery started shooting at the junction of my cul-de-sac and the trench. This went on for so long that I decided to run past as soon as a shell had fallen and before the next could arrive. The Germans

LEFT *Artillery officers and signallers direct battery fire, 1917.* IWM Q5095

must have seen me I think because this time a shell was followed very quickly by another which very nearly got me and my signaller. It fell just over the thrown-up earth of the communication trench and covered us with earth. Returned to find Squires looking pale and found that he also had been just missed by a shell. He said he had been bruised in the back so I had a look and found a minute hole in the middle of what looked like a slight bruise. When the doctor probed it, he found it was inches deep and Squires retired to England for good and all.

I heard afterwards that he had to undergo several operations before they could get him well again.

3rd April *I compared barrages with contiguous batteries, McKay and Richey, and found all correct. No. 6 gun was again knocked out that day.*

4th April *Start of bombardment [of the Battle of Arras].*

5th April *Went down to front line and inspected state of wire opposite our front. One of our aeroplanes was hit by one of our own shells and broke into many bits.*

6th April *Practice barrage to detect gaps and to cause casualties.*

9th April *Attack on large front up to Vimy Ridge. Zero hour 5.30 a.m. The attack appeared to proceed according to plan throughout. There was little interference by German guns near us till the advance to the brown line. Started when a battery started firing gas shell close to our control dug-out. At about 2.00 we limbered up and according to plan proceeded forward towards Athies. On arrival at the prearranged new position a message arrived to the effect that the progress on our front was greater than had been anticipated and directing us to a position further east. I rode on to Fampoux and, after consultation with the local infantry, selected a former German battery position as a good spot to come into action. Observation from the Fampoux ridge in front gave a good view of Greenland Hill, the chemical works and Monchy-le-Preux on the south bank of the Scarpe. Many abandoned German guns about and most*

of their equipment was left behind by the battery whose position we now occupied, including interesting maps and good instruments. This battery must have had an easy time in the past. Very cleverly hidden in the east end of Athies and just able to clear the buildings in front for shooting at our lines, it had concrete emplacements and concrete dug-outs for every gun all connected by tunnels so that it was unnecessary to go out at all, in visiting the guns. The emplacement, however, did not suit us well and for various reasons I made another position for the battery in a hedgerow at the boundary of the garden. The guns were excellently concealed and were I believe unspotted by the Germans for some time. A German aviator's target map had a query mark against our position, whereas all the other batteries of the brigade were marked in as identified.

Shelled all night by one of our own 4.5-inch howitzers which must have got a thousand yards or so wrong in its range, but without damage.

10th–11th April *Renewed attacks on Greenland Hill. Cavalry arriving all day at Fampoux but they are twenty-four hours too late. On the previous day they could have ridden onto Greenland Hill without opposition but unfortunately they were committed on the south side of the Scarpe and were held up at once at Monchy-le-Preux.*

The area in front of our guns was full of cavalry and in the afternoon a German aeroplane pursued one of ours which came down to about a height of perhaps fifty feet, straight over all the horses but the German never fired a shot at the ground targets but followed the aeroplane without a pause. He shot it down after it had passed us by 500 yards and then turned and bolted for home. Sleet and snow, and the wretched cavalry almost dead with cold and exposure.

The attacks on Greenland Hill were unsuccessful, as were various attempts by the cavalry to debouch from Fampoux. Many troopers and horses were killed by shellfire in the village.

13th April   *The battery area was deluged with gas shell. Dozens fell round the guns but the worst seemed to be coming to the left of the battery and shortly the 27th Battery reported many casualties. The air fairly hummed with projectiles for about an hour. Later on some HE was added by way of contrast.*

14th April   *Up early on a misty morning and went to Point du Jour to register some new points visible from there. Wandered on in the mist and fortunately became anxious about my position and retraced my steps when I came upon a post which the officer in charge said was the most advanced one in that sector. Waited about in the post until the mist cleared. Then ran out telephone line and carried out registration shoot.*

23rd April   *Another attack on Greenland Hill 4.45 a.m. Bombardier Houghton killed; Bombardier Fraser, Gunners Clark and Godden wounded. Attack unsuccessful.*

24th April   *Peaceful day, perhaps the German artillery is moving back. A French soldier arrived in the battery position and explained that he had come on leave from the Vosges to see how his farm was getting on. The battery was in action in what was once his garden and the house was just a rubble heap over our mess dug-out. Rather doleful about his home, he afterwards saw the humorous side and, after a drink, went away apparently cheerfully resigned.*

26th April   *Bombardier Hobbs killed. Milne joined the battery from G. I don't think he could stand Young any longer.*

27th April   *While [we were] playing cards in our dug-out a shell burst close and seemed to shake the place more than usual so we had a look out and found the most enormous hole outside our door. Shortly afterwards more shell could be heard coming, one of which struck the corner of the roof of one of the concrete shelters. Jenkins, Talboys, Brown and Holloway wounded. The head of the shell did not break up and we made it out to be an 8-inch armour-piercing shell.*

28th April   *Another attack on Greenland Hill. There are sixteen 60-pounders in line along the railway bank 800 yards behind and they go off like the noise of tearing a gigantic piece of calico, with a sheet of flame. One or more prematures always occur and the result usually comes bang into us. Bombardier Wade badly wounded today with one of them. The attack achieved slight success and stung the Hun into making a counter-attack in considerable force. This was clearly visible from the OPs and was repulsed mostly by shellfire with heavy losses. An official communiqué later even went so far as to admit the considerable effect of the guns on this occasion.*

3rd May   *Another unsuccessful attack on Greenland Hill. Three companies which penetrated to their objectives were cut off and have not returned.*

6th May   *Ordered to withdraw all but a guard from the guns and go for four days' rest to the wagon line. Marched out at dusk on the south bank of the Scarpe to avoid the main St-Laurent-Blangy Road which is always shelled by the Germans at night, but just as we reached the outskirts of Arras a terrific flare-up occurred and proceeding we found the big ammunition dump near the bridge burning merrily. Crossing there was out of the question and we had to retrace our steps to the next bridge up and got to bed very late.*

11th May   *Up to guns again for attack on Chemical Works by 4th Division. The barrage arranged was a very thick one, one 18-pounder per six yards, and as the attack was timed for the evening, it was an easy matter to ensure great accuracy by shooting slowly at the starting line of the barrage until the last moment. The sun was well in the west and observation perfect. The barrage came down at zero with a splendid crash and was quite the best I have yet seen in accuracy and thickness. The attack was a success.*

12th May   *A further attack on our left by the 17th Division which we watched from our OP on Orange Hill. In the evening a shell crashed into our tunnel leading into the mess and we were suddenly half smothered in gas fumes. Luckily everyone* had his gas mask ready and on in next to no time but the fumes hung about for a long time and everything tasted very bad for several days.

13th–16th May   *German shelling much increased on our front, especially in Chemical Works area, Fampoux and the support line. I stupidly chose one of these days to wander out in front with Cockle to reconnoitre possible forward positions and had many times to shelter from bursts of shelling. The shelling was followed at 3.30 a.m. on 16th May by a counter-attack in force. Detachments of Germans broke our line at Chemical Works but were afterwards driven out everywhere except from Cupid Trench. Hostile counter-battery work was heavy but we were lucky in only having a few close, though a very large number fell in our area. I think that our battery is still not located. A lorry on the road by the 86th Battery was hit direct and burst into flames. During the morning we counted fourteen ammunition dumps go up from the group of batteries north of the 27th Battery. The attack failed with great loss to the Germans who appeared to lose direction in their assault on the left of the sector. After the attack, the situation quieted down to a certain extent. Most of our shooting was by night. We used to send out two guns at dusk to previously prepared places to do the shooting and thus avoid giving away the main position. It was difficult to find a spot to which no one had some objection as the shooting often drew back a reply then or later. Several times every night a large concentration was fired at selected communications behind the German line:*

Altogether the enemy must have had a poor time from our artillery, as ammunition now seems quite unlimited. In fact one gets almost sick of shooting so continuously. Much aeroplane activity all the time. We saw one excellent fight when five Huns attacked one artillery machine of ours in the dusk when the tracer bullets could easily be seen. The fight had just reached a point a couple of hundred of feet over the battery when a triplane suddenly dived out of the sky and shot up one of the Huns who burst into flames and fell close by the guns. The artillery on the Fampoux ridge in front got very careless and used to replenish ammunition by day and take no precautions as to concealment. One day I was crossing the Athies bridge in the afternoon when I heard a stream of shells coming and saw the whole of the ridge in front a mass of shell bursts. Several wagons were there at the time. They stampeded and galloped wildly about, dragging the dead horses until the harness broke and the survivors charged off the scene. There were many casualties and the following day much digging was started. I had great fun one day shooting at a small length of trench near Cupid Trench into which several Huns disappeared just as it got light. Two guns with HE bolted them and the remaining four with shrapnel were ready to catch them as they appeared. They had only about a dozen yards to go to reach the main trench and I don't suppose I got one, though the bursts completely obliterated them, but it frightened them properly, and one extra fat German who doubled across at an amazing speed presented a most entertaining sight.

20th May   *To wagon line. The first chance I have had of seeing the horses properly since I joined six months ago. We sent a digging party to dig a new forward position in front of the 134th Battery, otherwise carried out normal training and generally cleared up.*

9th–20th June   *Went on leave to England.*

20th June–22nd July   *Spent a good deal of time at the wagon line trying to smarten that department up for the 4th Division Horse Show which was held on 2nd July outside Arras.*

The 32nd Brigade was placed in every event and I won the jumping with a clear round on my bay mare. Things were very quiet on our front and the normal life went on of shooting and liaison. On 7th July I had a telephone message to say that I was posted to the Ministry of Munitions.

Spent my last night at the OP and returned to the battery at daybreak, when

I said goodbye and rode back to the wagon line. Thence to Arras station and so home. The end of a most enjoyable three years.

The 4th Division artillery were in August moved to the Ypres Salient where in the 3rd Battle of Ypres they, together with most other artillery units employed there, lost nearly 100 per cent of their personnel.

So that was the end of Francis Foljambe's war at the front. He had been mobilised and sent out to the front in August 1914, had fought at the very first British battle of the war at Mons, and had spent the next three years in France and Belgium with only three visits back to England for leave. He spent the rest of the war at the Ministry of Munitions and there are no records of what he did there for the war effort.

Dora, Madya and George all spent some time with Ted in early 1917. Ted had proposed to Madya (although we do not know when) and they had all gone to discuss arrangements. George had come out after the

death of his father to see Ted and then went back. Dora and Madya stayed on longer and then Dora went home whilst Madya stayed on so they could get married as soon as it was possible to arrange.

Madya wrote to Dora regularly during that spring and summer. Most of the letters are gossipy, discussing social events in Switzerland, problems with domestic servants and similar matters. Only those dealing with wider issues are reproduced in the following pages:

20th March 1917
Dear Mrs Foljambe,
Madame Greyet just left and I gave Louise leave for the afternoon.
It was ever so kind of you to write to me from Vendiatil and I thank you heartily for it. I do hope the rest of the journey was easier than the start. Wasn't this horrible man at the customs a horrible nuisance.
I must thank you again for your kindness towards me all the time here and

beg you to forgive me if in any way I did even ill please you. My intentions were always very good and I know you will understand it and just try and consider me as your future and very loving daughter-in-law.

Please remind me to Colonel Foljambe and tell him how grateful I am to him to have so easily accepted me as a member of his family. I will try and deserve the honour made me, by making his son as happy as possible and being very happy myself I expect.

You will be interested to know that Edmond is to have your room as bedroom and his room as sitting room. I am to have Avice's, though in the meantime it will be my little Polish friend's.

It's rather lonely here, but I am very busy and time runs. If it was not for my cold and windy weather I believe I would be quite content. As it is, Flick [her dog] and me keep close to the stove in the hall, which is almost red-hot and keeps all the house warm.

I am sending you Edmond's note as to the things he liked to be sent to him – I found it when looking through my papers.

Remind me please to Mrs Warre when you see her and allow me to kiss you fondly and send you my very respectful wishes.

1st April 1917
Dear Mrs Foljambe,

I got your letter from Eton and the note included in Edmond's letter all right and thank you ever so much for it. I am very glad to hear that you crossed safely and it is a great relief to one's mind. I am as you see at Leysin for the day. As my little Polish friend did not get leave I have been fearfully lonely this fortnight except for Edmond coming twice for lunch and as if to spite one and make one more unhappy still it never stopped raining since you left and such an awful wind too that I simply shiver physically and mentally at the thought of it.

Otherwise everything is going on fairly well. Edmond went to Berne to see the lawyer and give him my papers to look through. And we are only waiting for his professional advice to start the necessary applications as his birth certificate came yesterday. It can't be but a satisfactory one as I spent no [little] time and trouble in Paris to get everything in order before I came here. If it is not, it never shall be. Of course Edmond was scolded severely by me as he ought to have gone through all this a long time ago as I don't think it's very fair of him to leave me fearfully lonely at Remnay for so long. I work all the day time but the evenings are wicked.

7th May 1917
Dear Mrs Foljambe,

You must have got Edmond's telegram letting you know we were married last Friday in Lausanne. I am so glad Mr Cockburn found everything correct. I thought it was but of course one always fears the unexpected.

The amount of difficulties raised before the event were not at all in ration to the facilities of the event itself. We walked into the town hall at 10.15 and at 10.30 had already had drinks on the strength of it with our witnesses.

The only misadventures were Mr Middlestone's red nose, due to his having been dragged out of bed and nearly missing the ceremony and Major Alexander dropping his stick with an awful row at the most crucial moment during the deathly pause in the proceedings.

Here we are back again at the Chalet Chausse which welcomed us with all its charms, a glory of white blossom and fresh green; it does change the little house for the best.

You were most kind to remember our housekeeping difficulties and it really is rather dull starting a new marriage without both ends meeting. I think also Cook's address is the best.

I am so awfully sorry to hear your eyes are not satisfactory and I do hope it is only temporary. Yes you must be really anxious about Major Francis, but they are doing such splendid work there. Although the last reports of killed and wounded are simply too awful to read.

Edmond is feeling rather tired after his hard work at Leysin before he left and I think a good complete cure down here will do him any amount of good. We got some huge basket chairs in Lausanne and we are awaiting these anxiously.

You told me once you were on the best of terms with your sons-in-law. I do hope you will not refuse to look kindly on your first daughter-in-law and that you will believe my looking on you as the mother I have missed all my life. You have already been so kind to me when I was but a stranger to you so that I do live in hopes and the best for the future.

Well I end my letter today and hope to hear from you soon. Don't forget about us in your prayers and ask God to bless our marriage for the present and the future.

Naturally Ted was writing home as well:

13th May 1917
My dear Mother,
Here we are back again at Chausson fighting penury and servants. Everything is perfectly delightful now, all the trees out and the village practically out of sight. The lilac is just out and the roses won't be long, at least the ones on the walk. We have

ABOVE *Ted and Madya in Switzerland.*

hopes for the kitchen garden and water it carefully every day and night, mostly for the benefit of the slugs. We slugged one night and saved 10/- on the butcher's bill. Cockchafers and narcissi are in great abundance and the fields are covered in one and the trees in another. My bedroom with the balcony we have turned into a sitting room and will have sweet peas on the balcony if they'll grow. All the floors have been stained dark and it's really quite comfortable. The only thing that is wanting really badly now is pictures and they are fearfully hard to get here. I was wondering if you had any sketches to spare that we could frame locally and hang up. We should be very glad of them if you had.

It's been really too hot to do anything exciting and I have only played golf once during the last age. We looked around for someone else to come and live here with us but without much success. There aren't very many people down here that I know and even some that I do, I wouldn't have here for anything in the world.

We have attempted to do away with the kitchen fire and substitute primus stoves but have been fearfully unlucky with them so far. Ours was broken on arrival and the

BELOW *Chalet Chausse in Switzerland, where Ted and Madya lived until his return to England.*

one we had in exchange has only lit once properly out of about twenty trials.

Best of love to all.

Your loving son,

Edmond

8th June 1917

Dear Mrs Foljambe,

We are very happy down here. The house is simply covered with roses and beautiful ones. We have about five or six bouquets in each room and there never seems to be one less. Our window boxes seem to be doing very well too and the begonias are already in bud. All the vegetables are beginning to behave very nicely and we feed on these almost completely. No butcher for a fortnight except for his roly polys and cottage pies.

We are really doing very nicely and I bless God everyday for the happiness and peace he sent us – it is all so undeserving alas! By me at least.

Rumours again about exchanges of prisoners, but everyone is very cagey about it. Experience has taught us not to rely on rumours too much.

I must end this as the cook has called me to show me some dish. I will write again soon. My respect to the colonel and love to Avice.

At the beginning of the year George was still working for the Red Cross. He felt that he was still helping the war effort but it was telling on his health. His letters home were cheerful and he continued to write to Rachie, as in this example from 20 January:

Dearest Rachie,

I am wondering much how you are getting on with Nino and Co on your own at Stonehill. I hope you manage to keep yourselves warm this bitter weather. They say the frost is the sharpest known to living men here, and it is certainly mighty chilly, but it is bright and, though the wind pretty near cuts one's ears off, it is better than the horrible wet and damp cold we had before.

Thank goodness we appear to have got over the coal crisis, but one never knows what is going to happen next in this house. First an occupant of the bath was shot out by a hot water pipe which burst. Then the cold water tap froze and one of the typists here this morning found her jug cracked in two and the water frozen solid. This lump of ice was requisitioned to cool the boiling water in the bath.

Our neighbours, the Fitzpatricks, were flooded out this morning and found the dining room converted into a skating rink. Toilet having to be performed on the bed.

I suppose you have heard nothing of the travellers beyond Paris as yet. It took a letter nearly four days from there before it was delivered here, so I fear they did not get one there from me before starting south.

This frost will have brought some wild duck in at Osberton and I suspect your Uncle Godfrey too. Did they think to send you any? I am afraid rabbits will be hard to come by this frost and they will be very thin, like I hope the Hun is getting. This submarine business is getting serious and the late government are terribly to blame for their want of foresight. It was not as if they were not warned. Now seriously drastic measures will be necessary or we might be crippled before we can bring the fight to a finish, which will be disastrous and unthinkable.

I think it would be as well if you could get a few, say three or four bottles, of whisky in from the stores if you can get it. What I used to get was about 19/- a gallon which would be I suppose 5/- a bottle. I see the price has gone up a lot but it may come down again. I should ask them what they think. If you can get it for 8/- I think I should get a little and I will refund it.

Not a line from Francis. I expect he has moved and never got my card which I sent off when I started. Ted, of course, is absolutely silent.

I heard of some farmer who had been given an Austrian as a substitute on his farm. Was most polite and made a most graceful bow to his employer, his previous trade was a ladies' hair draper and he might perhaps be able to put in a few potatoes! You can imagine the poor beggar's hands after the first day's work!

I see the government are going to requisition a lot more securities. I hope they let my savings alone, or at any rate be content with the loan of them. If they demand to buy at present prices it means a loss of about 20 per cent which is no joke, although probably the increase in interest one can now get will compensate in a way as far as income is concerned, but the capital will be gone.

Goodbye dear. My love to the children.

6th February 1917
Dearest Rachie,

I daresay you may have been told I have been telegraphed for from Osberton. The wire was sent Saturday and did not reach me until after midday on Sunday, too late to do anything. However, I put a move on on Monday but thanks to the blizzard we were much delayed on the drive there and consequently, though we had thirty-five minutes in hand, there was such a crowd at the passport inspection that many including myself got left behind. I missed the boat literally by inches and now I can't get off until this afternoon and no chance of getting to Osberton till midday tomorrow. I much fear I will be too late as the wire said your dear grandfather was dangerously ill. Well, grievous as the prospect of hurting is with one, with whom one has perhaps the happiest recollections of one's life, one cannot be altogether sorry to think that he may now be released from the burden of infirmity and I fear pain that has been his lot for too long.

You will hardly be able to leave the children, but I should be pleased if you would send me four fairly thick flannel shirts (two each of two colours) narrow stripes, and four collars to match them, and also four white soft ones. I also think I have at Stonehill my long grey ulster coat with check lining which I should also be glad of, and also a fairly thick dark morning trouser suit, but not the one that looks rusty – you know which I mean!

Should you come to Osberton, you might bring my despatch box. Love to the children and yourself.
Your affectionate father,
G. F. Foljambe

George was still in touch with some officers from the 1st/8th Sherwood Foresters and Lieutenant R. Whitton wrote to him in March:

I have intended to write for some time to congratulate you on receiving the CB. I am so glad to that at last your services to the country have been recognised.

Great events have been happening here lately which you will have seen in the papers, and [I] think and hope they are the beginning of the end. Can't believe the Germans would go back unless forced to and from what [I] have seen they must have had a terrible time lately. About ten days ago was brought out of the line and made town major of one of the captured villages. There isn't one brick left standing and their trenches are in a terrible state, but their dug-outs are splendid. Am living in one at the moment which would stop anything up to a 15-inch gun. One of the dug-outs here has three floors and the one which was apparently brigade HQ is a tremendous place, and will hold about 100 men.

I hope you are now feeling much fitter, and that your legs don't give you any trouble.

The next great adventure for the Sherwood Foresters was the arrival of the 2nd/8th Battalion in France. Their details have not been followed closely here, but they had already seen fighting and taken casualties during the war – though not in France. At Easter 1916 the 2nd/8th had been deployed to Ireland at the start of the Easter Rising and had played a large part in attacking the rebel forces in Dublin and putting down the rising and then providing garrison troops on the island. That is another story, but in 1917 the battalion was finally sent to the Western Front. The CO, Lieutenant-Colonel Oates, knew George well. Not only had George played a large part in raising the battalion, but he had been responsible for sending recruits to it until the end of 1915. Oates had written to George throughout the trouble in Ireland and now kept the news coming in from the front. On 4 April he wrote to his brother in England (also a family friend of George) who passed the letter around his regimental colleagues:

We have had a real hot time. [There are] several men who have served eight or ten months with the other battalion in France, and they say that the last four days are the hardest they have ever known. Up to the 30th we had just shelling with high

RIGHT *Captured Germans outside their destroyed bunker.*
IWM Q3013

explosive and shrapnel and had luck – one shell made a direct hit on a field kitchen and sent it and the men's dinner to the four winds. The cooks had just left to put on their steel helmets! In the afternoon B Company's headquarters was hit direct, and Woolley and about ten men had left the building two minutes before to watch the shelling.

Next day, 31st, the curtain came up.

An attack was ordered by another battalion on a strong point. I had to send one company to make a flank attack, and support with the rest. The flank attack was very difficult and I had to select John [Oates's son, a captain commanding a company in the battalion].

His men came splendidly through the enemy's barrage, and the village was taken. John lost two killed, eight wounded. Later I was ordered forward and found the force retiring on the captured village as they had come on very heavy enfilade fire. So the two regiments held on all night under very heavy shell fire, and with no support from our artillery, all night.

Last night I was ordered to capture a German strong point and this we did at 8 p.m. with two companies, taking one wounded prisoner. Following this I was ordered to organise an attack with my two remaining companies on another position in line with the strong point next morning. This was to be done at 5 a.m. and, as it was dark when we got the orders, I had to reconnoitre the position as best I could during the night. We attacked at 5 a.m. and took the position, and cleared our flank on which was an enemy machine gun and snipers. Then our trials began. First I had to site the position for the trenches we had to dig beyond the captured position, in broad daylight and then my two companies (one John's) had to dig in under shell and sniper fire as best they could. This was done. We all, I think, had equal risks, and the log I was sitting on was hit direct by a 5.9-inch HE shell two minutes after I had left it, and a sniper only just missed me when I was inspecting the position of our Lewis Guns. You will understand that the getting up to these strong points had to be done in broad daylight and in the open – snipers all round – officers and men utterly fearless. One man was heard to say of a sniper – 'That blighter is no good, he's missed me seven times'. We have been thanked in corps orders. At 3 a.m. yesterday morning I went round with Dryesdale and the snipers and got them dug in on the Germans' flank. Result, when day broke we killed three of their snipers and their fire was got under [control], but they fairly plastered us with shell, and my headquarters, a hole scraped in the bank close to the first-line trenches, was fairly plastered – four HE shells pitching within eight yards of it. We were relieved last night as the battalion was exhausted, and we are in a ruined village for two or three days to pick up. The sister county battalion has had a nasty reverse, and Martyn has left me to take command of it and Cursham and Dimock broke down from exhaustion yesterday. Logan has been wounded and three men killed and about eighteen wounded. Considering the gruelling, we have come off well. Men absolute heroes, but 100, at least, too exhausted to stand. A check to another battalion last night – heavy casualties. We have indeed been lucky. Am very well – John rather done.

W. C. Oates

8th April 1917
We have had a terrible experience. After capturing the last position, two battalions in this brigade were sent in succession against a terribly strong German position – both were badly punished. It was decided to launch a bigger attack on this position. The brigadier had left and the new one only just arrived. I was therefore told to command the brigade and carry out the operations under a plan mapped out entirely for me by higher authority. Martyn, who has been given command of the town battalion, was hurriedly brought back to command ours for the operation. It was a co-operative operation with the division on our right. An artillery preparation was to last forty minutes for wire

cutting etc., and then soon after midnight (12.40), in pitch darkness, the troops of the two divisions were to attack. Our battalion had had a night march of two hours up to the point of concentration for attack. It was pouring with rain for the whole of the operations and the country is in an awful state. We hear that the army commander nearly put the operation off. In my opinion, and I think in everybody else's almost, the artillery preparation ought to have lasted forty-eight hours to have any chance of cutting the wire. We have now driven the Huns back on to their entrenched positions. They are having all the advantage of trench warfare and we are advancing from considerable distances under the conditions of open warfare.

Well, the barrage lifted, and our battalion advanced to the attack. The two left companies had got within 100 yards of the German wire (John's and another) when suddenly our artillery shot down a terrible fire not on the German trenches to the left of our objective as ordered, but on my two companies. It was a horrible and inexplicable mistake, and inexcusable as the divisional orders were quite clear. Well, John's and the other company, not being able to get on owing to our own artillery fire, dug themselves in 100 yards from the German wire.

In the meantime, the left battalion of the other division, which was the directing battalion of the whole operation, retired and carried one company of mine with it. An officer of this battalion asked my commander of the second company from the right (Mr Warry who was so kind to Thelma) if he were not going to retire. He said 'No I am going to dig in and I advise you to do the same.' This battalion retired, leaving my right in the air. My right company, not having been under our artillery fire, reached the wire but, finding it twelve feet thick and uncut everywhere, dug themselves in. It was pitch dark and the telephone wire was cut so no message got through to me as brigadier until long afterwards, and the distance was too great for runners, and the first runner reached

me after the phone had been repaired.

I was proceeding to the spot to find out what the state of affairs was when I met the brigade intelligence officer who said that I could not get there before daylight, and if I did I could not withdraw the troops safely. In his opinion the trenches they had dug were quite untenable and they were already losing heavily from enfilade machine-gun fire. He thought the battalion would be annihilated. I therefore ordered their retirement, as the other division had retired long ago.

Casualties heavy and in the dark a number of officers and men left dead or wounded on the German wire. Huntsman, Mackinnon, Wilson, and Vinor all either killed or wounded prisoners, Huntsman only wounded we believe. Losses of men well over three figures, alas. The men were glorious and officers also. I am proud of them. I got home believing John killed (he is alright) and sadder than I had ever been in my life, thinking the men would blame me. In the result officers Martyn and Quibell just came up and said : 'We are sorry sir, we did our best.' All the men said was 'Have we failed, what will the colonel say.' I told them I was prouder of them than I had ever been in my life. They are not a bit down and one man was shot through the leg – he never moved or spoke the first two times, but swore the third! I never saw such men, and they told their officers that they would now follow them anywhere. Cursham is down from trench feet and Woolley from exhaustion.

After sleeping the clock round I am much better and ready to fight again. We had Holy Communion – just the bread – kneeling on a plank in a ruined garden. The brutes burn yew hedges – smash all fruit trees and wantonly and uselessly destroy everything: we must smash them. Think we may get a rest. Some of the men who joined us from the 1st/8th say we have had a far harder time than they experienced. This battalion has been in four actions in seven days.

Your most affectionate brother,
W. C. Oates

ABOVE *Lewis gun teams, April 1917.* IWM CO1146

29th April 1917

My dear old Chap,

The big fight is over, and we have won a marked victory. There is a certain important spot which gives artillery observation of a certain noted line: it is a place the army commander wanted taken. Although this battalion was heavily punished in the attack twenty days before, it was selected to carry out the left portion of the attack, a Derbyshire battalion taking the right sector. A large number of guns of all calibres had been collected, and at zero hour, just before daylight, the bombardment opened.

We took our first and second objectives straight away, but on reaching the second objective, it was found that the trench shown as A Trench by aeroplane photo, was only spitlocked, and the company comprising the first wave was mown down by enfilade machine-gun fire, and could not consolidate, as there was nothing to consolidate. Elliott accordingly withdrew them to the first objective, and reported that he was consolidating there. A Company under C. P. Elliott was in the first wave, C under Warry in the second, Woolley with B Company guarding the left flank, and John with D in reserve situated at the position of deployment. My battle headquarters selected

by brigade rather further back than I wanted, but connected up by a double wire, with the sunken road [which was] John's position.

The chief or one of the greatest difficulties had been the deployment for attack. It had to be done in darkness within 150 yards of the enemy, with no cover, and a ruined village within close rifle fire had to be passed through. Direction had to be changed several times and finally the whole battalion got through a single gap in the wire, and then deployed at five-pace intervals and got into battle formation, facing in a different direction, but not quite at right angles to that adopted when passing through the wire.

The slightest cough, or rattling of arms, rattling of accoutrements, unfilled water bottles or half-filled etc. was bound to put the enemy barrage down on us. My scouts had, of course, reconnoitred the ground for several days and then I laid out a map, life size, on some ground, as near the real thing as possible and practised the battalion on it in daylight and darkness. Then there were all the numerous details of carrying parties, formation of dumps for ammunition, bombs, etc., getting up the rations, and finally method of advance and consolidation. This was, of course, my work. Having done that I could do little once the action had begun. The deployment was well carried out. In the meantime A and C Companies had suffered heavily and John had reinforced them by two out of his three platoons having now only one left. Woolley had been killed and his subaltern wounded, and his company showed nervousness. On this John left his position and steadied NCOs and men and restored confidence. In the words of a wounded officer 'Captain Oates made all the difference.' B Company held the vital left flank and our objective was maintained. Then Warry (Thelma's friend) was killed and Page, Perry, Warren and Jameson all wounded. As the battalion only went into action with nine officers, we had only four company officers left, and the wire had been broken by shells in seven places. The signallers mended it and I could talk to John. His left was a bit exposed, and on the death of Woolley he took command of the battalion in the front line – reporting on the phone, or by runner if it was anything the enemy might overhear and derive advantage from. He blocked the trench on his left and then, taking the offensive with his bombers, established further blocks, and eventually got to the spot where the trenches from the German lines joined at an angle, then pushed forward to (a), and finally gravely informed me on the phone that he intended to raid a German post at 11 p.m.! This on the phone – his only slight slip all day. He begged for reinforcements but the general thought it impossible to get them to him by daylight, so the battalion had to do without.

Meantime the Derbyshire battalion had lost more heavily than we, but the two battalions were now in touch, and rapidly consolidating. Meanwhile our losses were very heavy, and will prove to be about 6 officers and 95 men; all the wounded men came back to our aid station and a terrible sight it was, which I shall never forget – nearly all very bad wounds, most men hit in three or four places.

During the afternoon I managed to get good observation of the battlefield, and could see about 16–20 of our dead in front of the line we were consolidating. A counter-attack was expected last night and two companies of a Lincoln battalion were placed under my orders. It did not come, and John, pursuing his victorious career, raided the German post at 12 (not 10.30). During the bombing operations a German officer was killed and a machine gun of theirs knocked to bits. It has been at terrible cost, but the battalion during the afternoon received the congratulations of the brigade, divisional, and corps commanders, and finally a telegram came through to me saying that the army commander was very pleased with the way my battalion had fought that day – so I must be content and not think too much of poor Mrs Woolley and Mrs Warry.

Of course I have only a ghost of a battalion.

W. C. Oates

Not much of Victor Yeats-Brown's war survives, but he had recovered from the breakdown following his early traumatic experiences in the trenches. He had worked in the signals section of a divisional headquarters and had served well in this role just behind the front line. He was a thoughtful and sensitive man and did his best and a letter to Rachie survives from April 1917:

Tiny my own child,

Well I had rather an interesting day yesterday up on top of Vimy Ridge with Unwin. I think perhaps what struck me most of all was that all of the country which until the show took place was absolutely desolate of human beings – at least [it] looked desolate because of course there were batteries with human beings serving them, and there were trenches with men in them, but by day none of these were visible of course – now over this same ground, which I knew so well as a desert, you see crowds of men, horses, wagons, tents, motor cars and all the many other things that go to make up an army. It makes the landscape look quite entirely different and makes it most difficult to recognise where you are. Quite an uncanny feeling in fact because you keep on saying to yourself 'It is absurd that I can't recognise this bit of ground, I was here for ages and only quite a short time ago, etc.' and yet presently you have to confess you simply don't recognise it. The next [thing] that impressed me very much indeed was the extent and severity of our shelling. All along where we walked, and beginning from about the old Bosche front-line sap heads, right down the eastern slopes of Vimy Ridge for nowhere less than ¾ of a mile I should think, there was practically not a square yard of ground anywhere which was not touched by shell fire, and as far as I could make out not an inch which had not either been blown away or covered from earth blown up by shells. It was certainly amazing to see the place. The German line had been so much blown to pieces it was very difficult to make out how it had run; trenches were practically non-existent. The best way of recognising where trenches probably ran was to follow a line of dug-outs.

The old mine craters were very interesting to see too, some of them enormous but except for one or two they seem to have been pretty well between the lines and cannot, I should think, have done much damage when they went up.

Oh my Tiny I was to have gone to the dentist at 12 noon today and have forgotten all about it thinking about my new switches and their fitting up. This is rather sad and very rude of me, not that the poor man would have to attend for me specially, he would be there in any case, but he may well have refused to give someone else his time who may have required his teeth done much more than me.

I also asked my own staff what they thought of ten days' leave for me very presently and they had no objections at all unless the situation alters, so that, my own wife darling, it really looks rather promising, though we must look at it with the greatest distrust for the present as it never does to imagine you have got leave

BELOW *Madya.*

*until you have actually landed in England!
If nothing much happens to our own crowd
therefore, my Tiny, I think you might expect
me on 2nd May sweetheart.*

*Goodbye wife mine darling, my whole
love to you and the small ones always and
God bless you.*

Your own husband

July–December 1917

Ted and Madya were still in Switzerland,
married, and looking forward to seeing how
they could get themselves repatriated to
England. Madya was writing to Dora
fairly regularly:

24th July 1917
Dear Mother,

*It is very kind of you to let me call you
like that. I was looking forward to it very
much.*

*I am sending you another photograph as
I think it is quite a good one.*

*They talk here again of sending back
English prisoners. Let us hope so and I am
longing badly to see my new home and
meet the rest of my new family.*

*Let's hope for the best about Russia, but
of course they are so mad that one can't
help being frightened at times.*

*We are so glad to hear that Francis got
a job in England now. Three years of it is
really enough for one and I wish everyone
had done his duty so well and modestly.*

*I am doing some more hats and
finishing two dresses. I am quite rich in
dresses now but frightfully poor in shoes,
as I can't get what I like in Switzerland.
(Do you think I could trouble you to order
me a pair in England? This is the shape I
want in suede, dark navy blue, with high
heels (about 4 or 5 cent) but not Louis XV,
square ones.)*

*Thank you so much if you do, I would be
so grateful as I can't match anything here.*

*We are going to Geneva on Sunday for
the races. I am biking as I am getting so
stout with happiness and good food. We are
really going quite well and spend very little,
never more than 10 francs a week for four*

*and no eggs as we have got our own hens
now, eight of them, and a cock. And they
are so good they started laying on the very
first day we got them which is I think quite
a record.*

*Well dear mother, goodbye and all my
best love and wishes of your health.*

Your ever loving daughter,
Madya

20th August 1917
Dear Mother,

*The frontier has been shut for a few
days so I got your two letters together.
Great news, Ted has passed and we are
going home in three weeks' time. I am so
overjoyed I can't write. We don't know yet
whether we go together or I go first or what.
Anyway I shall let you know all about it.*

*À propos the shoes do give them back
please if you can as I hate Glaa [?] shoes
and hate them pointed and never wear
Louis XV heels if I can avoid it. I will get
them when I am back home, though of
course it was so good of you to take the
trouble and I am so sorry I even worried
you with it.*

*We started packing this morning and
just fancy that I got my big trunk from
Paris with hats etc. only a week ago – pretty
quick isn't it. I have missed my hats most
terribly – anyway the trunk will be most
useful as five people could easily hide in
it. We want to send it by Cook's but I went
and enquired two days ago and they tell
me that no books are allowed, no pictures,
etc., etc., and nothing is insured – so we
will try and take all with us. After all the
customs are a good institution, but I think
that prisoners and interned ought to have
special conditions!*

*Excuse the awful writing and I send you
my very best love.*

Your loving daughter,
Madya

[Ted writing on the bottom of the letter]
*There seems to be a good chance of
getting home by the end of the year which
is really satisfactory. I don't think we shall
come together and I think probably M. will
come on ahead and if you could have her*

Lieut. G. W. Saville Foljambe

Rifle Brigade

BUCKINGHAM PALACE

1918.

The Queen joins me in welcoming you on your release from the miseries & hardships, which you have endured with so much patience & courage.

During these many months of trial, the early rescue of our gallant Officers & Men from the cruelties of their captivity has been uppermost in our thoughts.

We are thankful that this longed for day has arrived, & that back in the old Country you will be able once more to enjoy the happiness of a home & to see good days among those who anxiously look for your return.

George R.I.

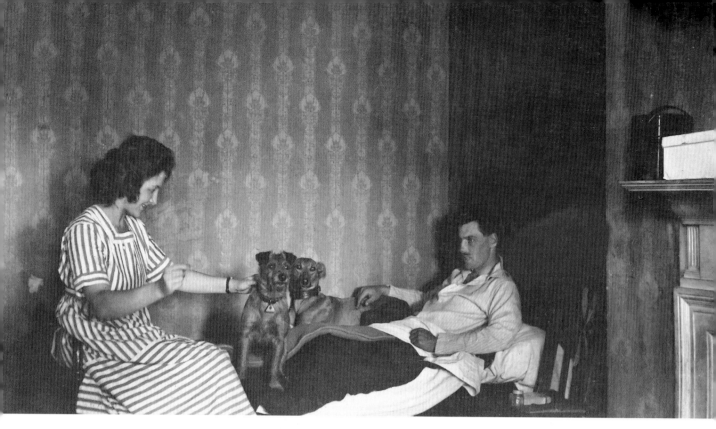

ABOVE *Ted and Madya at Oudenarde Barracks, Aldershot, in 1919.*

at Osberton she would be most grateful for a rest after the journey.

The postman is here so I must stop. Best of love to all and hoping to see you soon.

Your loving son,

E

The local Newark newspaper wrote the following slightly tongue in cheek article alongside a very bad photograph of Ted:

From Switzerland. – Here is Captain E. W. Savile Foljambe, of the Rifle Brigade, who is amongst this week's repatriated prisoners of war from Switzerland. While out there he became engaged to Mlle Madia Lis de Rudincki, of Siekierzynce, Podolia. (What an entry for a registrar of marriages to cope with: I hope I've got it right, anyway.) Captain Foljambe is the eldest son of Colonel George Foljambe of Osberton, Notts, and is heir to big estates in three counties. He claims Norman ancestry, is of the Earl of Liverpool's family, and calls himself 'Fulljam'. The pronunciation of the lady's birthplace I give up.

OPPOSITE *Madya and Olga at Osberton.*

Ted and Madya finally arrived back in England in early September and went to Osberton where they spent time with George and Dora. They then moved down to London. Ted was still recuperating:

16th December 1917
Dear Father,

We are coming up to Osberton on Friday to avoid the long crush of Saturday afternoon. It will be nice to get a change from London. It has been raining here for the last few days.

We are going to take a house after Christmas as this place is impossible for two. The only trouble is the big outlay in pennies, and, as you told me I could always rely on you in case of necessity, I am bold enough to ask you now if you could help us financially. The cost of furnished houses and the scarcity of them is such that it makes it completely impossible for us. It is true that in normal cases the bride's people do the furnishing etc. but you know the sad present circumstances of my family and I don't know if I shall ever see again my poor father alive.

I am going this very morning to a big sale to get some of the furniture. This sale seems a very good opportunity as all that kind of thing is very expensive now.

We shall be glad also if you let us have the silver now as we need it for settling down. I hope you and Mother will approve of it. We are both of us so tired of hotel and boarding-house life.

Thank you, dear Father, you have always been so kind to me and please believe in the secure love of your devoted daughter.

Madya

Although George was now completely retired from the war he still had a great interest in his regiment and continued to get the odd letter from his friends in the Sherwood Foresters. Captain Weetman wrote from France on 10 August:

I am more than sorry not to have written sooner after your two very kind letters.

At the moment I cannot for the life of me make out where we stand, but always hope for the best. They always say that things are going well on the Western Front, where after all the war will be decided, so that I suppose we must conclude that all is well. It's a long tedious business, and at present hardly looks like ending this year. We have had some rough times this year, and seen a good deal of fighting. I never want to go through anything quite like we had in April, May and June. General Shipley used to say it was worse than the Salient. It was certainly very rough. You know of course that he is now at home – we have a Gunner, General Carey, now commanding the brigade. I think he knows you. Poor old Shipley was about done, and really stayed on too long, I think. The new one is very keen and energetic in spite of his lameness.

I have never managed to run across Francis, but one never knows. If we are ever near one another I hope we may meet. I am glad indeed that he got his MC, which I'm sure he deserved. Goodbye and many thanks for your letters.

And a platoon commander George had trained in 1915, Lieutenant J. Johnston, wrote from hospital in September:

Very many thanks for your most welcome letter and sympathy. I am glad your son is

safely home again; I had been wondering
if he would be sent home and was bucked
to see his name in the paper. What an
anxious time it must have been for you.

I had a good innings in France, and
was a bit sick at being knocked out with a
working party! I had only to command the
company for one more week, and I should
have got my acting captaincy. However, I
am safer – which suits my wife better!

Finally, George heard indirectly from the
commanding officer of the 2nd/8th who had
had quite a rough time:

Dear George,
I think you would like to see the enclosed
letter from my brother. He came through
alright, but is now in hospital, suffering
from the effects of gas.
Yours ever,
F. H. Oates

In the Field
29th September 1917
The great battle of 26th and 27th
September is over, and I, and what is left
of my dear battalion, are on the march
back towards Ypres, and are then being
entrained for Boulogne and a week's sea
air, as nothing is considered too good for
us. I believe all the brigade follows, but we
have been taken out of the line first, as
we were right in front for three days and
suffered most.

Y-day was September 25th: YZ-night
the night of the 25th/26th and zero day
and hour September 26th at 5.50 a.m. The
Second and Fifth Army (General Gough)
– we belong to the latter – attacked on
a frontage of twelve miles. The portion
allotted to the 59th Division was from the
line of River Zonnebeke to Van Isackere
Farm and Decky Farm of the right flank.
The 3rd Division was on our right and
58th on our left. The portion allotted to
the brigade was from the Honnebeke to
Otto Farm. The plan of operations for the
Sherwood Foresters Brigade was for the
2nd/7th on the left and the 2nd/6th on the
right to advance at zero and capture the

first areas, then the 2nd/8th on the left and
the 2nd/5th on the right were to leap-frog
through them, and go for the final objective
being Riverside and the Honnebeke which
winds a good deal here. Troops had to be
in position by 3 a.m.: the 2nd/7th behind
Schuler Galleries, and the 2nd/8th close
up. An intense bombardment then took
place by 642 guns of all calibres lasting two
hours. We knew that the German barrage
must just catch the 2nd/8th rear, and as
they put it down eight minutes after ours
we suffered a good many casualties whilst
waiting, but we had to be the far side of
it, and there was no room further forward
as we were close to the enemy. The 2nd/7th
took their area without difficulty, and the
2nd/8th, although it was a foggy morning,
managed the difficult leap-frog manoeuvre
successfully and got so close to the barrage
that we had several casualties – always a
sign of a good battalion.

The frontage of the 2nd/8th was about
450 yards, and so close up were they that
they rushed Toronto before the Bosche
could get out. About fifty prisoners were
taken here. Meantime we lost heavily from
the German machine-gun barrage and, on
advancing on our final objective, Riverside
House, our Gunners made a mistake –
lifted off the objective for a time and then
returned. Broad, the captain of
D Company, and an old Artilleryman,
was hit in the back and several men. The
company retired to Toronto, reorganised,
and again advanced under 2nd Lieutenant
Rounds and took Riverside thus reaching
our last objective. It was cleared of prisoners
and a line of shell holes consolidated just in
rear of the place where the house and road
had been. There were seven tanks out but
they did no good, and Otto Farm, though
taken by the 2nd/5th (Derby Battalion),
could not be held. A very heavy counter-
attack was launched about 4 p.m. and
beaten off. 2nd Lieutenant Rounds with
great gallantry refusing to retire though
only five men were left in the front line. A
second counter-attack came at stand-to on
the 2nd/7th and was also beaten off. About
7 p.m. on the previous evening (26th) I saw

large forces coming in the direction of my headquarters. Quibell quite thought the Bosche had broken through. It turned out to be a large number of demoralised British troops returning.

I sent Quibell and Jefferies to the right to halt them and reorganise, whilst young Roe and I picked a line to stand on with the 2nd/8th headquarters, signallers, runners and officers' servants. The Bosche planes, however, spotted us and our very shallow trench got a very heavy shelling, and poor young Roe of Nottingham, who had done so well all day, was killed close to me by a direct hit from a shell, and three others were wounded. Eventually the disorganised troops advanced, and the position was restored. The 2nd/8th and 2nd/7th stood firm. I got a blow on my metal badges of rank from a piece of shell, but it only made me a little sore. Our battalion headquarters and that line were heavily bombarded and there were two direct hits. The 2nd/6th's colonel was hit and his adjutant killed. In the meantime the 2nd/8th had lost so heavily that the general allowed me to bring up my two reserve officers (C. P. Elliott and Macdonald), from the transport lines, and they and G. G. Elliott, the signalling officer, went into the line. Eventually at midnight on the 27th/28th, after beating off another counter-attack, the front line was so depleted that I decided to go down and see for myself how we stood. C. P. Elliott shortly after my visit sent a runner back to say that he had been buried twice and was not capable of commanding in an emergency, and that Heath was in the same condition. I decided to send Quibell and Cook to the line, my last two officers and got my sergeant-major to act as adjutant. An hour later Cook's arm was blown off and the Bosche planes, flying low, turned their machine guns on what was left of my dear old battalion.

They held on, however, and after suffering a rather heavy (mistaken) bombardment by one of our 18-pounder batteries, were relieved last night – the New Zealanders taking our place for the next push towards the Passchendaele Ridge just in front. This is what is wanted. Our troubles were not over as, after shelling us at 11 p.m. on the track home with HE, the Bosche put down a heavy mustard gas shell bombardment. I just got a

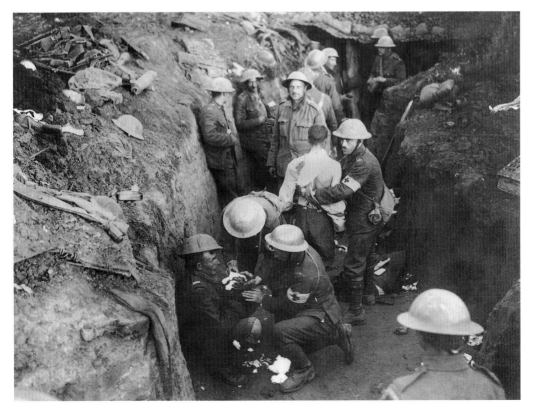

LEFT *Medics carry out emergency first aid at a regimental aid post. An aid post could typically deal with 20–30 men at a time.* IWM CO756

ABOVE *German prisoners-of-war help to load casualties into an ambulance.*

sniff but quickly got my respirator on, and feel all right, and two private soldiers led me (I couldn't see for the smoke) down to my new battalion headquarters. I regret to say that a large number of the 2nd/8th men are gassed – or rather large from what is left. We are just moving on. All 14 officers who went over the top are casualties. Heath slight (I hope) shell-shock, C. P. Elliott has come round, and of about 600 other ranks, of which the battalion consisted, I estimate we have lost 450 to 500 men. But the battalion has covered itself with glory, and you should see the general's face!

We took all our objectives and held them. *I am well; the excitement kills neuritis. I had no sleep for two nights and a day. Casualties Roe and Hadden killed; Mellows, Broad, Rounds, Hough, Bampton, Jones, Charlesworth, Cook, Lipscome, Lewis, Heath (shock), Cooper, Smith, wounded. I have only Quibell, Duncan and G. G. Elliott of the staff. With myself there are six officers in the battalion.*

W. Coape Oates

1918

1918 was a weary year and, although the war continued to rage in France and Belgium, the country was exhausted.

Most of the family was back in England, though Victor Yeats-Brown was still in France. Ted and Madya were now living in London whilst Ted recuperated, and Francis was still working at the Ministry of Munitions. George had inherited Osberton and had to deal with large death duties.

George's beloved regiment was still at the front and in January he got a letter from Colonel Oates, the old commanding officer of the 2nd/8th Sherwood Foresters:

My dear George,
Very many thanks for your kind letter. Yes, the 8th has done magnificently, and as I told my battalion in a letter today, I shall always feel deeply grateful for their gallantry, as it got me my DSO. This war has so far been good to me personally, and I feel I have got a second home in the dear

*old 8th. I'll certainly come and see you
when I next come to Nottingham.*

*I have a stiff job here: five companies
of young men, all between 18½ and 19¼:
all [fitness grade] A. After thirty weeks'
training with us, we send one complete
company to France, and Aldershot sends
us another, which begins at the bottom and
works its way up. Every six weeks we send
a company out. Fifty per cent of these are
trained bombers and rifle bombers and fifty
per cent trained Lewis gunners. The whole
are riflemen, and trained up to a very
advanced pitch, in rapid wiring, anti-gas,
etc., etc. The trouble is we are very short of
officers: only two per company. Smith is to
be my new adjutant. Well good luck
old chap.*

Britain was running out of men and all
of the battalions at the front were under-
manned. The toll of casualties over the
previous three years had been huge and
the expansion of the Army had created too
many strains to be managed. At the end of
January all the Territorial 2nd Battalions were
disbanded and the manpower distributed
amongst the rest of the units. Although there
were then fewer battalions, they could do
more as they were brought up to strength.
At the end of January the 2nd/8th Sherwood
Foresters was disbanded and many of the
officers and soldiers joined the 1st/8th which
was then simply called the 8th Battalion,
Sherwood Foresters. George was still in
occasional correspondence with some of the
officers and wrote to Captain J. P. Hales, who
replied:

29th January 1918
My dear Foljambe,

*I was glad to hear from you. It helps to
have a word of cheer from one of the old
crowd. I am one of the few survivors from
Hunmanby Camp. Do you remember our
walk that Sunday evening? I sometimes feel
a bit stale, and wonder if I ought to give
way to a fresher man – but I do want to
see the old division through. I saw the 8th
today. Blackwell has proved to be a capital
CO – in the trenches there is no one better.*

*I hope everyone at home is at our backs,
determined to see us through, and make
the peace one worthy of the men we have
to answer to who have gone west. How is
your boy?*

In June George heard again from Colonel
Oates, who had now decided to retire:

My dear George,

*I was very pleased to get your letter. I
don't think I have anything to complain of
in coming out, and it is a source of great
satisfaction to me to have been some use,
and I am very proud to have commanded
such a battalion as the 2nd/8th, and made
friends I shall never forget.*

*I shall certainly look you up at the first
opportunity, but I'm keeping very quiet.
My wound is healing well, but I am very
run down and have got out of the way of
sleeping properly. My battalion had thirty-
three consecutive days in the line without
a rest, and we were all pretty well used up
when I came away, young and old alike.*

*The chief trouble is plenty of officers
and men are coming out, but the men
are boys who want six months in a
quiet part of the line and are not fit to take
part in a battle yet – mostly boys of 18½
or 19, and the officers I got were mostly
without experience.*

*The whole trouble is we can't go on
retiring twenty-five miles any longer – there
isn't room.*

*The Americans look good, but where are
their senior officers coming from?*

*I hope you will get a good rest – you
certainly deserve it. Quibell has been
much knocked about, and has had his leg
amputated very high up. He is doing better
now I believe.*

The 8th Sherwood Foresters fought on
throughout 1918, losing another 127 officers
and soldiers killed during the attacks by the
Germans in their spring offensives and the
Allied advance in the autumn through the
German lines. In October 1918 the battalion
lost more killed than in any other month in
the war. At last, on 11 November 1918, the

Armistice was signed (even though one 8th Battalion man, poor Private Hand, died of wounds two days later), and the war was over. George wrote at once to the battalion and had the following reply from the CO:

14th November 1918
Dear Sir,

On behalf of myself and the 8th Sherwoods I wish to thank you for your very nice letter and congratulations. I have commanded the 8th since March last and I can assure you that I never wish to command a better battalion. Their fighting qualities, pluck and endurance during the past few months are beyond all praise and they have proved themselves second to none in the finest army in the world. And I am sure you can look back with pride on the work of your hands. For do we not know that a regiment is proved in the field by its early training? We have won fifty-odd decorations in the battalion during the recent fighting and the Hun knows that when he meets the Foresters Brigade the game is up. We are having a well-earned rest at present and hope soon to complete the job out here and get home once more. Again thanking you.

Yours very sincerely,
R. W. Currin

On 8 December George went out with the Duke of Portland, who was the colonel of the regiment, to visit the battalion and they had a parade, with the brigade band at the front, and the duke presented various medals. It was a good visit for George and they left the battalion preparing for Christmas.

But the Christmas planning did not go

BELOW *The Duke of Portland visits the 8th Battalion Sherwood Foresters at the end of the war. George took the photograph. From left: the Bishop of Southwell, the Duke of Portland, Colonel Mellish, Major Baines and one other.*

according to plan! In the words of the battalion journal:

> The only drawback to our Christmas celebration was that we were not able to celebrate it until Boxing Day, owing to the non-arrival of the necessary feeding stuffs and drinks. Something had gone wrong in the back regions, a thing which had been going on for some time, as canteen stores were always short, and rations at no other period of the war were so scarce and poor. We poured curses on the Royal Army Service Corps, and all connected with them, but to no purpose. Boxing Day, however, will live long in our memory. There was plenty of food and drink, and all sorts of other good things, towards the purchase of which we had been largely helped by money presents from friends at home.

George had sent money and got a very nice letter from Colonel Currin in reply:

> *29th December 1918*
> *Dear Colonel Foljambe,*
> *Very many thanks for your letter and cheque towards the men's Xmas dinner. Thanks to the noble response to our appeal, we were able to give the boys the best day they have had during the war, and for once they really enjoyed themselves to the full. A large number of people sent money, whose addresses I do not know, and I would be very glad if you would tell any whom you know what a good time the men had. Many thanks for congratulations. We have sent away all the miners now so the battalion is not very strong, but we still have enough to put up a fight with, should the Hun or anyone else care to have a cut. Wishing you a very prosperous New Year.*

During this period Madya was as usual keeping Dora up to speed with the news:

> *18th October 1918*
> *Dear Mother,*
> *I know you will be anxious to hear of Edmond's medical board, though they would not say anything of course, except*

that Edmond must be careful and eat a lot. This is one of the points of my letter as meat is very short in town just now and not mentioning the price. I got a ham the other day of about 5 to 7 pounds for 18/-! Could I ask then for an ample supply of game especially now that Avice is coming to stay? Our meat coupons just do for a joint on Sundays and perhaps one other meal in the week. Fish is also very difficult to get and not very nourishing so I would like to get about four brace of birds and one hare and two bunnies a week. This is an awful lot and I would gladly pay for it, or part of it if you would let me. I would not trouble about chickens in the game season and leave it for other times but I would like cream for Edmond, what you can spare of course. I tried to get some in London but it cannot be promised regularly.

> I would not ask if I was not sure that you wish to contribute towards Edmond's welfare. As it is his holiday has made another man of him. Also we have been saved so far from domestic troubles as our new servants seem to be quite satisfactory. I hope you will be satisfied with your butler. I am most anxious to hear how you are getting on and if he is a nice man.

> I would also like to hear about Victor's fate. He seemed rather worried about his future. I hope he has managed to secure some leave.

> The news gets better daily and I am in firm belief of the war ending very soon now. Thanks to the Lord for his help.

> Do tell me about the herbaceous border.
> Your loving daughter-in-law,
> *Madya*

1919

Ted was now back serving with the 1st Battalion, The Rifle Brigade, in Aldershot and he had recovered well after all his traumas of the war. Demobilisation was happening quickly as the extra Rifle Brigade battalions raised during the war were disbanded to get the regiment down to the previous four Regular battalions. Madya had gone up to live at Osberton whilst Ted was so busy. Dora had been spending time with her parents; her father, the ex-provost of Eton, was getting very old. Madya wrote to Dora:

12th May 1919
Dearest Mother,
I hear from Father that you might soon come back to Osberton and it worries me very much as the servant question is still acute and very likely to remain so. I have not, however, given up the struggle and perhaps luck will be on our side soon.
I have at last got a maid. She has never been one before but she is a dressmaker by profession, willing to maid, so it is really all I want. I have taken her temporarily as I do not know my next move and she might not be willing to follow me to Ireland or wherever it is going to be that Ted is going to be sent.
I hope I shall be here when you come; all is rather uncertain because of Teddy's movements. I hope you are quite all right by now in every possible way. Osberton is at its best, I think; at least I have never seen it so lovely as it is now. I am enjoying daily joy-rides but miss Teddy most frightfully!
Rachel is looking well and cheerful. Father has been rook shooting today and I am afraid his leg is bad tonight in consequence.

Victor Yeats-Brown was now a major and had played a full part after his early breakdown in the trenches. He was commanding a company at the Rifle depot in 1919 when he was pulled out to form No. 1 Special Company of the King's Royal Rifle Corps (which included three platoons of King's Royal Rifle Corps and one platoon of the Rifle Brigade). The company was to take part in the Allied intervention in north Russia during the civil war that had followed the Russian Revolution of 1917. Victor and his men arrived at the docks in Murmansk in late April 1919 and met with the rest of the force. This consisted of Victor's company, a special company from the Middlesex Regiment, a company of Royal Marines, the Malmoot Company of Canadian officers and sergeants, 250–300 Slavo-British (commanded by a Lieutenant Colonel Moore), a battalion of Serbians and two companies of Italians. Victor spent some months there, including, on 15 May, an 8-hour battle in which the Allied side took 2 officer and 8 other rank casualties, and killed 40 Red Russians and captured 2 machine guns and many prisoners. The battalion account says:

This action, which was fought over very difficult ground in face of very heavy fire from a confident enemy, was a very credible start for a company which had never previously done any field training together. Our success was due to Major Yeats-Brown's determined leading, as much to the endurance of the men, and the excellent shooting of the Lewis gunners.

Finally Victor returned to England, the last of the family to be home from the fighting. His return was welcomed by George:

6th September 1919
My dear Victor,
So glad you are home again; I quite agree with what you say as to the future. Now that the war is over, folks must look after themselves a bit. My advice has always been to everyone that asked me, to stick to the job they have, till a better or more permanent one turns up. Rachie has, as I rather feared, got run down again after having this [another baby]. The difficulties of life are very great now and it will be a great thing for her to get a home where she and you can be on a more permanent basis than has been possible these last five years. As regards the future of the Army I should personally endeavour at all costs to enlist the services of the senior regimental officers whom I could find available for the next two or three years, regardless if they were fit for active service or not. In spite of the League of Nations I hope that we may consider that war on a large scale for the next decade is not in the region of practical politics and what seems to me to be wanted is the services of men of experience and administrative ability to start the show again on sound lines. The daily papers

ABOVE *Rachie with her children Nino and Dora and with George at Osberton*

bore me to tears. They raise one's hair every morning and do you no good. I'm tired to death of it.

There was an excellent letter from a Dr Eaton in today's Times which about summed up the situation: that it was no use talking about nationalisation or any other fad as a means of getting increased production. The only way to get it was to dig. I am afraid Rachie had an awful journey down to Ramsgate. Maybe things may be quieter later and I am glad you have consulted old March at Westgate, as I think he would interest himself in any of the family.

We are definitely off on Tuesday from Liverpool. It has been rather a big job putting away everything and for mother and Avice to get their clothes ready. The latter has spent many hours preparing her kit, trousseau I was nearly calling it! Poor dear, I hope she won't be too disappointed, tied up with two worn-out and tired hulks.

It is with some regret that one leaves one's home for an indefinite spell, but apart from all other considerations it is quite inappropriate to keep this place going even in a small way, and with incompetent domestics the impossibility is increased. When estate duties are paid off, it will be time enough to see what can be done. My best love to Rachie and the youngsters.

Your affectionate

GSF

P.S. You will have heard about Francis's arrangements. I think he has gathered to himself quite a nice girl from what I could see.

George and Dora were exhausted and collected Avice, packed up Osberton and went abroad for the winter. They visited New Zealand, staying with the Governor-General Lord Liverpool (who was also a Foljambe and a cousin) and then went on to Fiji and back via Canada, arriving back in 1920.

Afterword, 1982

It is appropriate that the final part of the account should belong to Francis, who started the whole story:

It is now November 1982 and I have only to survive a few more days to reach age ninety, so before it is too late I had better draw upon memory to being up to date the diary, the last entry in which was July 1917. The only excuse for inflicting this diary on a possible reader is that I happen to have lived in a period during which a great number of changes have taken place in every aspect of life.

It was while I was at the Ministry of Munitions in London that I met Nell Priestman and her family, who were very friendly to me and invited me to visit them at their home at Shotley Park. The Priestmans, I found, were a clan of solid Quaker origin grouped in the still unspoilt area of north Durham. They lived in nice houses, all fairly adjacent, and mostly these were occupied by relations or friends of long-standing. It was a community quite self-contained and why the Priestmans should wish to include me in their family group I do not know. Nevertheless that was how it was, and in June 1919 Nell and I became engaged and the wedding was fixed for 14th January 1920. The wedding was a large local occasion and meanwhile my parents and near relatives were abroad, in New Zealand, India and elsewhere, and

the outcome was that my best man and my Uncle Godfrey were the only representatives on my side. Sixty years after the above event took place it seems appropriate to digress and say that on 14th January 1980 Nell and I were honoured to receive a telegram from the Queen, congratulating us on the occasion of our diamond wedding anniversary, and to record that over the many years I have never failed to have the kindness and help of the Priestman family.

After the honeymoon spent at Villars, Switzerland, we lived a regimental life for the next six years, half of this time in England and the other half in India. We had quite a number of different houses: Sind Gate; Flore Manor, Brighton; White Lodge, Colchester; and bungalows at Hyderabad, Sand and Kirkee. Dida was born in December 1920 but we did not take her with us to India. She had been a tiny baby and meanwhile the single battery station at Hyderabad had the reputation of having during the hot season the highest temperature in India. Nell used to spend part of this hot weather at the Carlton Hotel in Karachi. It was not always hot in Hyderabad; at about November each year there came a change in wind direction and since rain is almost unknown at Hyderabad, one could look forward to about three months of quite perfect weather – shirt-sleeves during the day, while in the evenings a small fire was very welcome. One could change then from sleeping on the flat roof to sleeping

OPPOSITE *Francis in his nineties.*

indoors. At Hyderabad we were not much bothered by visits by generals and such, who mostly preferred the overall better climate at Quetta and the overpowering social life there!

Army life in India, if one had no young family to look after and had a few hundred rupees to spend, could be for both officer and troops a grand time. For example, about six of us from Hyderabad went to Bubbak Station on the railway to Quetta where there was some wild country and countless acres of grass about two feet high inhabited by pig, and many sheets occupied by migratory duck. There we spent two days pig sticking and three days duck shooting. The government provided the train free, and as for the camp, no problem at all; under the supervision of a havildar [Indian Army sergeant], all necessary tents were taken, officers' mess and servants, horses, forage, horse lines, etc., etc. were loaded and all was ready for us when we arrived after the first day's shooting. Cost per individual apart from normal mess-bill was virtually nil, just the cost of cartridges! From Hyderabad itself one could in the cool season go in any direction for a shoot of quail or black partridge or sand grouse or duck.

We made friends in India, including the Gilberts; he was conservator of forests and had a steamer on the Indus to help reach places in the large area for which he was responsible. His work seemed to be mostly in settling disputes about grazing which arose each year because the Indus used frequently to change its course in the monsoon so that grazing changed banks so to speak. We accompanied the Gilberts on one of their trips going to several places on the Indus and camping out from these to visit people in the area. It certainly was camping de luxe; even if it was for a single night, everything was taken: tents, carpets, chairs, tables, crockery, proper meals, etc!

During our time in India, instead of using leaves to dash back to England as most officers seemed to do, we did try to see what India had to offer. We were invited to Lopea Christmas camp in the Central Province where Arthur Jelf was Resident Agent to the Begum of Bhopal and shot a

tiger there, skin now at Osberton. Another expedition was with friends, the Fosters, to Kashmir – unfortunately Captain Foster was taken ill in the middle of the trip and had to be taken back to Srinigar where he was operated on for appendicitis. I continued alone to fish in the Bringhi River and hunt for Barasingh (Kashmiri stag). I got two good heads which are now in the billiard room at Osberton. On shorter leaves I hired shooting blocks at various places: Kauaca, Coorg, Nilghiri Hills. The battery went for practice camp each year to Pishin on the Afghanistan border north of Quetta.

In 1926 we moved to Kirkee, a very social place near Poona; most people used to go in the evenings to the club for tennis and dancing. During that year there were several courts martial trying wretched subalterns who found themselves forced to steal battery or company funds to pay their bills at the club, incurred mostly by the vicious habit of having to offer rounds of drinks. I hated seeing people asking for expensive cocktails, etc., and many official efforts were made to stop treating, but without avail.

It was at about this time that the government decided that as a result of the conclusion of the 'war to end all wars' the Army could be reduced in numbers and officers were encouraged to leave and settle in such places as Rhodesia to help in the development there, and there certainly seemed to be little purpose in staying in the Army. We accordingly decided to leave and take up some new interest. Nell returned to England while I stayed to square up battery affairs and hand over, before I left for Dar es Salaam in Tanganyika territory where I had induced Ted to meet me for a month's safari. We took out a full licence to shoot all kinds of unfortunate animals from elephant, rhino and buffalo downward, and indeed came home with a fine collection to adorn the walls of the hall at Osberton.

Nell and I and Dida then returned to White Lodge and began to search for a farm, against the advice of everyone who warned us that we were just wasting our money. The country's grain was to come cheaply from the virgin soils of America,

ABOVE *Mary, Ted, Rachie, Francis and Avice in later life.*

and indeed nearly all arable land in this country tumbled down to weeds, as could be seen for mile after mile from the railway. We found and at once settled on Wormingford Grove, five miles north of Colchester. The property comprised the fair-sized house, set of farm buildings, large walled garden with moat and stream running through and 120 acres of good land capable of growing all crops, plus three cottages – price £5,000 the lot.

We gave notice to the existing tenant and started to stock up by buying a dozen Guernsey cows at about £30 each. I took the milk to Frinton each morning where we were paid 9d a gallon for a quota and 6d a gallon for the remainder. A labour force of foreman, horseman, and cowman plus three Suffolk Punches at a total wage of about £8 weekly (plus £5 for the harvest) were engaged to work the land on a strict four-course rotation. We did a good bit of manual work ourselves and I found so much of interest to attend to that I did not replace the three hunters I had sold on leaving for India and in fact never rode again for the rest of my life. Instead of hunting we spent a holiday each year visiting different parts of the world with Ted. Another visit to Africa with Nell and the Gibbins, who hived off at half time for a sightseeing cruise up the west coast. In subsequent years we went shooting or fishing to New Zealand (two good heads at Osberton), Red Sea Hill, Yugoslavia, while Nell paid a visit to Malaya, with Margot Waite, and to Ceylon. That brought us up to 1939 when Hitler started another war.

During these years we took opportunities to enlarge our farm, improve the buildings and cottages and increase the dairy herd. I was still on the reserve of officers at the outbreak of the war and was posted to a job in Movement Control at Southampton. I was glad at last to get back to the farm here where, with U-boats coming near to starving out this country, it would have been difficult not to make a good profit!

The farm continued to enlarge as more land came on the market and all went well until in 1958, when disaster struck. On 19th January of that year, Christopher [Francis's eldest son] had taken a friend and the latter's girlfriend for a morning's sail at Kirby Quay. A car came down the drive but instead of our party returning for lunch, a policeman got out to tell us that Cygnet had hit a mud-bank and gone over and that Christopher and the girl had been drowned. This was indeed a shattering blow from which we can never recover. His death, too, upset all the plans made by Ted for his inheritance and I am sure contributed to my brother's own death only two years later.

In due course, after the disaster in 1958, one had to pick up the threads and in a rather unenthusiastic way continue to enlarge and equip the farm to the extent appropriate for the management capability of a farm manager. This we have now more or less achieved and the estate now comprises 1,000 acres of good land, equipped with dairy buildings, grain stores, two silos, workshop, cattle yards, good cottages, etc., and two reservoirs which ensure ample grazing for the dairy cows and followers throughout the summer regardless of the weather. The reservoirs have proved a great success. A powerful pump on the lower one can send water right round a 4-inch pipe circling the farm, with take-off points so that most of the land can be reached for irrigation. We have stocked the lakes with trout and the lakes attract a great variety of birds especially when bad weather drives waterfowl from the sea to seek shelter. They would have been a delight to Christopher.

What I have written might well be taken as a success story.

However, some inevitable misfortunes have now come along. About the time of our diamond wedding anniversary Nell woke one morning to find her right leg paralysed. It has never recovered and among other disadvantages we can no longer undertake the journey to Hope [his estate in Scotland]. I too have suddenly during the past year begun to feel old with badly failing eyesight and am getting very unstable on the legs.

Anyway there will be very large taxes to pay due to the wicked capital robbery imposed by a spiteful Labour chancellor. It may be too that the Left will achieve their ambition for a Labour government kept permanently in power by the unions in return for doing whatever the latter want, which will no doubt include nationalisation of land without compensation, abolition of the House of Lords, etc., etc. Certainly the world would seem to be as unstable as it could well be. On the other hand there are still quite a number of good people in this country and it is difficult to think up any better part of the world to retreat to. Meanwhile I am glad that I have lived long enough to remember the great British Empire under Queen Victoria when we had a dominant say in all world affairs, when London was the financial centre of the world, all countries still enjoyed the peace of Pax Britannica and when the word British was the hall-mark of integrity and good quality.

Concluding the Family Story

George Foljambe died in 1920, shortly after his return from his trip around the world. Dora was convinced it was the hard work he had done during the war and the strain he had been under, particularly inheriting the estates and their responsibilities in 1917 at such a difficult time, which led to his early death. Ted took over the estates and was invalided out of the Army. He, Madya and Francis made several visits to Africa during the 1920s. They enjoyed big-game hunting and collected trophies for the hall at Osberton. Madya once shot a pride of eight lions before breakfast and the albums are full of her with elephant, rhino and other trophies. They kept meticulous accounts and diaries of these trips and others. She was in Africa on a trip on her own when she died in 1931. The cause of her death was possibly malaria but my mother (born in 1929 and Madya's god-daughter) was always told that Madya was eaten by a lion! Ted and Madya did not have children, possibly as a result of Ted's injuries during the war. However, after Madya's death Ted married Judith Wright (not the same lady who had been married to his Uncle Godfrey). Ted died in 1960.

Francis's account has already explained what he did after the war. He was devastated when his elder son Christopher died in a sailing accident. Francis died in 1987. Michael, Francis's second son, inherited the estates direct from Ted and is a very keen horseman and eventer, starting the well-known Osberton horse trials, the East Midlands dressage group and supporting younger riders by hosting pony club camps since 1961. He is also a passionate farmer and has kept the Osberton Jersey herd, which was started in 1869 and restarted the Osberton beef shorthorn herd. He has cared for and looked after the estates for almost 50 years.

ABOVE *Ted with the chickens at Osberton.*

LEFT *Ted and Madya host a shooting party in 1919 at Osberton.*

INDEX